Lecture Notes in Computer Science

Edited by G. Goos, J. Hartmanis, and J. van Leeuwen

Springer

Berlin
Heidelberg
New York
Barcelona
Hong Kong
London
Milan
Paris
Tokyo

Craig A. Lee (Ed.)

Grid Computing – GRID 2001

Second International Workshop
Denver, CO, USA, November 12, 2001
Proceedings

 Springer

Series Editors

Gerhard Goos, Karlsruhe University, Germany
Juris Hartmanis, Cornell University, NY, USA
Jan van Leeuwen, Utrecht University, The Netherlands

Volume Editor

Craig A. Lee
The Aerospace Corp., High Performance Computing
2350 East El Segundo Blvd., El Segundo, CA 90245, USA
E-mail: lee@aero.org

Cataloging-in-Publication Data applied for

Die Deutsche Bibliothek - CIP-Einheitsaufnahme

Grid computing : GRID 2001 ; second international workshop, Denver, CO,
USA, November 12, 2001 ; proceedings / Craig A. Lee (ed.). - Berlin ;
Heidelberg ; New York ; Barcelona ; Hong Kong ; London ; Milan ; Paris ;
Tokyo : Springer, 2001
  (Lecture notes in computer science ; Vol. 2242)
  ISBN 3-540-42949-2

CR Subject Classification (1998): C.2, D.1-4

ISSN 0302-9743
ISBN 3-540-42949-2 Springer-Verlag Berlin Heidelberg New York

Typesetting: Camera-ready by author
Printed on acid-free paper   SPIN: 10845876   06/3142   5 4 3 2 1 0

Preface

The term "grid computing" is based on an analogy with the electrical power grid: computing capabilities should be ubiquitous and easy to use. While the development of what we now call grid computing is, in many ways, part of a natural progression of work done in the last decade, what's special about it is that all of its enabling technologies are converging at once: (1) a widely deployed, network infrastructure will connect virtually every device in the world, (2) an interface technology is widely understood and embraced by virtually every segment of science, technology, commerce, and society, and (3) there is a wide-spread, and growing, understanding of the properties, capabilities, and services that are necessary and *possible* to utilize this infrastructure. Information services and resource brokers will allow the dynamic sharing of resources for applications large and small and enable virtual organizations. These properties, capabilities, and services will be used in different contexts to enable different styles of computing such as Internet computing and Peer-to-Peer computing. To facilitate the adoption of standard practices, the Global Grid Forum (www.gridforum.org) was formed to identify common requirements and push for eventual standardization.

The phenomenal growth of grid computing and related topics has created the need for this workshop as a venue to present the latest research. This year's workshop builds on the success of last year's. Grid 2000, chaired by Rajkumar Buyya and Mark Baker, was held in conjunction with HiPC 2000, in Bangalore, India, and attracted participants from 15 countries. This year's workshop was held in conjunction with Supercomputing 2001, the world's premier meeting for high-performance computing. We sincerely thank Sally Haerer, David Culler, and Ian Foster for making this happen.

This year's Program Committee represented 12 countries on 4 continents and authors submitted papers from 7 countries on 3 continents. This certainly attests to the wide-spread, international importance of grid computing. We heartily thank all of the authors and the members of the Program Committee. It is the contribution of their valuable time and effort that has made this workshop a success. A very special thanks is extended to Dennis Gannon for his stimulating keynote address. Dennis has a long history of identifying the important issues and clearly elucidating them.

We thank our sponsors, the ACM, the IEEE, the IEEE Computer Society, the IEEE Task Force on Cluster Computing, and also Supercomputing 2001 for making the workshop and these proceedings possible. We are very grateful to Prof. Cauligi Raghavendra and Prof. Viktor Prasanna for allowing Grid 2001 to host its web site at the University of Southern California. Using WIMPE from Dartmouth College for managing the workshop through the web site from wherever I was proved to be invaluable. (Just make sure no other project fills up the disk partition with /tmp. ;-) We also wish to thank Jan van Leeuwen of Utrecht University (LNCS Series Editor) and Alfred Hofmann of Springer-Verlag

(Executive Editor) for publishing the proceedings. A special thanks goes to Anna Kramer of Springer-Verlag (Computer Science Editorial Assistant). Her prompt help made prefecting these proceedings as easy as \addtocounter{one}{2+3}.

Finally we wish to thank all who attended Grid 2001 in Denver. We now invite you to study these proceedings and their contribution to the further development of grid computing.

August 2001

Craig A. Lee
Grid 2001 Program Chair
www.gridcomputing.org

Grid 2001 Sponsoring Institutions

Association for Computing Machinery
(ACM SIGARCH)
http://www.acm.org

Institute of Electrical and Electronics
Engineers (IEEE)
http://www.ieee.org

IEEE Computer Society
http://www.computer.org

Supercomputing 2001
http://www.sc2001.org

IEEE Task Force on Cluster
Computing (TFCC)
http://www.ieeetfcc.org

Grid 2001 Organization

Workshop Chair

Craig A. Lee
The Aerospace Corporation, El Segundo, California, USA

Program Committee

David Abramson, Monash University, Australia
Ishfaq Ahmad, The Hong Kong University of Science and Technology, China
Giovanni Aloisio, University of Lecce, Italy
Ruth Aydt, University of Illinois, Urbana-Champaign, USA
David Bader, University of New Mexico, USA
Mark Baker, University of Portsmouth, UK
Rajkumar Buyya, Monash University, Australia
Henri Casanova, University of California, San Diego, USA
Steve Chapin, Syracuse University, USA
Frederica Darema, National Science Foundation, USA
Jack Dongarra, University of Tennessee/ORNL, USA
Wolfgang Gentzsch, Sun Microsystems, USA
Jonathan Giddy, Monash University, Australia
Sergi Girona, Polytechnic University of Catalunya, Spain
Ken Hawick, University of Wales, UK
Hai Jin, Huazhong University of Science and Technology, China
William Johnston, Lawrence Berkeley National Laboratory, USA
Domenico Laforenza, Institute of the Italian National Research Council, Italy
Gregor von Laszewski, Argonne National Laboratory, USA
Miron Livny, University of Wisconsin, USA
Satoshi Matsuoka, Tokyo Institute of Technology, Japan
Jarek Nabrzyski, Poznań Supercomputing and Networking Center, Poland
Lalit Patnaik, Indian Institute of Science, India
Thierry Priol, IRISA/INRIA, France
Alexander Reinefeld, ZIB, Germany
Mitsuhisa Sato, Real World Computing Partnership, Japan
Peter Sloot, University of Amsterdam, The Netherlands
Alan Sussman, University of Maryland, USA
Domenico Talia, ISI-CNR, Italy
Yoshio Tanaka, NIAIST, Japan
Mary Thomas, San Diego Supercomputing Center, USA
Brian Tierney, Lawrence Berkeley National Laboratory, USA

Additional Referees

Vishwanath P. Baligar, Indian Institute of Science, India
Christian Pérez, INRIA, France
Alexandre Denis, INRIA, France
Dave DiNucci, Elepar, USA
Jason R. Mastaler, Albuquerque High Performance Computing Center, USA
Florian Schintke, ZIB, Germany
Otto Sievert, University of California, San Diego, USA
James Stepanek, The Aerospace Corporation, USA

Table of Contents

Invited Presentation

Grid Application Design Using Software Components and Web Services ..   1
Dennis Gannon

Object Middleware

Design and Implementation of a CORBA Commodity Grid Kit   2
Snigdha Verma, Manish Parashar, Jarek Gawor, Gregor von Laszewski

Towards High Performance CORBA and MPI Middlewares for Grid
Computing   14
Alexandre Denis, Christian Pérez, Thierry Priol

An Integrated Grid Environment for Component Applications   26
*Nathalie Furmento, Anthony Mayer, Stephen McGough,
Steven Newhouse, Tony Field, John Darlington*

Resource Discovery and Management

KNOWLEDGE GRID: High Performance Knowledge Discovery on the
Grid   38
Mario Cannataro, Domenico Talia, Paolo Trunfio

On Fully Decentralized Resource Discovery in Grid Environments   51
Adriana Iamnitchi, Ian Foster

An Adaptive Service Grid Architecture Using Dynamic Replica
Management   63
Byoung-Dai Lee, Jon B. Weissman

Identifying Dynamic Replication Strategies for a High-Performance
Data Grid   75
Kavitha Ranganathan, Ian Foster

Scheduling

Ensemble Scheduling: Resource Co-Allocation on the Computational Grid   87
Jon B. Weissman, Pramod Srinivasan

JobQueue: A Computational Grid-Wide Queuing System   99
*Dimitrios Katramatos, Marty Humphrey, Andrew Grimshaw,
Steve Chapin*

A Scheduling Model for Grid Computing Systems 111
Anuraag Sarangi, Alok Shriram, Avinash Shankar

Grid Architecture and Policies

Exposed vs. Encapsulated Approaches to Grid Service Architecture 124
Micah Beck, Terry Moore, James S. Plank

A Methodology for Account Management in Grid Computing
Environments 133
Thomas J. Hacker, Brian D. Athey

Policy Engine: A Framework for Authorization, Accounting Policy
Specification and Evaluation in Grids 145
Babu Sundaram, Barbara M. Chapman

Performance and Practice

Performance Contracts: Predicting and Monitoring Grid Application
Behavior 154
Frederik Vraalsen, Ruth A. Aydt, Celso L. Mendes, Daniel A. Reed

Production-Level Distributed Parametric Study Capabilities for the Grid   166
Maurice Yarrow, Karen M. McCann, Edward Tejnil, Adrian DeVivo

The D0 Experiment Data Grid - SAM 177
*Lee Lueking, Lauri Loebel-Carpenter, Wyatt Merritt, Carmenita Moore,
Ruth Pordes, Igor Terekhov, Sinisa Veseli, Matt Vranicar, Steve White,
Vicky White*

Author Index 185

Grid Application Design
Using Software Components and Web Services

Dennis Gannon

Indiana University
Bloomington, Indiana

Abstract. Software Component systems are widely used in the commercial world for designing desktop applications and multi-tier business systems. They have not been widely used in large scale scientific computation. However, as our computing platform has evolved into Grid systems, a distributed component architecture is gaining support as a programming model for building heterogeneous, wide-area application. There are several interesting Grid component architectures that are currently being used. Some are derived from the Corba component model and others are based on EJB or other object systems. The DOE CCTTSS organization has developed a model that supports parallel applications as well as distributed computation called CCA. Components in CCA are defined by public interfaces called "ports" which define the endpoints in the communication channels that link an application's components together.

Over the past year a number of companies have defined another approach to designing distributed application based on a concept called "Web Services." A Web Service is a process that provides a network-accessible interface of "services" that is described by an XML specification called WSDL (Web Services Description Language). The Grid Forum is currently working on several projects which allow Grid services to be defined and accessed as webservices.

In this talk we will describe the simple duality that exists between component-based programming and web services. We will also discuss the difficult problems of integrating web services protocols like SOAP into high performance distributed systems.

Design and Implementation of a CORBA Commodity Grid Kit

Snigdha Verma[1], Manish Parashar[1], Jarek Gawor[2] and Gregor von Laszewski[2]

[1] The Applied Software Systems Laboratory,
Department of Electrical and Computer Engineering,
Rutgers University, 94 Brett Road, Piscataway, NJ 08854-8058, U.S.A
{snigdha,parashar}@caip.rutgers.edu
http://www.caip.rutgers.edu/TASSL/CorbaCoG/
[2]Mathematics and Computer Science Division
Argonne National Laboratory, 9700 S. Cass Ave, Argonne, Il, 60440, U.S.A.
{gawor,gregor}@mcs.anl.gov
http://www.globus.org/cog/

Abstract. This paper reports on an ongoing research project aimed at designing and deploying a CORBA Commodity Grid (CoG) Kit. The overall goal of this project is to explore how commodity distributed computing technologies and state-of-the-art software engineering practices can be used for the development of advanced Grid applications. As part of this activity, we are investigating how CORBA can be integrated with the existing Grid infrastructure. In this paper, we present the design of a CORBA Commodity Grid Kit that provides a software development framework for building a CORBA "Grid domain." We then present our experiences in developing a prototype CORBA CoG Kit that supports the development and deployment of CORBA applications on the Grid by providing them access to the Grid services provided by the Globus toolkit.

1. Introduction

The past decade has seen the emergence of computational Grids aimed at enabling programmers and application developers to aggregate resources[1] scattered around the globe. However, developing applications that can effectively utilize the Grid still remains a difficult task. Although, there exist Grid services that enable application developers to authenticate, access, discover, manage, and schedule remote Grid resources, these services are often incompatible with commodity technologies. As a result, it is difficult to integrate these services into the software engineering processes and technologies that are currently used by application developers. Recently, a number of research groups have started to investigate Commodity Grid Kits (CoG Kits) to address this problem. Developers of CoG Kits have the common goal of developing mappings and interfaces between Grid services and a particular

---

[1] In this paper we use resources to collectively refer to computers, data stores, services and applications.

commodity technology (such as Java platform [1] [2], Java Server Pages [3], Python [4], and Perl [5]). We believe that CoG Kits will encourage and facilitate the use of the Grid, while at the same time leveraging the benefits of the commodity technology. Recent years have also seen significant advances in commodity distributed technologies aimed at easing application development in distributed environments. One such technology is the **Common Object Request Broker Architecture (CORBA)** [6] defined by the Object Management Group (OMG). CORBA specifies an open, vendor independent and language independent architecture for distributed application development and integration. Furthermore, CORBA defines a standard interoperability protocol (i.e. GIOP and IIOP) that enables different CORBA implementations and applications to interoperate and be portable across vendors. CORBA has emerged as a popular distributed computing standard and meets the necessary requirements to be considered by application developers as part of the Grid infrastructure. It is therefore natural to investigate the development of a CoG Kit that integrates CORBA with the Grid such that CORBA applications can access (and provide) services on the Grid. Such an integration would provide a powerful application development environment for high-end users and create a CORBA "Grid domain".

This paper presents the design and implementation of a CORBA CoG Kit that provides CORBA application with access to Grid services provided by the Globus toolkit [7]. In this paper we first give a brief overview of the Grid and its architecture and introduce the services and protocols that we intend to integrate within the CORBA CoG Kit. We then briefly outline requirements, advantages and disadvantages of CORBA technologies from the point of view of Grid application developers. Next, we present the architecture of the CORBA CoG Kit, and describe the design, implementation, and application of a prototype. Finally, we conclude our paper and identify the directions of ongoing and future activities.

2. The Grid

The term "Grid" has emerged in the last decade to denote an integrated distributed computing infrastructure for advanced science and engineering applications. The Grid concept is based on coordinated resource sharing and problem solving in dynamic multi-institutional virtual organizations [8]. Grid computing not only provides access to a diverse set of remote resources distributed across different organizations, but also facilitates highly flexible sharing relationships among these resources, ranging from client-server to peer-to-peer. An example of a typical client-server relationship is the classical model where a remote client submits jobs to batch queues for resources at a supercomputer center. An example of peer-to-peer relationship is the collaborative online interaction and steering of remote (distributed) high-end applications and advanced instruments [9].

Grids must support different levels of control ranging from fine-grained access control to delegation and from single user to multi user, and different services such as scheduling, co-allocation and accounting. These requirements are not sufficiently

4

addressed by the current commodity technologies, including CORBA. Although sharing of information and communication between resources is allowed, it is not easy to coordinate the use of distributed resources spanning multiple institutions and organizations. The Grid community has developed protocols, services and tools, which address the issues arising from sharing resources in peer communities. This community is also addressing security solutions that support management of credentials and policies when computations span multiple institutions, secure remote access to resources, information query protocols that provide services for obtaining the configuration and status information about the resources. Because of the diversity of the Grid it is difficult to develop an all-encompassing Grid architecture. Recently, a layered Grid architecture representation has been proposed [8] that distinguishes a

- *fabric layer*, that interfaces to local control including physical and logical resources such as files, or even a distributed file system,
- *connectivity layer*, that defines core communication and authentication protocols supporting Grid-specific network transactions,
- *resource layer*, that allows the sharing of a single resource while using a
- *collective layer* that allows to view resources as collection,
- and an *application layer* that uses the appropriate components of each layer to support applications.

Each of these layers may contain protocols, APIs, and SDKs to support the development of Grid applications. This general layered architecture of the Grid is shown in the left part of Fig. 1.

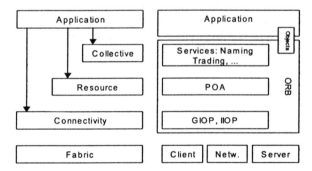

Fig. 1. The Grid Architecture and CORBA (The figure on the left shows the Grid architecture. The figure on the right shows how CORBA fits into the Grid Architecture).

3. CORBA and Grid Computing

CORBA provides advanced capabilities and services for distributed computing and can support the Grid architecture as shown in Fig. 1. Features of CORBA that makes it a suitable candidate for a CoG Kit include its high-level modular programming model, availability of advanced services (e.g. security, naming, trading, event, transaction, etc.) and readymade solutions, interoperability, language independence, location transparency and an open standard supported by industry and academia. The interest in CORBA within the Grid Community has led to a number of efforts aimed at combining functionalities of CORBA and Globus [10]. While most of these efforts address specific problems encountered in individual applications, the goal of this work is to examine the affinities of these two models as well as the breadth of functionality they cover, and to define a consistent set of functionality that would fulfil the needs of CORBA Grid applications.

Integration and interoperability between CORBA and Grid applications/services can be achieved at atleast two levels – a high-level integration where CORBA interfaces are wrapped around Grid services, and a low level integration wherein CORBA services are extended (and new services added) to support Grid applications. While our final solution will combine these approaches, the design and implementation presented in this paper focuses on a high-level integration. Furthermore, the discussion in this paper concentrates on providing CORBA applications access to Grid services. Our approach however, enables true interoperability between CORBA and Grid services.

4. CORBA Interfaces to Globus Grid Services

This section describes the development of CORBA interfaces to Grid services provided by the Globus toolkit [7]. The section focuses on information management, security, remote job submission, and data access services, as these services are elementary and essential to enabling computational Grids and provide the foundation for building more advanced Grid services. The corresponding Globus services are Meta-computing Directory Service (MDS) [11], Grid Security Infrastructure (GSI) [12], Grid Resource Allocation Manager (GRAM) [13] and Globus Access to Secondary Storage (GASS) [14].

4.1 CORBA CoG Kit Architecture

In the overall CORBA CoG Kit architecture, the CORBA ORB (object resource broker) forms the middle-tier providing clients access to CORBA server objects that interface to services on the Grid. Our current implementation provides server objects for the Globus MDS, GSI, GRAM and GASS services. Each of these server objects is a wrapper around the corresponding Globus service. Clients access these server objects using the CORBA naming service, which maps names to object references. The CORBA security service is used for authenticating clients and enabling them to interact securely with server objects. The server objects notify clients of any status changes using the CORBA event service.

4.2 Grid Information Service

The Globus Meta-computing Directory Service (MDS) provides the ability to access and manage information about the state of Grid resources. The current implementation of MDS consists of a distributed directory based on LDAP [15]. A Grid application can access information about the structure and state of the resource through the uniform LDAP API. Information in the MDS is structured using a standard data model consisting of a hierarchy of entities. Each entity is described by a set of "objects" containing typed attribute-value pairs.

4.2.1 The MDSServer Object
The CORBA MDSServer object implements a CORBA object wrapper to MDS providing a simple interface with the following functionality:
1. Establishing connection to the MDS server.
2. Querying the MDS server.
3. Retrieving results from an MDS query.
4. Disconnecting from the MDS server.

The CORBA MDSServer object accesses Globus MDS using JNDI (Java Naming and Directory Interface) [16] libraries, i.e. it essentially replicates the approach used by the Java CoG Kit [1]. Fig. 2 presents the IDL used for this purpose. The data types returned by the calls to the MDSServer are very specific to the JNDI libraries. As CORBA is a language independent middleware, it is necessary to map these specific data types into a generic data type. This is achieved by the structures (i.e. *Result, ListResult, MDSList, MDSResult*) defined within the MDSServer object IDL in Fig. 2. For example, when the *getAttributes()* method is invoked on the CORBA MDSServer object, the JNDI libraries return an array of *NamingEnumeration* objects which have to be mapped into a *Result* data variable. This is done by retrieving the *id* and *attribute* for each *NamingEnumeration* object in this array as string types, and storing the string array as the value variable in the *Result* object. An array of this *Result* object forms the *MDSResult* data variable. Similarly *MDSList* data variable is created by mapping the values returned by the *search()* and *getList()* methods.

```
module MDSService {
   struct Result {string id; sequence<string> value; };
   typedef sequence<Result> MDSResult;
   struct ListResult {string id; MDSResult value; };
   typedef sequence<ListResult> MDSList;

   interface MDSServer {
     exception MDSException{string mdsMessage;
                            string ldapMessage;}};
     void connect(in string name, in long portno,
                  in string username,
                  in string password)
          raises MDSException);
     void disconnect()
          raises (MDSException);
     MDSResult getAttributes(in string dn)
          raises (MDSException);
```

```
        MDSResult getSelectedAttributes (in string dn,
                                     in Attributes attrs)
            raises (MDSException);
        MDSList getList(in string basedn)
            raises (MDSException);
        MDSList search (in string baseDN, in string filter,
                                     in long searchScope)
            raises (MDSException);
        MDSList selectedSearch (in string baseDN, in string
                filter, in Attributes attrToReturn,
                in long searchScope)
            raises (MDSException);
};};
```

Fig. 2. The IDL for accessing CORBA MDS Service.

4.2.2 Grid Domain Trading Service

The CORBA Trader Service is used to store service advertisements from remote objects. In the CORBA CoG Kit, we use the CORBA trader to provide service offers from Grid resources. For example, Fig. 3 presents the interface for a trader that returns information about the number of free nodes at a compute resource. The trader obtains this information from the MDS either using direct access or using the CORBA MDSService. More sophisticated and customized trader services can be similarly defined. These traders provide bridges between different information sources and form the basis for a more sophisticated information service within the Grid. Such a trading server has been successfully prototyped and implemented as part of [10].

```
module GlobusMachineTrader {
    struct MachineType {string dn;  string hn; string
      GlobusContact; long freenodes; long totalnodes;};
    typedef sequence<MachineType>  MachineTypeSeq;
    ...
    interface GetMachineInfofromMDS {
      void update_seq();
      void initialize_trader();
      void update_trader();
      void refresh_trader();
};};
```

Fig. 3. A simple example for a CORBA trader accessing selected MDS information

4.3 Accessing Grid Security

Providing access to Grid security is an essential part of the CORBA CoG Kit. We base our current implementation on the Globus Grid Security Infrastructure (GSI) [12]. GSI provides protocols for authentication and communication and builds on the Transport Layer Security (TLS) protocols. It addresses single sign-on in virtual organizations, delegation, integration with local security solutions, and user-based trust relations, and is designed to overcome cross-organizational security issues.

One can integrate Grid security at various levels of the CORBA architecture. In order to maintain portability across ORBs, we have not considered the modification of the protocol stack in this work, but have placed an intermediary object between the CORBA client and Grid services called the CORBA GSIServer object. This GSIServer object creates a secure proxy object, which allows other server objects, i.e. MDSServer, GRAMServer and GASSServer objects, to securely access corresponding Globus services. The creation of the secure proxy object consists of the following steps:

1. The client and the CORBA server mutually authenticate each other using the CORBA security service (CORBASec) [17][18]. One of the basic requirements for mutual authentication in CORBASec is to have private credentials i.e. a public certificate signed by a trusted certificate authority (CA), at both the client and server side. In our architecture both the CORBA client and server use Globus credentials where the trusted certificate authority is Globus CA.
2. As Globus services, such as gatekeeper [13] and gasserver [14], only accept connections from clients with secure Globus credentials, the CORBA client delegates the GSIServer object to create a secure proxy object that has the authority to communicate with the gatekeeper/gasserver on the clients' behalf.
3. After successful delegation, the GRAMServer and GASSServer objects use the secure proxy object to set up secure connections to the corresponding Globus servers (gatekeeper/gasserver) and access required Globus services.

The process of delegation from the CORBA client to the CORBA GSIServer object involves the following steps. First, the client sends over its public certificate in an encoded form to the server object. Next, the server object generates a completely new pair of public and private keys and embeds the new public key and the subject name from the client certificate in a newly generated certificate request. The certificate request is signed by the new private key and sent across to the client. The client retrieves the public key from the certificate request and embeds it a newly generated certificate. This new certificate is called a proxy certificate. It is signed by the client's original private key (not the one from the newly generated pair), and is sent back to the server object in an encoded form. The server object thus creates a chain of certificates where the first certificate is the proxy certificate, followed by the client certificate and then the certificate of the CA. It can then send this certificate chain to the gatekeeper as proof that it has the right to act on behalf on the client. The gatekeeper verifies the chain by walking through it starting with the proxy certificate, searching for trusted certificates and verifying the certificate signatures along the way. If no trusted certificate is found at the base of the chain the gatekeeper throws a *CertificateException* error. The IDL interface for the GSISever object is shown in Fig 4. Its methods are described below:

• setClientCredentials(): This method is called by the client to send its public certificate to the server in an encoded form. The client can access this method only after mutual authentication has been successful.
• getCertificateRequest(): This method provides the client access to the certificate request generated at the server end.

- setDelegatedCertificate(): Using the certificate request obtained from the server, the client generates a new certificate called the proxy certificate for delegating to the server the right to access the Globus services on its behalf. By invoking this method the client can send this proxy certificate in an encoded form to the server.

```
module GSIService {
  interface GSIServer{
    typedef sequence<octet> ByteSeq;
    void setClientCredentials(in ByteSeq certificate);
    ByteSeq getCertificateRequest();
    void setDelegatedCertificate(in ByteSeq
                                  certificate);
};};
```

Fig. 4. The IDL for accessing CORBA GSI Service.

4.4 Job Submission in a Grid

Remote job submission capabilities are provided by the GRAMServer object using the Globus GRAM service as described below.

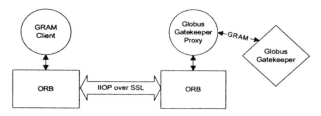

Fig. 5. Accessing a Globus Gatekeeper from a CORBA client.

Job submission using GRAM consists of the following steps: First, the client authenticates with the CORBA server object using CORBASec. After mutual authentication is successful, the client subscribes to the CORBA event channel on which the server is listening. Next the client gets a handle to the GSIServer object from the naming service and delegates the CORBA GSIServer object as described in the process above. Once delegation is successful, the client obtains a reference to GRAMServer object (using the CORBA naming service) and submits a job submission request specifying the name of the executable and the name of the resource on which the job is to be executed. On receiving the request, the GRAMServer uses the secure proxy object created by GSIServer during delegation to set up a secure connection with the GRAM gatekeeper. It then forwards the request to the gatekeeper and waits for status updates from the job via the CORBA event channel. The implementation of the GRAMServer object in the CORBA CoG Kit provides a simple interface with the following methods (see Fig. 6):

- setProxyCredentials() : This method sets the reference to the proxy secure object created by the GSIServer object.
- jobRequest(): This method is used by the client to request a job submission on a remote resource.

Additionally the following data structure is used to monitor the status of the job:

- JobStatus: This data structure is used by the CORBA event service to notify the client of changes in the job status. The structure consists of two string data types – *jobid* and *jobstatus*. *jobid* identifies the id of the submitted job and *jobstatus* is one of the following values – PENDING, DONE, ACTIVE, FAILED, or SUSPENDED.

```
module GRAMService {
    exception GramException{short errorcode;};
    exception GlobusProxyException{short errorcode;};
    struct JobStatus{string jobid;string currstatus;};
        interface GRAMServer{
            void setProxyCredentials();
            void jobRequest(in string rsl, in string
            contact, in boolean batchjob);
};};
```

Fig. 6. The IDL for accessing CORBA GRAM Service

4.5 Data Transfer on the Grid

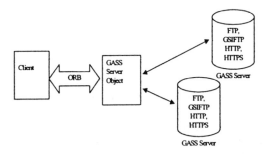

Fig. 7. The CORBA CoG Kit interface to GASS.

A frequent problem that needs to be addressed by Grid applications is access to remote data -- for example, when the application may want to pre-stage data on remote machines, cache data, log remote application output in real time or stage executables on a remote computer. In our current implmentation we use Globus GASS [14] for data transfer between resources on the Grid. The goal of GASS is not to build a general-purpose distributed file system but to support I/O operations commonly required by Grid applications. The strategy employed is to fetch the file and cache it on first read open, and write it to disk when it is closed.

The objective of the CORBA GASSServer object is to provide an interface to the Globus GASS service as shown Fig 7. The client gets a handle to the GASSServer object from the naming service, and then the server object forwards the request to the appropriate GASS servers using the protocol specified by the client. GASS supports FTP, HTTP, HTTPS, and GSIFTP. Both the FTP and GSIFTP protocol allows third-party file transfers; that is they allow file transfers from a sender machine to a receiver machine to be initiated by an third initiator machine. Both the sender and receiver machines have to provide a GASS server. Authentication is performed using GSI. The methods defined by the CORBA GASSServer object is defined in the IDL as shown in Fig. 8.

```
module GASSService {
    interface GASSServer {
        void setProxyCredentials();
        void setSourceURL(in string sourceurl);
        void setDestinationURL(in string destnurl);
        void allowThirdPartyTransfer(in boolean value);
        void URLcopy()
    };
};
```

Fig. 8: The IDL for accessing CORBA GASS Service.

5. Applications

We believe that many applications can benefit from the CORBA CoG Kit presented in this paper. One example is the Numerical Propulsion System Simulation (NPSS) [10], which is part of NASA IPG and provides an engine simulation using computational fluid dynamics (CFD). It consists of 0 to 3-Dimensional engine component models responsible for examining aerodynamics, structures and heat transfer. Previous studies have shown that NPSS's engine components can be encapsulated using CORBA to provide object access and communication from heterogeneous platforms, while at the same time enable coordination of multiple modeling runs across the Grid. In this application a large number of NPSS jobs (1000+) are submitted from a desktop interface using the CORBA CoG Kit. The longer-term goal of the application is to deploy computationally intense (3-Dimensional) NPSS jobs across the Globus-enabled NASA Information Power Grid (IPG). The primary benefit of the CORBA CoG Kit to this project is being able to access Globus functionality directly from the CORBA application.

6. Status

The current implementation of the CORBA CoG Kit provides server objects for MDS, GSI, and GRAM services. The performance of the CoG implementation with different

ORBs is currently being evaluated. We have also made significant progress in integrating the CORBA CoG Kit with DISCOVER[19], a collaboratory for interaction and steering. The current status of the CORBA CoG project and the software can be obtained from http://www.caip.rutgers.edu/TASSL/CorbaCoG/CORBA/.

7. Conclusion

This paper reports on an ongoing project aimed at designing, implementing and deploying a CORBA CoG Kit. The overall goal of this project is to provide a framework that will enable existing Grid Computing Environments and CORBA Service Providers to interoperate. CORBA is an accepted technology for building distributed applications and is widely used and supported by academia and industry. Its features include a high-level modular programming model, availability of advanced services (e.g. security, naming, trading, event, transaction, etc.) and readymade solutions, interoperability, language independence, location transparency and an open standard, making it a suitable candidate for developing Grid applications. Developing a CORBA CoG Kit facilitates this integration. The demand for such a CoG Kit has been expressed by various projects ranging from the creation of CORBA based control systems for advanced instruments to the collaborative interaction and computational steering of very large numerical relativity and fluid dynamics applications. Our current efforts are focused on enabling applications to combine and compose services on the Grid – e.g. combining services provided by Globus, with the collaborative monitoring, interaction, and steering capabilities provided by DISCOVER [19]. For example a scientific application can use CORBA CoG Kit to discover the available resources on the network, use the GRAM Service provided by CoG to run his simulation on the desired high end resource, and use DISCOVER web-portals to collaboratively monitor, interact with, and steering the application.

8. Acknowledgement

We would like to acknowledge Brian Ginsburg, Olle Larsson, Stuart Martin, Steven Tuecke, David Woodford, Isaac Lopez, Gregory J. Follen, Richard Gutierrez and Robert Griffin for their efforts towards providing a C++ based CORBA interface for the NPSS application performed at the NASA Glenn Research Center. We would also like to thank Kate Keahey and Nell Rehn for valuable discussions.
This work was supported in part by the National Science Foundation under Grant Number ACI 9984357 (CAREERS) awarded to Manish Parashar, by the Mathematical, Information, and Computational Sciences Division subprogram of the Office of Advanced Scientific Computing Research, U.S. Department of Energy, under Contract W-31-109-Eng-38; by the Defense Advanced Research Projects Agency under contract N66001-96-C-8523, and by the NASA Information Power Grid program.

9. References

[1]G. v. Laszewski, I. Foster, J. Gawor, and P. Lane, "A Java Commodity Grid Kit," Concurrency and Computation: Practice and Experience, vol. 13, pp. 643-662, Issue 8-9, 2001. http://www.globus.org/cog/documentation/papers/

[2]V. Getov, G. v. Laszewski, M. Philippsen, and I. Foster," Multi-Paradigm Communications in Java for Grid Computing," ACM Communications, October 2001 (to appear). http://www.globus.org/cog/documentation/papers/

[3]"The Grid Portal Development Kit," 2001, http://dast.nlanr.net/Features/GridPortal/.

[4]"The Python CoG Kit," 2001, http://www.globus.org/cog.

[5]"The Perl CoG Kit," 2001, http://hotpage.npaci.edu.

[6] CORBA: Common Object Request Broker Architecture, http://www.omg.org.

[7] I. Foster, and C. Kesselman, "Globus: A Metacomputing Infrastructure," International Journal of Supercomputer Applications, 11(2): pp. 115-128, 1997

[8]I. Foster, C. Kesselman, and S. Tuecke, "The Anatomy of the Grid: Enabling Scalable Virtual Organizations," International Journal of Supercomputing Applications, 2001 (to appear). http://www.globus.org/research/papers/anatomy.pdf.

[9]Y. Wang, F. D. Carlo, D. Mancini, I. McNulty, B. Tieman, J. Bresnahan, I. Foster, J. Insley, P. Lane, G. v. Laszewski, C. Kesselman, M.-H. Su, and M. Thiebaux, "A high-throughput x-ray microtomography system at the Advanced Photon Source," Review of Scientific Instruments, vol. 72, pp. 2062-2068, 2001.

[10] Numerical Propulsion System Simulation NPSS),http://hpcc.lerc.nasa.gov/npssintro.shtml.

[11]K. Czajkowski, S. Fitzgerald, I. Foster, and C. Kesselman, "Grid Information Services for Distributed Resource Sharing," Proc. 10th IEEE International Symposium on High Performance Distributed Computing, August 2001.

[12]I. Foster, C. Kesselman, G. Tsudik, and S. Tuecke, "A Security Architecture for Computational Grids," Proc. 5th ACM Conference on Computer and Communications Security Conference, pp. 83-92, 1998.

[13]K. Czajkowski, I. Foster, N. Karonis, C. Kesselman, S. Martin, W. Smith, and S. Tuecke, "A Resource Management Architecture for Metacomputing Systems," Proc. IPPS/SPDP'98 Workshop on Job Scheduling Strategies for Parallel Processing, 1998.

[14]J. Bester, I. Foster, C. Kesselmaz, J. Tedesco, and S. Tuecke, "GASS: A Data Movement and Access Service for Wide Area Computing Systems," 6th Workshop on I/O in Parallel and Distributed Systems, May 1999.

[15]Netscape Directory and LDAP Developer Central, http://developer.netscape.com/tech/directory/index.html.

[16]JAVA Naming and Directory Interface (JNDI), http://java.sun.com/products/jndi. V1.2.

[17]U. Lang, D. Gollmann, and R. Schreiner, "Security Attributes in CORBA," Submitted to IEEE Symposium on Security and Privacy, 2001.

[18]B. Blakley, R. Blakley, and R. M. Soley, "CORBA Security: An Introduction to Safe Computing With Objects," The Addison –Wesley Object Technology Series

[19]S. Kaur, V. Mann, V. Matossian, R. Muralidhar, and M. Parashar, "Engineering a Distributed Computational Collaboratory," Accepted for publication at the 34th Hawaii Conference on System Sciences, January 2001.

Towards High Performance CORBA and MPI Middlewares for Grid Computing

Alexandre Denis[1], Christian Pérez[2], and Thierry Priol[2]

[1]IRISA/IFSIC, [2]IRISA/INRIA,

Campus de Beaulieu - 35042 Rennes Cedex, France
{Alexandre.Denis,Christian.Perez,Thierry.Priol}@irisa.fr

Abstract. Due to the high level of heterogeneity in a computational Grid, designing a runtime system for such computing infrastructure is extremely challenging, for example regarding the ability to exploit transparently and efficiently various networking technologies. Programming a computational Grid often requires the use of several communication paradigms (RPC, RMI, DSM, Message passing) that have to share these networking resources. This paper presents the first step towards a runtime system that allows efficient communication for various communication-oriented middlewares. We introduce a CORBA implementation that reaches 240 MB/s, which is as far as we know the best CORBA performance. Thus, CORBA can be as efficient as MPI on high performance networks. Moreover, we show that different communication middlewares, like CORBA and MPI, can efficiently co-habit within the same runtime system taking full benefit of various networking resources (SAN to WAN).

1   Programming the Grid

Due to the high level of heterogeneity in a computational Grid, designing a runtime system for such computing infrastructure is extremely challenging. In this paper we focus on a particular facet that a grid runtime has to tackle: managing various communication resources and hiding them so that middlewares can use them transparently and efficiently.

Beside various communication technologies, the design of grid applications requires different middlewares allowing programmers to use programming models that are most suitable for their applications. Although first implementations of Grid infrastructures, such as Globus[8], support mainly the execution of message-based applications, it is foreseen that future grid applications will require much more advanced programming models based on either distributed objects or components. Among such grid applications, multi-physics applications are good examples. They are made of several high-performance simulation codes coupled together to simulate several physics behaviors. Each phenomenon is simulated by a parallel simulation code. This kind of application appears well suited for the Grid because many of its codes need either a parallel machine or a vector supercomputer to run in order to keep the computation time within reasonable bounds. The codes that compose a coupling application are generally independently developed. It appears very constraining to require that all codes are based on the same communication paradigm, like for example MPI to be able to run on a computational grid. We advocate an approach that lets the application designer choose the most suitable communication paradigm. Within a parallel code, it may be MPI, PVM, a distributed shared memory system (DSM), a parallel language like OpenMP[7], etc. The coupling of the simulation codes could be carried out through the use of a Remote Method Invocation mechanism (Java RMI or CORBA) to transfer the control between the simulation codes.

Such an approach requires several communication middlewares to exploit various networking technologies. Depending on the computing resource availability, several simulation codes could be mapped onto a WAN or onto the same parallel machine. In the later case, the RMI mechanism should be able to exploit the underlying network of a parallel machine. Current implementations of existing RMIs (Java RMI or CORBA) do not support such specific network so that the coupling application cannot fully exploit the communication resources.

In this paper, we advocate the choice of the CORBA technology to couple simulation codes. CORBA has some very interesting features. It has been designed for distributed communication. So, it harnesses adequately the heterogeneity of the different computers. Moreover, it offers an object oriented framework. Last, it offers binding for most languages[1]. CORBA has to fulfill two important requirements: efficiency on high speed networks, and interconnect two parallel codes. This paper aims at giving a positive answer to the performance of CORBA on high speed networks.

The answer to the second requirement is twofold. First, the OMG[2] has issued an RFP[14] (Request For Proposal) that solicits proposals to extend CORBA functionality to conveniently and efficiently support parallel processing applications. A response[13] was submitted by a consortium of several industrial companies and a supporting organization. The proposed approach shares some similarities with previous works [10, 16]. Second, we are working on providing similar functionalities – i.e. CORBA support for parallel applications – but based on standard CORBA 2 [6]. Our motivation is that normalization is a long process and it is not clear whether most ORB will implement it.

The remainder of this paper is divided as follows. Section 2 presents the challenges that our approach has to face. In section 3, the first challenge, a high performance CORBA, is overcome. Our second challenge, concurrent support of several middlewares, is the subject of section 4. All these results are gathered in a coherent platform Padico which is sketched in section 5. Then we conclude in section 6.

---

[1] The mapping to FORTRAN9x is not official but a study that has been carried out within the Esprit PACHA project has shown that such a mapping is possible
[2] Object Management Group – the consortium that defines CORBA

2 Communication Issues in a Grid Environment

2.1 Grid Infrastructures

Grid computing infrastructures cover a wide range of machines, going from supercomputer to cluster of workstations. While the former is still a platform of choice for computing-intensive applications, the success of the latter is always growing due to their competitive performance/price ratio. A grid computing middleware must be portable enough to run on every machine of the grid.

The Grid is composed of several kinds of networks: SAN on clusters of workstations (eg. Myrinet, SCI, VIA), dedicated interconnection networks on supercomputers, and WAN. Multi-threading is more and more required by middlewares like MPI or CORBA. Also, it is an efficient paradigm to support concurrently several middlewares. So, it is challenging to design a grid computing runtime system that is both *portable* and *efficient*.

2.2 CORBA

As CORBA is a corner stone of our approach, it is critical to have a high performance CORBA implementation (ORB) able to exploit various networking technologies (from dedicated networks within supercomputers to SAN). However, such an implementation must overcome some challenges.

A high performance CORBA implementation will typically utilize SAN with a dedicated high-performance protocol. It needs to be interoperable with other standard ORBs, and thus should implement both high-speed protocol for SAN and standard IIOP (Internet Inter-Orb Protocol) for interconnecting with other ORBs over TCP/IP. From the application, the high-speed ORB must behave as any other ORB. We aim at using standard CORBA applications on our high-performance ORB. Network adapter selection, protocol selection and address resolution must be automatic and fully hidden.

There is a network model discrepancy between the "distributed world" (eg. CORBA) and the "parallel world" (eg. MPI). Communication layers dedicated to parallelism typically use a static topology[3]: nodes cannot be inserted or removed into the communicator while a session is active. On the other hand, CORBA has a distributed approach: servers may be dynamically started, clients may dynamically contact servers. The network topology is dynamic. It is challenging to map the distributed communication model onto SAN that are biased toward the parallel communication model.

2.3 Supporting Several Middlewares at the Same Time

Supporting CORBA and MPI, *both running simultaneously*, is not not as straightforward as it may seem. Several access conflicts for networking resources

---

[3] PVM and MPI2 address this problem but do not allow network management on a link-per-link basis.

may arise. For example, only one application at a time can use Myrinet through BIP [17]. If both CORBA and MPI try to use it without being aware of each other, there are access conflicts and reentrance issues. If each middleware (eg. CORBA, MPI, a DSM, etc.) has its own thread dedicated to communications, with its own policy, communication performance is likely to be sub-optimal. In a more general manner, resource access should be cooperative rather than competitive.

2.4 Madeleine and Marcel

To face the heterogeneity of the Grid, a portability layer for network and multi-threading management should be adopted. At first look, it may seem attractive to use a combination of MPI and PosixThreads as foundation. However, [4] shows that this solution has drawbacks. To deal with portability as well as low level issues, we choose the Madeleine communication layer [2] and the Marcel multi-threading library [5]. The Madeleine communication layer was designed to bridge the gap between low-level communication interfaces (such as BIP [17], SBP or UNET) and middlewares. It provides an interface optimized for *RPC-like* operations that allows zero-copy data transmissions on high-speed networks such as Myrinet or SCI. Marcel is a multi-threading library in user space. It implements an N:M thread scheduling on SMP architectures. When used in conjunction with Marcel, Madeleine is able to guarantee a good reactivity of the application to network I/O.

3 High Performance CORBA

3.1 Related Works

Previous works have already be done about high performance CORBA. TAO [11] (the ACE ORB) focuses on high performance and real-time aspects. Its main concern is predictability. It may utilize TCP or ATM networks, but it is not targeted to high performance network protocols found on clusters of PCs such as BIP or SISCI. OmniORB2 had been adapted to ATM and SCI networks. Since the code is not publicly available, we only report published results. On ATM, there is a gap of bandwidth between raw bytes and structured data types [15]. The bandwidth can be as low as 0.75 MB/s for structured types. On SCI, results are quite good [12] (156 μs, 37.5 MB/s) for messages of raw bytes; figures for structured types on SCI are not published. CrispORB [9], developed by Fujitsu labs, is targeted to VIA in general and Synfinity-0 networks in particular. Its latency is noticeably better, up to 25 % than with standard IIOP.

OmniORB2 was developed in 1998. In the next version, OmniORB3, there is only TCP support. Support of high-speed networks did not seem promising and thus had been discontinued. CrispORB is interesting but restricted to VIA. TAO is targeted to predictability and quality of service. As far as we know it has not been deployed on high speed networks.

3.2 CORBA Performance Analysis

This section analyzes the performance of available CORBA implementations so as to understand where are the overheads. Copy limitations are also validated thanks to two prototypes on top of high speed networks.

We will first analyze a remote method invocation. The steps are: a) build and send a header to notify to the remote object it has to invoke a method. This is the invocation latency, t_1. b) marshal and send the *in* parameters of the method. This is described by the bandwidth, B_{in}. c) execute the remote method with duration t_{exec}. d) marshal and send the *out* parameters, with bandwidth B_{out}. e) notify to the caller that the remote invocation is finished. The termination notification is t_2.

Our measurements are $RTT = t_1 + t_2$ (round trip time), which is the time needed for the remote invocation of an empty method, and the bandwidth B. If a method takes parameters of size S bytes and is invoked in time T, then $T = RTT + \frac{S}{B}$, and then $B = \frac{T - RTT}{S}$.

Coupled codes of numerical simulation handle huge amounts of data. The bandwidth is thus an important performance factor. It is determined by two factors: the marshaling/demarshaling speed and the network bandwidth.

Marshaling/demarshaling is the action of encoding/decoding data into an interoperable format called CDR – Common Data Representation – in order to put it into GIOP requests. Some ORBs use a straightforward approach; they assemble and disassemble requests by making an explicit copy of all the parameters. Some ORBs use a zero-copy strategy. Depending on the memory bandwidth/network bandwidth ratio, the copy can be a negligible or a very cost effective operation. The overall bandwidth B is given by the formula:

$$B = \frac{1}{\frac{1}{B_{marshal}} + \frac{1}{B_{net}} + \frac{1}{B_{demarshal}}}$$

We realized a minimal, not-fully functional porting of two open-source COR-BA implementation on top of Madeleine : MICO [18] and OmniORB3 [1]. We were then able to measure the performance we could get from a complete implementation. We ran benchmarks on our dual-Pentium II 450 based PC cluster with Ethernet-100, SCI, and Myrinet network adapters.

Table 1 shows the peak bandwidth analysis of MICO. On high-speed networks such as SCI and Myrinet, $\frac{1}{B_{marshal}}$ and $\frac{1}{B_{demarshal}}$ become dominant. Thus, be-

Table 1. MICO's peak bandwidth analysis in MB/s

network	$B_{marshal}$	$B_{demarshal}$	B_{net}	B	$B_{measured}$	$B_{measured}/B_{net}$
Ethernet-100	129	80	12	9.6	9.4	78%
SCI	129	80	86	31	27.7	32%
Myrinet	113	72	99	30.4	26.2	26%

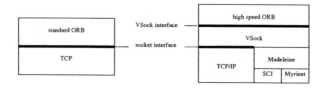

Fig. 1. Porting scheme overview

cause of the high overhead introduced by copies, the overall bandwidth B is only about 30% of the network bandwidth B_{net}.

OmniORB3 does not always copy on marshaling/demarshaling. It implements a "zero-copy" transfer mode and pre-allocated buffers as often as possible. Thanks to this strategy, it can achieve a higher bandwidth, even if theoretically the more complex marshaling methods cause a higher latency. Our OmniORB/Madeleine reaches 86 MB/s on SCI and 91 MB/s on Myrinet. $B_{marshall}$ and $B_{demarshall}$ do not make sense in zero-copy strategy. Overall performance results are given in Section 3.4.

3.3 Porting OmniORB on Top of Madeleine

The previous section has shown that OmniORB3 is well suited for high performance thanks to its efficient marshaling/demarshaling strategy. In this section, we present a complete port of OmniORB3 on top of Madeleine, our approach is to modify OmniORB as little as possible to be able to follow its next versions with virtually no supplementary work. We only modified OmniORB transport and threads layer. Porting the OmniORB thread system on top of Marcel is straightforward since Marcel implements the subset of PosixThreads API that OmniORB needs. For the transport layer, our approach relies on the concept of *virtual socket*, or VSock, as shown on Figure 1. VSock implements a subset of the standard socket functions on top of Madeleine, for achieving high-performance (ie. only datagram, no streaming). It performs zero-copy datagram transfer with a socket-like connection handshake mechanism using standard IP addresses. Then, porting OmniORB on top of VSock is straightforward. We realized a fully-functional porting of OmniORB on top of VSock.

Interoperability Interoperability is one of our main concerns. We need our high-speed ORB to be interoperable with other "non-Madeleine aware" ORBs. This implies the VSock module to be transparent in three ways:

Protocol auto-selection. The CORBA application built on top of the ORB is a standard application. It does not have to know that there are several underlying network protocols. Thus, VSock should automatically select the adequate protocol to use according to the available hardware.

IIOP pass-thru. For interoperability issues, our ORB must be able to communicate with the outside world using the CORBA standard IIOP protocol. VSock should determine itself whether an object may be reached using Madeleine or if it should revert to standard TCP.

Address mapping. Since we do not modify much the ORB, and for compatibility reasons, contact strings are always IP addresses. VSock translates, when needed, IP addresses into Madeleine logical node number using a reverse address resolution table.

VSock's strategy for managing both TCP and Madeleine is the following: when a client tries to connect to a server, it resolves the provided IP address into a Madeleine address. If it fails, then the object is outside the cluster, and it reverts to standard IIOP/TCP. If it succeeds, then it asks the server if this particular object is handled by Madeleine – a machine being in a VSock cluster does not imply that all its CORBA servants are VSock-enabled! This is performed by comparing the corresponding TCP port numbers.

Dynamicity. The network topology of CORBA is dynamic, client-server oriented. The network topology of Madeleine (like most communication library for SAN) is static. A solution is to use a unique bootstrap binary that is started on each node. Thus, it satisfies the "SPMD" approach of the communication library. Then, this bootstrap process dynamically loads the actual application binaries stored into dynamically loadable libraries. Thanks to this mechanism, different binaries can dynamically be loaded into the different nodes of a grid system.

3.4 Performance

The bandwidth of our high-performance CORBA implementation is shown on Figure 2. We ran our benchmark on "old" dual-Pentium II 450 machines, with Ethernet-100, SCI and Myrinet 1, and "up to date" dual-Pentium III 1GHz with Myrinet-2000. The benchmark consists in a remote invocation of a method which takes an *inout* parameter of variable size. The peak bandwidth is 86 MB/s on SCI, 101 MB/s on Myrinet 1 (not shown on figure), and 240 MB/s on Myrinet-2000. This performance is very good. We reach 99 % of the maximum achievable bandwidth with Madeleine.

Figure 2 shows a comparison of the bandwidth of MPI/Madeleine [3] and our OmniORB/Madeleine. For small messages, CORBA is a little slower than MPI, because of the software overhead introduced by the ORB. For larger messages, our CORBA implementation outperforms MPI on SCI and has the same performance than MPI on Myrinet. The overall performance of CORBA is thus comparable to MPI. This validates our approach of using both MPI and CORBA for a better structuration of the applications without performance loss.

On the "old" machines (Pentium II 450, SCI or Myrinet 1), the latency of our CORBA is around 55 μs. It is a good point when compared to the 160 μs latency of the ORB over TCP/Ethernet-100. However, MPI/Madeleine latency is 23 μs. On the "up to date" machines (Pentium III 1GHz, Myrinet-2000), the latency

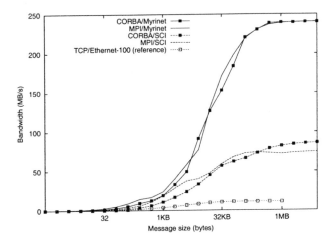

Fig. 2. Bandwidth (in MB/s) of OmniORB and MPICH over SCI and Myrinet-2000

of CORBA is 20 μs where MPI gets 11 μs. This high-performance CORBA uses the GIOP protocol. GIOP is very time-consuming and is not needed inside a homogeneous part of a grid system. CORBA enables us to write other protocols than GIOP, called ESIOP. Thus, to lower the latency, it is possible to write a high performance network ESIOP. However, figures show that the increase of the CPU power narrows the latency gap between CORBA and MPI.

4 Concurrent Support of CORBA and MPI

4.1 Problem Overview

This section exposes the problem of concurrently supporting both CORBA and MPI interface active. An ORB or a MPI implementation, and in a more general way every networkable middleware, takes an exclusive access on the resources. For example, the ORB uses the Myrinet network with the BIP protocol and Marcel threads. It is correct as a standalone package. Assume that MPI uses the Myrinet network with BIP, and Posix threads; it is fine as a standalone package. But, if this ORB and this MPI are used together, several problems arise:

- cluster-oriented protocols (BIP on Myrinet, SISCI on SCI) are most of the time single-user. They cannot be used concurrently by several packages that are not aware of the others;
- an application runs into trouble when mixing several kinds of threads;
- if ever we are lucky enough and there is no resource conflict, there is probably a more efficient way than putting side by side pieces of software that do not see each other and that act in an "egoistic" fashion.

We aim at making it work in a *coherent rather than competitive* way. The main points are: network multiplexing and common thread management.

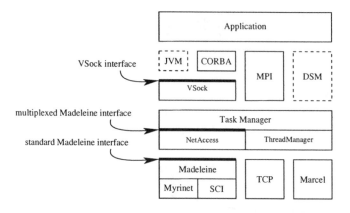

Fig. 3. Concurrent access to resources through a Task Manager

4.2 Network Access

There is a need for a multiplexing method. If both the ORB and MPI access
the network resources without being aware they do not have exclusive access,
there will be conflicts. The ORB is our VSock-based OmniORB; as an MPI
implementation, we choose the Madeleine-based port of MPICH [3] for its good
overall performance and its portability. We manage two level of multiplexing as
shown on Figure 3:

– low-level multiplexing, provided by the Task Manager on top of Madeleine.
  It enables several modules to use Madeleine native communications;
– high-level multiplexing, provided by VSock. It enables several modules to
  use virtual socket on top of Madeleine. VSock itself is a module that uses
  low-level multiplexed Madeleine communications.

Multiplexing on top of Madeleine is performed by adding a tag into headers.
We centralize the global operations such as initialization and channel management. Very few changes have to be done to existing Madeleine-based modules
to obtain multiplexed Madeleine modules. As for the VSock porting, this can be
automated with a script acting on the source code.

4.3 Threads Management

When it comes to multi-threading, every standalone package has its own library,
compatibility layer, and policy. When we put side by side such packages that
are not aware of each other, some problems arise: at best, the efficiency is sub-
optimal; at worst, incompatibilities appear at run-time or compile-time.

We propose that the Task Manager centralizes threads execution, and in
particular threads dedicated to communications. We chose Marcel threads for
their efficiency and good integration with Madeleine. Then, we are able to have
a unified thread policy:

- If every module (ORB, MPI) has its own communication thread, resources are wasted. Latency is increased because of the thread scheduler overhead. The Task Manager runs a *polling thread*. Each module may register its polling action that will be called by the Task Manager. There are, for example, Madeleine callbacks for Madeleine multiplexing.
- Since the Task Manager knows every polling function, it is able to decide on a coherent polling policy. It interleaves the several actions in a coherent way. It adapts the polling frequency to the network performance. For example, control channels are polled less often so that they do not interfere with time-critical data channels. TCP sockets are polled less often than SCI or Myrinet channels since their polling is more time-consuming.

Performance The result of this coherent concurrent support of both CORBA and MPI has a good overall performance. Every level of interface (multiplexed Madeleine, VSock) is zero-copy, thus the bandwidth remains unchanged at any level of multiplexing. Thanks to header piggy-backing, multiplexing does not increase latency. We are able to keep CORBA and MPI at the same performance level as when they were standalone packages as described in Section 3.4.

5 Padico

Padico is our research platform for parallel and distributed computing. In particular, it targets code coupling applications based on the concept of parallel CORBA objects [6]. The runtime environment is called Padico Task Manager, shortened in PadicoTM. The role of PadicoTM is to provide a high performance infrastructure to *plug in* middlewares like CORBA, MPI, JVM, DSM, etc. It offers a framework that deals with communication and threads issues, allowing different middlewares to efficiently share the same process. Its strength is to offer the same interface to very different networks.

The design of Padico, derived from the software component technology, is very modular. Every module is represented as a component: a description file is attached to the binary (in a dynamically loadable library form) that describes it. PadicoTM implements the techniques described in Section 4, namely network multiplexing, provided by the Padico NetAccess module and thread management, provided by the Padico ThreadManager module. Padico NetAccess and Padico ThreadManager, built on top of Madeleine and Marcel, are the core of PadicoTM. Then, services are plugged in PadicoTM core. These services are: a) the virtual socket module VSock, used by CORBA. It may be used by several other modules at the same time; b) the CORBA module, based on OmniORB3, on top of VSock as described in Section 3; c) the MPI module, derived from MPICH/Madeleine [3]; d) a basic CORBA gatekeeper that allows the user to dynamically load modules upon CORBA requests.

Currently, we have a functional prototype with all these modules available. Its performance is reported in Section 3.4. Padico is just in its beginning phase. Several important issues like security, deployment and fault tolerance are not yet addressed.

6 Conclusion

The Grid offers an heterogeneous environment, in particular with respect to communication protocols. At the programming level, it is not realistic to consider all links as similar as they are not. A better solution seems to keep the structure of the applications to have some knowledge about the performance requirement of the links. For example, a parallel MPI code expects low latency and high bandwidth communications while a code coupling communication do not expect to be so efficient. Targeting code coupling applications, our choice is not to constraint the communication paradigm used inside parallel code and to use CORBA for coupling communications. As coupling communications can be mapped on high performance networks, it is important that CORBA could efficiently exploit them. Also, as applications may simultaneously use for example MPI for its internal communications and CORBA for coupling, it is also mandatory that both middlewares efficiently co-habit. This paper shows that both requirements can be fulfilled.

First, this paper has shown that CORBA can be as efficient on high performance network as MPI. We measure 240 MB/s bandwidth for CORBA on top of Myrinet-2000. This is the same bandwidth than MPI. The latency is less than twice the MPI latency. This is mainly due to GIOP related overhead. Second this paper shows that different middlewares can efficiently co-habit in a high performance environment. This paper has given some insight on the different interactions, mainly related to network access and thread issues. This co-habitation has been obtained without loss of efficiency neither for CORBA nor for MPI. These contributions have been integrated into an operational research platform, called Padico.

These works have several perspectives. The first direction is related to CORBA. In order to reduce the latency of CORBA requests, customized CORBA protocol based on ESIOP should be studied. This can be directly be done by porting TAO on top of PadicoTM. The other direction is to plug other middlewares on top of PadicoTM as applications may want other middlewares than MPI. This also allows us to evaluate whether the concepts handled by the PadicoTM layer are adequate to DSM middleware or to Java Virtual Machine middleware. Last, we plan to use Padico as a experimental platform for parallel CORBA objects.

Acknowledgments We would like to thank the PM2 developer team for their efficient support of Madeleine and Marcel.

References

1. AT&T Laboratories Cambridge. OmniORB Home Page. http://www.omniorb.org.
2. O. Aumage, L. Bougé, J.-F. Méhaut, and R. Namyst. Madeleine II: A portable and efficient communication library for high-performance cluster computing. *Parallel Computing*, March 2001. To appear.

3. O. Aumage, G. Mercier, and R. Namyst. MPICH/Madeleine: a true multi-protocol MPI for high-performance networks. In *Proc. 15th International Parallel and Distributed Processing Symposium (IPDPS 2001)*, San Francisco, April 2001. IEEE. To appear.

4. L. Bougé, J.-F. Méhaut, and R. Namyst. Efficient communications in multithreaded runtime systems. In *Parallel and Distributed Processing. Proc. 3rd Workshop on Runtime Systems for Parallel Programming (RTSPP '99)*, volume 1586 of *Lect. Notes in Comp. Science*, pages 468–482, San Juan, Puerto Rico, April 1999. In conj. with IPPS/SPDP 1999. IEEE TCPP and ACM SIGARCH, Springer-Verlag.

5. V. Danjean, R. Namyst, and R. Russell. Integrating kernel activations in a multithreaded runtime system on Linux. In *Parallel and Distributed Processing. Proc. 4th Workshop on Runtime Systems for Parallel Programming (RTSPP '00)*, volume 1800 of *Lect. Notes in Comp. Science*, pages 1160–1167, Cancun, Mexico, May 2000. In conjunction with IPDPS 2000. IEEE TCPP and ACM, Springer-Verlag.

6. A. Denis, C. Pérez, and T. Priol. Portable parallel corba objects: an approach to combine parallel and distributed programming for grid computing. In *Proc. of the Intl. Euro-Par'01 conf.*, Manchester, UK, 2001. To appear.

7. The OpenMP Forum. OpenMP fortran application program interface, version 1.1, November 1999. available from www.openmp.org.

8. I. Foster and C. Kesselman. Globus: A metacomputing infrastructure toolkit. *The International Journal of Supercomputer Applications and High Performance Computing*, 11(2):115–128, Summer 1997.

9. Yuji Imai, Toshiaki Saeki, Tooru Ishizaki, and Mitsushiro Kishimoto. CrispORB: High performance CORBA for system area network. In *Proceedings of the Eighth IEEE International Symposium on High Performance Distributed Computing*, pages 11–18, 1999.

10. K. Keahey and D. Gannon. PARDIS: A Parallel Approach to CORBA. In *Supercomputing'97*. ACM/IEEE, November 1997.

11. F. Kuhns, D. Schmidt, and D. Levine. The design and performance of a realtime I/O subsystem. In *Proceedings of the 5th IEEE Real-Time Technology and Applicati ons Symposium (RTAS99)*, Vancouver, Canada, June 1999.

12. Sai-Lai Lo and S. Pope. The implementation of a high performance ORB over multiple network transports. Technical report, Olivetti & Oracle Laboratory, Cambridge, March 1998.

13. Mercury Computer Systems, Inc. and Objective Interface Systems, Inc. and MPI Software Technology, Inc. and Los Alamos National Laboratory. Data Parallel CORBA - Initial Submission, August 2000.

14. Object Management Group. Request For Proposal: Data Parallel Application Support for CORBA, March 2000.

15. S. Pope and Sai-Lai Lo. The implementation of a native ATM transport for a high performance ORB. Technical report, Olivetti & Oracle Laboratory, Cambridge, June 1998.

16. T. Priol and C. René. COBRA: A CORBA-compliant Programming Environment for High-Performance Computing. In *Euro-Par'98*, pages 1114–1122, September 1998.

17. L. Prylli and B. Tourancheau. Bip: a new protocol designed for high performance networking on myrinet. In *1st Workshop on Personal Computer based Networks Of Workstations (PC-NOW '98)*, Lect. Notes in Comp. Science, pages 472–485. Springer-Verlag, apr 1998. In conjunction with IPPS/SPDP 1998.

18. A. Puder. The MICO CORBA Compliant System. *Dr Dobb's Journal*, 23(11):44–51, November 1998.

An Integrated Grid Environment for Component Applications

Nathalie Furmento, Anthony Mayer, Stephen McGough,
Steven Newhouse, Tony Field, and John Darlington

Imperial College Parallel Computing Centre, Department of Computing,
Imperial College of Science, Technology and Medicine, London, SW7 2BZ, UK
icpc-sw@doc.ic.ac.uk
http://www-icpc.doc.ic.ac.uk/components/ **

Abstract. Computational grids present many obstacles to their effective exploitation by non-trivial applications. We present a grid middleware, implemented using Java and Jini, that eliminates these obstacles through the intelligent use of meta-data relating to the structure, behaviour and performance of an application. We demonstrate how different problem sizes and selection criteria (minimum execution time or minimum cost) utilise different implementations for the optimal solution of a set of linear equations.

1 Introduction

Computational grids, federations of geographically distributed heterogeneous hardware and software resources, are emerging in academia, between national research labs and within commercial organisations. Eventually, these computing resources will become ubiquitous and appear transparent to the user, delivering computational power to applications in the same manner as electrical energy is distributed to appliances through national power grids [1]. This can only be achieved when an application is fully integrated with the *grid middleware* which provides access to the underlying hardware and software resources.

The grid middleware has to mask the heterogeneous nature of the resources and provide:

- **A secure execution environment** that is scalable in terms of the number of users and resources.
- **Virtual organisations**, formed through the federation of real resources. Resource owners will only contribute their resources to these federations if they are able to ensure access to their own local community [2].
- **Information** relating to the grid's resources, the application's performance and behaviour and the user's and resource provider's requirements.
- **Effective resource exploitation** by exploiting information relating to the structure, behaviour and performance of the application.

** Research supported by the EPSRC grant GR/N13371/01 on equipment provided by the HEFCE/JREI grants GR/L26100 and GR/M92455

In this paper, we present an overview of a grid middleware that supports resource federation through locally defined access and usage policies and the exploitation of application meta-data to optimise execution. The paper makes the following contributions:

1. We describe a federated grid architecture, implemented using Java and Jini, which supports management of a collection of computational resources and which provides scalable secure access to those resources by registered users.
2. We present a component-based application development framework which associates performance meta-data with each component enabling composite performance models to be built for complete applications.
3. We show how application performance models can be used within the grid framework to determine optimal resource selection under minimum resources cost and minimum execution time constraints.

2   Federated Grid Architecture

2.1   Overview

To support our grid related research activities into application composition and resource exploitation, we have defined a middleware that supports the federation of hardware and software resources [3] as shown in Figure 1. Central to our grid architecture is the notion of a public Computational Community. It represents a virtual organisation (comprising individuals and organisations with a common goal) to which real organisations can contribute their resources. These are made available to all users, satisfying access control restrictions specified by the resource provider through the Computational Community. Information relating to the resources in the Computational Community (such as the current resource load, operating system, access and usage policies, etc.) are accessed through a published API or a GUI such as the Resource Browser by the user. At this level, the functionality of the Resource Browser is comparable to that of a federated virtual machine room [4].

The resources within an organisation are managed through a private Administrative Domain by the Resource Manager. Static and dynamic attributes on each resource provide information on demand to services in the Computational Community (e.g. the Application Mapper). This information service is critical to resource selection and updates can be pulled on demand to the services in the Computational Community. The Domain Manager acts as a gateway between the public and private areas of the grid middleware, the Administrative Domain and Computational Community, by enforcing the locally defined access and usage policies. Authentication of the resource request is delegated to the Identity Manager which is described in Section 3.1.

The Computational Community on its own provides a low-level homogeneous interface to the grid's heterogeneous resources that is similar to Globus's toolkit of services [2] and Legion's object model [5]. Our infrastructure provides a toolkit of software objects that can be extended and specialised by the user to provide

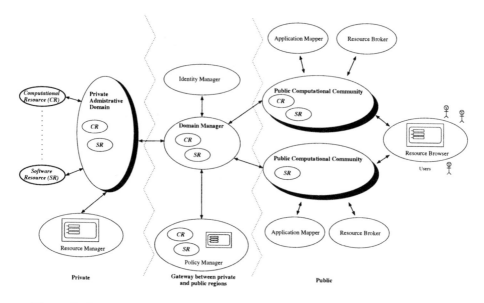

Fig. 1. Building a public Computational Economy through Federated Resources.

higher level services such as an Application Mapper (to generate optimal application decomposition) and a Resource Broker (to maximise throughput using computational economics).

2.2 Implementation

This architecture is being implemented using a combination of Java [6] and Jini [7]. Jini's leasing mechanism allows transient grid resources, represented by Java objects, to connect and re-connect over time while allowing unexpected failures to be handled gracefully. We use Jini's look-up server to provide dynamic registration of grid objects in the public Computational Communities and private Administrative Domains. This behaviour could also be achieved, for example, through the use of an LDAP server [8]. The initial stages of this work were described in [9] and are expanded in this paper. Other Java computing infrastructures such as Javelin [10], Popcorn [11] (using computational economics) and those based on Jini [12] have not addressed the usage and access policies which are essential in building virtual organisations.

3 Security Infrastructure

3.1 Authentication

All user interaction with the private Administrative Domain from the Computational Community has to pass through the Domain Manager. The authentication of the users (their identity, organisation and group memberships) is delegated

```
<identificationOrganisation publish="jini://jini.doc"
    name="ICPC" keystore="./data/security/keystore.ICPC">
  <group name="ala">
    <user name="aem3Signed"/>
    <user name="nfurSigned"/>
    <user name="sjn5Signed"/>
  </group>
  <group name="ra">
    <user name="asm100Signed"/>
    <user name="sjn5Signed"/>
  </group>
  <knownOrganisation name="rwth"/>
  <knownOrganisation name="inria"/>
</identificationOrganisation>
```

Fig. 2. Example of a Identity Manager XML configuration file.

by the Domain Manager to a trusted Identity Manager. The user's identity and organisation are encapsulated within an X509 certificate [13] associated with the resource request. No transport level security is currently implemented, however several SSL implementations exist for Java. The Identity Manager therefore has two roles: to authenticate users and to act as a Certification Authority by issuing certificates to its local user community. In doing so, it maintains a list of local users which is used to group individuals within the organisation and to mark certificates as revoked if an user leaves an organisation.

The configuration is maintained as a disk-based XML schema which lists the trusted organisations, local individuals and the membership of each group within the organisation. The example in Figure 2 shows an organisation (ICPC) with 4 users split into 2 groups (ala and ra). Users from two trusted non-local organisations (rwth and inria) are accepted by the Identity Manager. The certificates of the trusted organisations are exchanged through off-line resource sharing agreements or are a recognised Certification Authority.

A user's X509 certificate contains the public parts of their own key signed by a succession of other organisations (Certification Authorities). The Identity Manager compares these signatures with those of the local organisation and the known trusted organisations (see point (1) in Figure 3). If no match is found, the authentication fails. Following validation of the organisation's signature on the user's certificate by the local Identity Manager, authentication then passes to the known Identity Manager of the trusted non-local organisation to retrieve the user's group memberships and to validate if the user is still part of the organisation (see point (2) in Figure 3). These responses (see point (3) in Figure 3) are stored in a time-limited cache to reduce inter-organisation authentication traffic. Finally, the Identity Manager returns to the Domain Manager an authenticated user, groups and organisation identities (see point (4) in Figure 3). The Identity Manager sits outside the private Administrative Domain but is administered, like the Domain Manager, by the local organisation and will only interact with known and trusted Identity Managers. This ensures that no user interaction takes place with the private Administrative Domain until the user is authenticated and the request authorised.

30

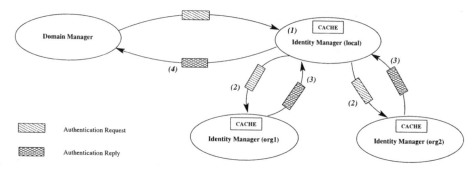

Fig. 3. Authentication Flows between the Domain Manager and the Identity Manager(s).

3.2 Authorisation

The Domain Manager uses the authenticated user, groups and organisation entities to determine if the request complies with the local access and usage policy. A simplified access control policy has already been implemented that accepts or rejects a request on the basis of the user, group or organisation [14]. The policy can be applied throughout the week or be restricted to specific periods. This functionality will be extended to include polices based on the number and identity of remote users (e.g. no more than 5 users from the Physics department) or the current resource load (e.g. if the utilisation is less than 50% then accept remote users). The Domain Manager allows the formulation of fine-grained control policies to specify how local and non-local users are permitted to use the resources.

3.3 Execution

After the Domain Manager has authenticated and authorised the request, it is passed to the resource. A request to access a resource's dynamic attribute (defined in Section 2.1) is fulfilled by the Domain Manager invoking the attribute's service function (e.g. Remote Method Invocation server to return the current queue status) and passing the result back to the Computational Community. If the request requires access to a computational resource, a session is provided through a secure shell (ssh) implementation [15]. The Domain Manager uses a pool of standard user accounts to provide access to the computational resource. A session can be mapped to a specific account (if the incoming request is from a local user) or to a generic account (from the available guest accounts) if one is available. The guest accounts are stateless with files staged in and out of the account before and after each session depending on the user's request. Any authenticated and authorised user from a remote organisation is able to gain access to a computational resource without having a specified account on each of the available resources. This is essential if any grid computing system is to scale.

On startup, all jobs have access to their own execution plan. This allows user specified configuration information to be passed into the application. If a job

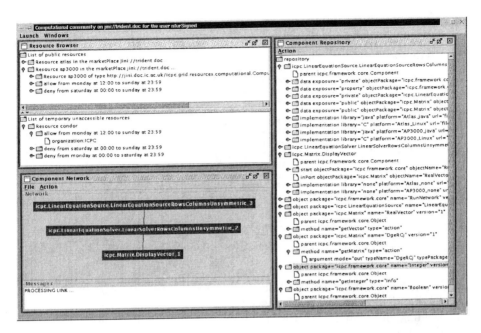

Fig. 4. Building a Component Network from the Resource Component Repositories.

spans multiple resources in potentially several Administrative Domains, it will be able to extract the location of the other distributed components from the execution plan and initiate contact with the other components.

4 The Computational Community

The Resource Browser is the primary user interface to the resources within the Computational Community. See the top left quadrant of Figure 4. On start up, the Resource Browser uses Jini's automatic discovery and join protocols to find a local Computational Community. Alternatively, the Jini URL relating to the Computational Community can be specified explicitly. Depending on the user's identity, a resource within the Computational Community will be:

1. *Available* - it will be shown with all of its public attributes and resource related information. The users are able to obtain the current value of each displayed dynamic attribute or to request a direct connection to the resource.
2. *Temporary unavailable* - the access policies relating to the resource, which the user is currently unable to satisfy, will be shown. The users therefore know when they will be allowed to access the resource.
3. *Always unavailable*, no information about this resource is shown to the users as they will never be permitted access to the resource.

For users to access resources within the Computational Community through a Resource Browser, they need a valid X509 certificate. This is obtained by:

```
<application>
 <network>
  <instance componentName="DisplayVector" componentPackage="icpc.Matrix" id="1"/>
  <instance componentName="LinearSolverRowsColumnsUnsymmetric"
        componentPackage="icpc.LinearEquationSolver" id="2"/>
  <instance componentName="LinearEquationSourceRowsColumnsUnsymmetric"
        componentPackage="icpc.LinearEquationSource" id="3">
   <property name="unknowns">10</property>
  </instance>
  <dataflow sinkComponent="2" sinkPort="unknowns"
        sourceComponent="3" sourcePort="unknowns"/>
  <dataflow sinkComponent="2" sinkPort="matrix"
        sourceComponent="3" sourcePort="matrix"/>
  <dataflow sinkComponent="2" sinkPort="vector"
         sourceComponent="3" sourcePort="vector"/>
  <dataflow sinkComponent="1" sinkPort="vector"
         sourceComponent="2" sourcePort="solution"/>
 </network>
</application>
```

Fig. 5. The XML definition of a Component Network.

1. Generating a certificate and the associated Certificate Signature Request (CSR) with a Certificate Manager tool,
2. Sending the CSR file to the administrator of their local organisation (or Certification Authority),
3. Importing the reply - a signed certificate - into their own certificate database.

The definition and membership of groups is currently controlled by the organisation's local administrator and maintained within the Identity Manager. To ensure unique group names between organisations, each name is appended with the organisations domain name e.g staff@doc.ic.ac.uk.

Any organisation can contribute a resource to a Computational Community (if it is already registered within their private Administrative Domain) by supplying their Domain Manager with the URL of the Jini look-up service and by defining their local access and usage policies.

5 Application Specification

5.1 Component eXtensible Markup Language

The key to the effective mapping of an application to heterogeneous computational resources is an understanding of its structure and behaviour. Application structure is exposed through the use of a component-based design pattern in its specification. To support this aspect of our work, we have defined a Component eXtensible Markup Language (CXML) that encapsulates meta-data describing the application structure. There are three distinct classes of meta-data described by the CXML.

Application Specification Document. This CXML document represents an application, consisting of component instances and connectors indicating the composition of the instances (through a simple port mechanism) and of their properties. Figure 5 shows an application network with three component instances, one with a user customised property, that declares the data flows between components.

Repository Data: Interfaces & Behaviour. Each abstract component type is defined by its interface and behaviour. The interface indicates how the component may be composed with others, and what data is accessible. The behaviour of the component is the explicit context dependencies of the component's methods, i.e. a limited semantics of the dependencies between a component's ports. This information together with default values for properties is described in CXML and stored within the repository.

Repository Data: Implementations. Alongside the abstract component definitions is the meta-data for the component implementations. This includes binding code and performance models relating execution time and memory usage to data size for the implementation's methods.

The details of both the component mechanism and the CXML used to encapsulate the component meta-data are discussed in [14, 16]. The separation between component interface and implementation allows the composite application to be deployed across multiple platforms, and enables the selection of the most appropriate implementation for the given resource environment. The choice of implementation and platform is determined by performance modelling. In general an application is an assembly of fine grain components, it is possible to build a composite performance model of a complete application by examining the behaviour specification of the components and composing their individual performance models.

5.2 Composition

We have developed a visual programming environment that enables users to define their component application. The components and implementations installed on a local resource are made available to the Computational Community through a dynamic attribute. The current contents of each local Component Repository (provided by the dynamic attribute) are used to build a global Component Repository representing all the available and accessible components within the Computational Community. This community-wide Component Repository allows the users to build their application by dragging the components from the "Component Repository" window to the "Component Network" one. (Figure 4)

The users are able to build an application from the components in the Component Repository without having to know on which resources the implementations exist. If the same component is available with different implementations on more than one resource, the component will only appear once in the "Component Repository" window. The composed application is matched to the available implementations (and their corresponding resources by the Application Manager). This process is discussed in the following section.

```
<application>
 <network>
  <instance componentName="DisplayVector" componentPackage="icpc.Matrix" id="1">
   <implementation library="java" platform="java" url="file:."
        className="icpc.DisplayVector" resource="hotol@jini://jini.doc"/>
  </instance>
  <instance componentName="LinearSolverRowsColumnsUnsymmetric"
        componentPackage="icpc.LinearEquationSolver" id="2">
   <implementation library="C" platform="Linux" url="file:."
        className="icpc.LinearEquationSolver.DgeRCluC_EO"
        resource="hotol@jini://jini.doc" />
  </instance>
  <instance componentName="LinearEquationSourceRowsColumnsUnsymmetric"
        componentPackage="icpc.LinearEquationSource" id="3">
   <implementation library="C" platform="Linux" url="file:."
        className="icpc.LinearEquationSource.DgeRCddC_EO"
        resource="hotol@jini://jini.doc"/>
   <property name="unknowns">10</property>
  </instance>
  <dataflow> .... </dataflow>
  ....
 </network>
</application>
```

Fig. 6. The Execution Plan for a Component Network.

6 Application Execution

The preceding sections have demonstrated how we can build up meta-data relating to the resources in the Computational Community, the structure of a component application and the available component implementations. We are now able to exploit this rich meta-data to optimally distribute the application within the Computational Community.

This process starts with the user placing the CXML definition of their application (as shown in Figure 5) into the Computational Community for analysis by the Application Mapper(s). The Application Mapper constructs a global Component Repository from the resources in the Computational Community which it matches with the CXML application definition to find implementations that produce viable execution plans. The execution plan shown in Figure 6 extends the definition of the component network by adding to each instance the selected implementation. In this example, the Application Mapper has selected a C implementation of each component on the Linux machine hotol.

The execution plans are scored according to both the user's criteria (e.g. minimum execution time) and resource provider's criteria (e.g. resource access and loading). The users can either select one of the better execution plans generated by the Application Mapper or automatically execute the best plan.

Our initial implementation of an Application Mapper performs an exhaustive search on all feasible implementation options on all of the available resources. We find the best combination of component implementations for this specific instance of the application by incorporating information such as the specified problem size [14,16]. An alternative approach to application partitioning, used by the AppLeS project, is to define the resource and user constraints as a linear programming problem and maximise a user supplied objective function [17].

Both approaches can also be used to configure the best implementation to yield optimal performance by selecting, for example, matrix blocking size and parallel data partitioning.

7 Demonstration

We illustrate the use of the complete grid environment with an example for solving a system of linear equations. Such computation regularly occurs in a wide range of scientific computing problems. When this application is represented as a component system, it consists of three component instances: a simple linear equation generator, a solver, and a display component. These components are connected as shown in the lower left quadrant of Figure 4.

Having defined the component network, the Application Mapper automatically selects the best algorithm, implementations and resource from those that are available within the Computational Community for various problem sizes. The AP3000 is an cluster of Sun SPARC Ultra II 300MHz processors running Solaris 2.6 with a proprietary Fujitsu interconnect. Atlas is a cluster of EV67 Alpha processors with a proprietary Quadrics interconnect running Tru64 Unix. Hotol is a 800MHz AMD processor Linux machine running Redhat 6.2.

Two cost models were evaluated. In both cases the relative costs of the different systems were based on the cost of a single processor on the AP3000. The Linux machine (hotol) was set to 80% of the cost of a processor on the AP3000 in both models to bias small jobs towards this system. The cost of each processor on Atlas was set to 475% (Cost Model 1) and 425% (Cost Model 2) of the cost of a processor on the AP3000. The best execution time and resource cost required to solve a system of linear equations is shown in Figures 7 and 8 (key to symbols in Table 1) for two different selection policies: minimum execution time and minimum resource cost. It can be seen in Figure 7 that different resource costs (an inevitable consequence of any demand driven computational economy) result in the selection of different implementations on different resources if the overall costs are to be minimised. The two graphs show that minimising cost produces significantly longer (on average 5 times) execution times while minimising execution time increases the resource cost (on average 1.6 times) with the current cost models.

Symbol	Source Implementation	Solver Implementation	Processors
◇	C	Hotol, BCG	1
+	Java	AP3000, BCG	4
□	Java	AP3000, BCG	9
×	Java	AP3000, BCG	16
○	Java	Atlas, BCG	1
△	Java	Atlas, BCG	4
⋆	Java	Atlas, BCG	9
∘	Java	Atlas, BCG	16
•	C	Atlas, BCG	16

Table 1. Key to Graphs.

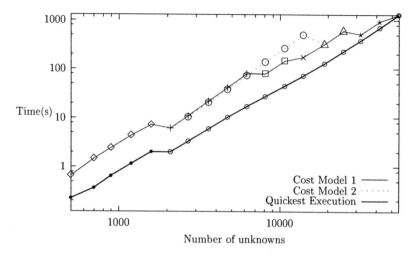

Fig. 7. Execution Time for the Composite Application Network with Different Number of Unknowns.

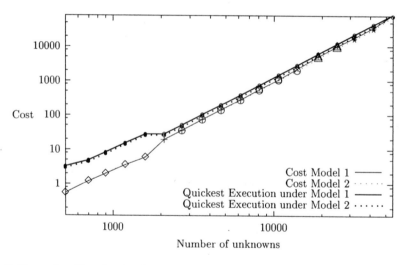

Fig. 8. Execution Cost for the Composite Application Network with Different Number of Unknowns.

8 Summary & Future Work

We have shown how the integration between the application and grid middleware is essential in the effective exploitation of grid resources from both the user's and resource provider's perspective. We use Java and Jini to build a fault tolerant grid middleware that supports the federation of resources into a Computational Community while the local organisation retains full control of access and usage policy. We have illustrated how the optimal solution of a set of linear equations with various implementations is dependent on both the resource selection criteria and the overall problem size.

The Computational Community will be extended to include an Application Mapper based on solving the resource allocation problem as an integer linear programming problem (e.g. [17]). We will also be implementing Computational Economics through a Resource Broker and banking system to explore resource pricing within high throughput federated grid environments. This work will continue with motivating applications in high throughput computing and distributed supercomputing applications.

References

1. I. Foster and C. Kesselman, editors. *The Grid: Blueprint for a New Computing Infrastructure.* Morgan Kaufmann, July 1998.
2. I. Foster, C. Kesselman, and S. Tuecke. The Anatomy of the Grid: Enabling Scalable Virtual Organizations. *Intl. J. Supercomputer Applications*, 2001.
3. S. Newhouse and J. Darlington. Computational Communities: A Market Place for Federated Resources. In *High-Performance Computing and Networking, HPCN*, volume 2110 of *LNCS*, pages 667–674, 2001.
4. The Virtual Machine Room. http://www.ncsa.uiuc.edu/SCD/Alliance/VMR/.
5. A. S. Grimshaw and W. A. Wulf *et al.* The Legion vision of a Worldwide Virtual Computer. *Communications of the ACM*, 40:39–45, 1997.
6. K. Arnold, J. Gosling, and D. Holmes. *The Java Programming Language.* Addison-Wesley, 3rd edition, 2000.
7. Sun Microsystems. Jini(tm) network technology. http://java.sun.com/jini/.
8. OpenLDAP Project. http://www.openldap.org.
9. N. Furmento, S. Newhouse, and J. Darlington. Building Computational Communities for Federated Resources. Accepted for Euro-Par 2001.
10. M. O. Neary, B. O. Christiansen, P. Cappello, and K. E. Schauser. Javelin: Parallel computing on the Internet. In *Future Generation Computer Systems*, volume 15, pages 659–674. Elsevier Science, October 1999.
11. O. Regev and N. Nisan. The Popcorn Market - Online Markets for Computational Resources. In *The 1st Int. Conference On Information and Computation Economies. Charleston SC*, 1998.
12. Z. Juhasz and L. Kesmarki. Jini-Based Prototype Metacomputing Framework. In *Euro-Par 2000*, pages 1171–1174, 2000.
13. Sun Microsystems. X.509 certificates. http://java.sun.com/products/jdk/1.2/docs/guide/security/cert3.html.
14. N. Furmento, A. Mayer, S. McGough, S. Newhouse, and J. Darlington. A Component Framework for HPC Applications. Accepted for Euro-Par 2001.
15. Mindterm, the java secure shell client. http://www.mindbright.se/mindterm/.
16. N. Furmento, A. Mayer, S. McGough, S. Newhouse, and J. Darlington. Optimisation of Component-based Applications within a Grid Environment. Accepted for SuperComputing 2001.
17. H. Dail, G. Obertelli, F. Berman, R. Wolski, and A. Grimshaw. Application-Aware Scheduling of a Magnetohydrodynamics Application in the Legion Metasystem. In *The 9th Heterogeneous Computing Workshop*, May 2000.

KNOWLEDGE GRID : High Performance Knowledge Discovery Services on the Grid

Mario Cannataro[1], Domenico Talia[2], Paolo Trunfio[1]

[1]ISI-CNR
Via P. Bucci, cubo 41-C
87036 Rende (CS), Italy
cannatar@si.deis.unical.it
trunfio@si.deis.unical.it

[2]DEIS
Università della Calabria
Via P. Bucci, cubo 41-C
87036 Rende (CS), Italy
talia@deis.unical.it

Abstract. Knowledge discovery tools and techniques are used in an increasing number of scientific and commercial areas for the analysis of large data sets. When large data repositories are coupled with geographic distribution of data, users and systems, it is necessary to combine different technologies for implementing high-performance distributed knowledge discovery systems. On the other hand, computational grid is emerging as a very promising infrastructure for high-performance distributed computing. In this paper we introduce a software architecture for parallel and distributed knowledge discovery (PDKD) systems that is built on top of computational grid services that provide dependable, consistent, and pervasive access to high-end computational resources. The proposed architecture uses the grid services and defines a set of additional layers to implement the services of distributed knowledge discovery process on grid-connected sequential or parallel computers.

1   Introduction

Data and information stored in computers is growing at a very fast rate. Computer-based data sources contain a huge amount of information that it makes hard to deal with. Often it is very complex to understand what is the important and useful information in data. To sift large data sources, computer scientists are designing software techniques and tools that can analyze data to find useful patterns in them. These techniques contribute to define the so called *knowledge discovery in databases* (*KDD*) process. The basic component of the KDD process is *data mining*: a set of methods for the semi-automatic discovery of patterns, associations, changes, anomalies, events and semantically significant structures in data. Typical examples of data mining tasks are data classification and clustering, event and values prediction, association rules discovery, and episodes detection [3].

Early attempts to automate the process of knowledge extraction date from at least the 1980s, with the work on statistical expert systems. Today new techniques, such as rule induction, neural networks, bayesian networks and genetic algorithms are used.

The size of data sources mean that we cannot do detailed analysis unaided, but must use fast computers, applying sophisticated software tools from statistics to artificial intelligence. Today data mining is used in commerce, scientific data analysis, banking, medicine and economics with very interesting, and sometime surprising, outcomes. Industries, finance companies, public administrations, scientific laboratories and Web-based enterprises are benefiting from this technology. They are gaining positions over competitors by discovering knowledge in their own databases.

Recently, several KDD systems have been implemented on parallel computing platforms to achieve high performance in the analysis of large data sets that are stored in a single site. However, KDD systems that must be able to handle and analyze multi-site data repositories. The combination of large data set size, geographic distribution of data, users and resources, and computationally intensive analysis demand for a parallel and distributed data management and analysis infrastructure for *parallel and distributed knowledge discovery* (PDKD).

Advances in networking technology and computational infrastructure made it possible to construct large-scale high-performance distributed computing environments, or *computational grids* that provide dependable, consistent, and pervasive access to high-end computational resources. These environments have the potential to fundamentally change the way we think about computing, as our ability to compute will no longer be limited to the resources we currently have on our desktop or office. The term *computational grid* refers to an emerging infrastructure that enables the integrated use of remote high-end computers, databases, scientific instruments, networks, and other resources. Grid applications often involve large amounts of computing and/or data. For these reasons, we think grids can offer an effective support to the implementation and use of PDKD systems.

Recently have been proposed a few PDKD systems that address knowledge discovery issues in a distributed framework, however at the best of our knowledge, there is no work in designing an integrating PDKD architecture that makes of use of the *grid computing* resources for data-mining petabyte-scale applications that both address high-performance and wide area operations.

This paper introduces and discusses a reference software architecture for geographically distributed PDKD systems called *Knowledge Grid*. The proposed architecture is built on top of a computational grid that provides dependable, consistent, and pervasive access to high-end computational resources. The proposed architecture uses the basic grid services and defines a set of additional layers to implement the services of distributed knowledge discovery on world wide connected computers where each node can be a sequential or a parallel machine. The *Knowledge Grid* enables the collaboration of scientists that must mine data that are stored in different research centers as well as executive managers that must use a knowledge management system that operates on several data warehouses located in the different company establishments.

The paper aims to represent an initial step towards the design and implementation of a PDKD architecture that integrate data mining techniques and computational grid resources. The rest of the paper is organized as follows. Section 2 discusses the requirements of parallel and distributed data mining on grids and what basic services the grid offers as basic support for PDKD. Section 3 describes the *Knowledge Grid* architecture and defines the features and services of each layer of the proposed architecture. Section 4 describes related existing approaches in the implementation of PDKD systems. Section 5 presents the current status of implementation of our architecture. Section 6 describes a simple case study and section 7 draws some conclusions.

2   Parallel and Distributed Data Mining on Grids

Traditional sequential KDD typically requires local (central) storage of data, which may not always be stored in a single repository. Their collection in some cases is not feasible because of their large size, limited network bandwidth, security concerns, scalability problems, or just because they are have different owners or are geographically distributed. PDKD is the application of the KDD techniques to distributed, large, possibly heterogeneous, volumes of data that are residing over computing nodes distributed on a geographic area. Several parallel algorithms for single data mining tasks such as classification, clustering and rules association have been designed in the past years. However, it lacks a proposal for integrated environments that use novel computing platforms to support PDKD environments that integrate different sources, models, and tools.

Parallel and distributed knowledge discovery is based on the use of high-bandwidth communication networks and high-performance parallel computers for the mining of data in a distributed and parallel fashion. This technology is particularly useful for large organizations, environments and enterprises that manage and analyze data that are geographically distributed in different data repositories or warehouses [5]. The *Grid* has recently emerged as an integrated infrastructure for high-performance distributed computation. Grid applications often involve large amounts of data and/or computing, and are not easily handled by today's Internet and Web infrastructures. Grid middleware targets technical challenges in such areas as communication, scheduling, security, information, data access, and fault detection [11]. However, mainly because of the recent availability of grid middleware, till today no efforts are devoted to the development of PDKD tools and services on the computational grid. Because of the importance of data mining and grid technologies, it is very useful to develop data mining environments on grid platforms by deploying grid services for the extraction of knowledge from large distributed data repositories. The only effort that has been done in the direction of data intensive applications on the grid is the *Data Grid* project that aims to implement a data management architecture based on two main services: storage system and metadata management [2]. This project is not concerned with data mining issues, but its basic services could be exploited to implement higher-level grid services for knowledge discovery from large and distributed data repositories such as the ones we intend to develop.

Motivated by these considerations, we designed a reference software architecture, which we call the *Knowledge Grid*, for the implementation of PDKD systems on top of grid toolkits such as Globus and Legion. We attempt to overcome the difficulties of wide area, multi-site operation by exploiting the underlying grid infrastructure that provides basic services such as communication, authentication, resource management, and information. To this end, we organize the *Knowledge Grid* architecture so that more specialized data mining tools are compatible with lower-level grid mechanisms and also with the *Data Grid* services. This approach benefits from "standard" grid services that are more and more utilized and offers an open PDKD architecture that can be configured on top of grid middleware in a simple way. In the following two subsection we first identify the main requirements of the framework we propose, then list the generic grid services, with a particular emphasis on Globus that can be used in the implementation of the *Knowledge Grid* operations.

2.1   Requirements

Here we identify the basic principles that motivate the architecture design of the grid-aware PDKD system we propose.

1. *Data heterogeneity and large data size*
   The system must be able to cope with very large and high dimensional data sets that are geographically distributed and stored in different types of repositories as structured data in DBMS, text in files or semi-structured data in Web sites.

2. *Algorithm integration and independence*
   The architecture must allow the integration of different data mining algorithms and suites and must be as independent as possible from the data mining algorithms used for knowledge extraction. A data interface that is orthogonal to the data mining tools so that data access will be uniform is to be defined.

3. *Compatibility with grid infrastructure and grid awareness*
   The higher levels of the architecture use the basic grid services for implementing wide area communication, cooperation and resource management of a PDKD system. Thus the data mining services are interfaced with the lower levels of the grid infrastructure. The interface is aware of the grid services and accesses them for supporting the data mining components in the distributed execution of knowledge discovery tasks.

4. *Openness*
   The system architecture must be open to the integration of new data mining tools and knowledge discovery packages. Sequential and parallel analysis models will be added to extend the knowledge discovery services without affecting the lower levels of the *Knowledge Grid* architecture.

5. *Scalability*
   The architecture must be scalable both in terms of number of nodes used for performing the distributed knowledge discovery tasks and in terms of performance achieved by using parallel computers to speed up the mining task.

6. *Security and data privacy*
   Security and privacy issues are vital features in wide area distributed systems. The grid services offer a valid support to the PDKD system to cope with user authentication, security and privacy of data. Basic grid functionality (e.g., Globus security infrastructure - GSI) are able to support secure client-server interactions without impacting on the usability of the grid infrastructure and services.

2.2 Basic grid services

As mentioned before, grid infrastructure tools, such as Globus [4] and Legion [6], provide basic services that can be effectively used in the development of the *Knowledge Grid* handling distributed, heterogeneous computing resources as a single virtual parallel computer. Just to outline the type of services, in figure 1 we list the core Globus services [4] and the *Data Grid* services [11]. These services address several PDKD requirements discussed before and need to support the *Knowledge Grid* architecture.

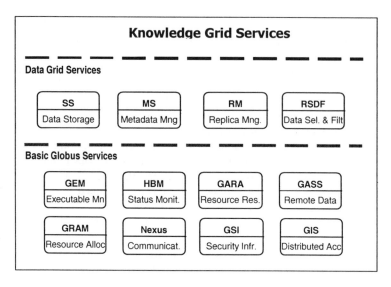

Fig 1. Basic Globus services and Data Grid services.

For each of the listed services, a C and/or Java application programming interface (API) is defined for use by developers, thus the higher-level components of a PDKD system will use these services by calling the corresponding APIs.

3 The Knowledge Grid Architecture

The *Knowledge Grid* architecture is defined on top of grid toolkits and services, i.e. it uses basic grid services to build specific knowledge extraction services. Following the Integrated Grid Architecture approach, these services can be developed in different ways using the available grid toolkits and services, such as Globus, Legion, SNIPE, etc. However, in this paper we discuss an architecture based on the Globus toolkit. As in Globus, the *Knowledge Grid* offers global services based on the cooperation and combination of local services.

3.1   Knowledge Grid services

The *Knowledge Grid* services (layers) are organized in two hierarchic levels: *core K-grid layer* and *high level K-grid layer*. The former refers to services directly implemented on the top of generic grid services, the latter are used to describe, develop and execute PDKD computations over the *Knowledge Grid*. The *Knowledge Grid* layers are depicted in figure 2. The figure shows layers as implemented on the top of Globus services, moreover, the *Knowledge Grid* data and metadata repositories are also shown.

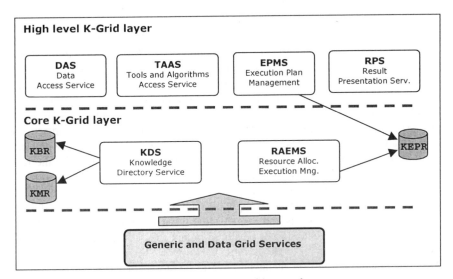

Fig. 2. *Knowledge Grid* architecture layers.

3.1.1   Core K-grid layer

The core K-grid layer has to support the definition, composition and execution of a PDKD computation over the grid. Its main goals are the management of all metadata describing characteristics of data sources, third party data mining tools, data management, and data visualization tools and algorithms. Moreover, this layer has to coordinate the PDKD computation executions, attempting to match the application requirements and the available grid resources. This layer comprises the following basic services:

Knowledge Directory Service (KDS)
This service extends the basic Globus MDS service and it is responsible for maintaining a description of all the data and tools used in the *Knowledge Grid*. The metadata managed by the KDS regard the following kind of objects:

- data source providing the data to be mined, such as databases, plain files, XML documents and other structured or unstructured data. Usually data to be mined are extracted from their sources only when needed;
- tools and algorithms used to extract, filter and manipulate data (data management tools);
- tools and algorithms used to analyze (mine) data (data analysis tools);
- tools and algorithms used to visualize, store and manipulate PDKD computations results (data visualization tools);
- PDKD execution plans, they are graphs describing the interaction and data flow between data sources, DM tools, visualization tools, and result storing. An execution plan is an abstract description of a PDKD grid application;
- PDKD results, i.e. the "knowledge" discovered after a PDKD computation.

The metadata information are represented by XML (eXtensible Markup Language) documents and are stored in a *Knowledge Metadata Repository (KMR)*. For example, they describe features of different data sources that can be mined, as location, format, availability, available views and level of aggregation of data.

Whereas it could be infeasible to maintain the data to be mined in an ad hoc repository, it could be useful to maintain a repository of the "knowledge" discovered after a PDKD computation. These information (see below) are stored in a *Knowledge Base Repository (KBR)*, but the metadata describing them are managed by the KDS. The KDS is so used not only to search and access raw data, but also to find pre-discovered knowledge that can be used to compare the output of a given PDKD computation when varying data, or to apply data mining tools in an incremental way.

Data management, analysis and visualization tools are usually pre-existent to the *Knowledge Grid*, so they should not be stored in any specialized repository (i.e. they resides over file systems or code libraries). However, to make them available to PDKD computations, relevant metadata have to be stored in the KMR. In a similar way, metadata are to be stored to allow the use of data sources. Another important repository is the *Knowledge Execution Plan Repository (KEPR)* storing the execution plans over the grid of PDKD computations.

Resource Allocation and Execution Management Service (RAEMS)
These services are used to find a mapping between an execution plan and available resources, with the goal of satisfying requirements (computing power, storage, memory, database, network bandwidth and latency) and constraints. The mapping has to be effectively obtained (co-) allocating resources. After the execution plan has been started, this layer has to manage and coordinate the application execution. Other than using the KDS and the MDS services, this layer is directly based on the GRAM services. Resource requests of single data mining programs are expressed using the Resource Specification Language (RSL). The analysis and processing of the execution plan will generate global resource requests that in turn are translated into local RSL requests for local GRAMs and communication requirements for Nexus or other high level communication services.

3.1.2 High level K-grid layer

The high-level K-grid layer comprises the services used to compose, to validate, and to execute a PDKD computation. Moreover, the layer offers services to store and analyze the knowledge discovered by PDKD computations. Main services are:

Data Access Service (DAS)

The Data Access services are responsible for the search, selection (*Data search services*), extraction, transformation and delivery (*Data extraction services*) of data to be mined. The search and selection services are based on the core *KDS* service. On the basis of the user requirements and constraints, the Data access service automates (or assists the user in) the searching and finding of data sources to be analyzed by the DM tools.

The extraction, transformation and delivery of data to be mined (*Data extraction*) are based on the GASS services and use the KDS. After useful data have been found, the data mining tools can require some transformation, whereas the user requirements or security constraints can require some data filtering before extraction. These operations can usually be done after the DM tools are chosen. The extraction functions can be embedded in the data mining programs or, more usefully, can be coded and stored in a utility repository, accessible by the KDS.

Tools and Algorithms Access Service (TAAS)

This layer is responsible for the search, selection, downloading of data mining tools and algorithms. As before, the metadata regarding their availability, location, configuration, etc., are stored in the KMR and managed by the KDS, whereas the tools and algorithms are stored in the local storage facility of each K-grid node. A node wishing to "export" data mining tools to other users has to "publish" them using the KDS services, which store the metadata in the local portion of the KMR. Some relevant metadata are parameters, format of input/output data, kind of data mining algorithm implemented, resource requirements and constraints, and so on.

Execution Plan Management Service (EPMS)

An execution plan is an abstract description of a PDKD grid application. It is a graph describing the interaction and data flows between data sources, extraction tools, DM tools, visualization tools, and storing of knowledge results in the KBR. In simplest cases the user can directly describe the execution plan, using a visual composition tool where the programs are connected to the data sources. However, due to the variety of results produced by the Data Access and Tool Access services, different execution plans can be produced, in terms of data and tools location, strategies to move or stage intermediate results and so on. Thus, the Execution Plan Management Service is a semi-automatic tool that takes the data and programs selected by the user, and generates a set of different, possible execution plans that satisfy user, data an algorithms requirements and constraints.

Execution plans are stored in the *Knowledge Execution Plan Repository* to allow the implementation of iterative knowledge discovery processes, e.g. periodical analysis of the same data sources that vary during time. More simply, the same execution plan can be used to analyze different set of data. Moreover, different execution plans can be used to analyze in parallel the same set of data, and to compare the results using different point of views (e.g., performance, accuracy).

Results Presentation Service (RPS)

This layer specifies how to generate, present and visualize the PDKD results (rules, associations, models, classification, etc.). Moreover, it offers the API to store in different formats these results in the Knowledge Base Repository. The result metadata are stored in the KMR to be managed by the KDS. The KDS is so used not only to search and access raw data, but also to find pre-discovered knowledge that can be used to compare the output of a given PDKD computation when varying data, or to apply data mining tools in an incremental way.

4   Related work

A few PDKD systems that support high-performance distributed data mining have recently been proposed. Those systems operate on clusters of computers or over the Internet, but, none of those we know make use of the computational grid infrastructure for the implementation of the basic services of authentication, data access, communication and security. Here we very shortly list their basic features.

Papyrus [7] is a distributed data mining system developed for clusters and super-clusters of workstations as composed four software layers: data management, data mining, predictive modeling, and agent or Bast. Papyrus is based on mobile agents implemented using Java aglets. Another interesting distributed data mining suite based on Java is PaDDMAS [12], a component-based tool set that integrates pre-developed or custom packages (that can be sequential or parallel) using a dataflow approach. Each system component is wrapped as a Java or CORBA object with its interface specified in XML. Connectivity to databases is provided thorough JDBC bridges. Kensington Enterprise data mining [1] is a PDKD system based on a three-tier client/server architecture in which the three tiers include: client, application server and third-tier servers (RDBMS and parallel data mining service). The Kensington system has been implemented in Java and uses the Enterprise JavaBeans component architecture. JAM [13] is an agent-based distributed data mining system that has been developed to mine data stored in different sites for building so called meta-models as a combination of several models learned at the different sites where data are stored. JAM uses Java applets to move data mining agents to remote sites. A sort of meta-learning, called *collective data mining*, is implemented also in the BODHI system [8]. BODHI is another agent-based distributed data mining system implemented in Java.

Besides the systems we discussed here, other distributed data mining systems that have recently been developed or are in development are WoRLD, MASSON [9], PADMA and DMA. Alongside with these research work on distributed data mining, several research groups are working in the computational grid area developing algorithms, components, and services that can be exploited in the implementation of distributed data mining systems. Thus, this work could be useful integrated with work on parallel and distributed data mining to obtain world-wide grid based PDKD systems for the analysis of large data collections in scientific and commercial areas.

5   Implementation

We are implementing a prototype of the basic *Knowledge Grid* components and services on top of Globus. Each node of the grid declares the availability of KGrid objects (resources, components and services) by publishing specific entries into the *Directory Information Tree* (DIT) maintained by a LDAP server, such the *Grid Resource Information Service* (GRIS) provided by Globus Toolkit.

For instance, by publishing the following LDAP entry:

```
dn: kgr=KMR, hn=telesio.isi.cs.cnr.it, dc=isi, ...
objectclass: KGridRepository
kgr: KMR
description: Knowledge Metadata Repository
hn: telesio.isi.cs.cnr.it
storedir: /opt/kgrid/KMR
lastupdate: Thu May 3 00:07:05 UTC 2001
 ...
```

the grid node `telesio` declares the availability of a Knowledge Metadata Repository accordingly to the definition of the objectclass `KGridRepository`, which stores, in the filesystem directory specified by the `storedir` attribute, metadata about KGrid resources, such as data sources and data mining tools, provided by that node.

Metadata are implemented by XML documents, on the basis of a set of specified schemas, and provide specific information for the discovery and the use of resources. For instance, metadata about data mining tools provide information about the implemented task (e.g., classification, clustering), complexity of the used algorithm, location of executables and manuals, syntax for running the program, format of input data and results, etc.

The discovery of interesting resources over the grid is accomplished in two step: the metadata repositories are first located, searching LDAP directories for KGrid entries. Then the relevant XML metadata are downloaded from the specified location and analyzed to find more specific information. We implemented the basic tools to find, retrieve and select metadata about KGrid resources (e.g., data sources, data mining software), on the basis of different search parameters and selection filters.

Moreover, we are modeling the representation of Knowledge Execution Plans as labeled graphs where nodes represent computational elements such as data sources, software programs, results, etc. and arcs represent basic operations such as data movements, data filtering, program execution and synchronization, and result storing. We consider different network parameters, such as topology, bandwidth and latency, for PDKD program execution optimization.

6   A case study

We can envision several classes of PDKD applications over the grid. In the following we discuss an example that is not representative of every possible scenarios, however it can be useful to show how the different *Knowledge Grid* services could be exploited for the execution of a simple distributed data mining application.

We assume that on the grid node $node_0$ is stored the data set DS_0, on which we need to perform a clustering algorithm to identify homogeneous clusters in data. To do this we use the parallel clustering algorithm P-AutoClass [10] that is available on the grid nodes $node_1...node_n$ (fig. 3).

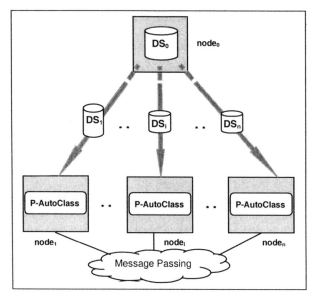

Fig. 3. Parallel data clustering application over the *Knowledge Grid*.

Data set DS_0 is divided in a set of partitions $DS_1..DS_n$ that are moved respectively to the nodes $node_1..node_n$ before to start the data mining process. The size of the *i-th* subset is obtained on the basis of the expected performance of the target node and of the communication bandwidth between the origin and the target nodes, according to the following formula:

$$size(DS_i) = size(DS_0)\frac{F_i}{\sum_{j=1}^{n}F_j} \quad \text{where} \quad F_i = \frac{f_1(cpuspeed(node_i),bandwidth(link_{0,i}),...) \cdot}{f_2(cpuload(node_i),latency(link_{0,i}),...)}$$

Inter-process communication among the P-AutoClass processes running in parallel is performed using the Message Passing Interface (MPI) primitives.

The execution of the data mining application is based on the following steps:

1. *Metadata about the data set DS_0 and the P-AutoClass tool are published by corresponding owners.* Publication of metadata of a specific resource is done by a specific tool of KDS that after getting information about a resource, it generates an XML metadata document according to the specific schema for that resource and it publishes that document on the KMR. Hence, metadata about DS_0 are published in the KMR of $node_0$, and they contain information about number, names and types of attributes, data format, data size (number of tuples) and data set location. Metadata about P-AutoClass are published in the KMRs of

$node_1..node_n$ specifying the performed data mining task, program syntax, data set input format, and other details about the program execution.

2. ***Users find data set DS_0 and P-AutoClass data mining tools.*** Resource finding is performed by means of search tools of the DAS and TAAS services. Search tools select, on the basis on the user provide parameters, interesting resources by analyzing XML metadata stored in KMRs of remote sites. For example, a user can specify a search of a data sets containing attributes with a specified name and type. The search tool will provide a list of candidate data sets that can be searched again to select the resources to be used. In the same way, needed tools can be searched and selected.

3. ***An execution plan is built of the data mining application.*** In this case study the execution plan generated by the EPM service defines the data set partitioning strategy, the transfer of each partition to the target node, the parallel execution of the P-AutoClass programs and the result (clustering model) collection. The EPM service uses processor and network monitoring features that are used to compute different execution strategies.

4. ***Data mining application execution and result collection.*** Execution of the parallel data mining application is supported by the RAEMS that, on the basis of the execution plan, allocate resources and provide the application start. Output of the data mining computation, that is the classified data, are moved to the user KBR and visualized by means of the RPS tools.

7   Conclusions

The *Knowledge Grid* represents a first step in the process of studying the unification of PDKD and computational grid technologies. The main goal is defining an integrating architecture for distributed data mining and knowledge discovery based on grid services. The design of such an architecture will accelerate progress on very large-scale geographically distributed data mining by enabling the integration of currently disjoint approaches and revealing technology gaps that require further research and development.

References

1. Chattratichat J., Darlington J., Guo Y., Hedvall S., Köler M. and Syed J., An architecture for distributed enterprise data mining. *HPCN Europe 1999, Lecture Notes in Computer Science,* **1593**, 1999, pp. 573-582.
2. Chervenak A., Foster I., Kesselman C., Salisbury C. and Tuecke S., The Data Grid: towards an architecture for the distributed management and analysis of large scientific data sets. *Journal of Network and Computer Appls*, 2001.

3. Fayyad U.M. and Uthurusamy R. (eds.), Data mining and knowledge discovery in databases. *Communications of the ACM* **39**, 1997.
4. Foster I. and Kesselman C., Globus : a metacomputing infrastructure toolkit. *International Journal of Supercomputing Applications* **11**, 1997, pp. 115-128.
5. Freitas A.A. and Lavington S.H., *Mining Very Large Databases with Parallel Processing*, Kluwer Academic Publishers, 1998.
6. Grimshaw A.S., Ferrari A., Knabe F., and Humphrey M., Wide-area computing: resource sharing on a large scale. *Computer* **32**, 1999, pp. 29-37.
7. Grossman R., Bailey S., Kasif S., Mon D., Ramu A. and Malhi B., The preliminary design of papyrus: a system for high performance, distributed data mining over clusters, meta-clusters and super-clusters. *International KDD'98 Conference*,1998, pp. 37-43.
8. Kargupta H., Park B., Hershberger, D. and Johnson, E., Collective data mining: a new perspective toward distributed data mining. In H. Kargupta and P. Chan (eds.) *Advances in Distributed and Parallel Knowledge Discovery*, AAAI Press 1999.
9. Kimm H. and Ryu T.-W., A framework for distributed knowledge discovery system over heterogeneous networks using CORBA. *KDD2000 Workshop on Distributed and Parallel Knowledge Discovery,* 2000.
10. D. Foti, D. Lipari, C. Pizzuti, D. Talia, "Scalable Parallel Clustering for Data Mining on Multicomputers", *Proc. of the 3rd Int. Workshop on High Performance Data Mining HPDM00-IPDPS*, LNCS, Springer-Verlag, Cancun, Mexico, May 2000.
11. Moore R., Baru C., Marciano R., Rajasekar A. and Wan M., Data-intensive computing. In I. Foster and C. Kesselman (eds.) *The Grid: Blueprint for a Future Computing Inf.*, Morgan Kaufmann Publishers, 1999, pp. 105-129.
12. Rana O.F., Walker D.W., Li M., Lynden S. and Ward M., PaDDMAS: parallel and distributed data mining application suite. *Proc. International Parallel and Distributed Processing Symposium (IPDPS/SPDP)*, IEEE Computer Society Press, 2000, pp. 387-392.
13. Stolfo S.J., Prodromidis A.L., Tselepis S., Lee W., Fan D.W., Chan P.K., JAM: Java agents for meta-learning over distributed databases. *International KDD'97 Conference*, 1997, pp. 74-81.

On Fully Decentralized Resource Discovery in Grid Environments

Adriana Iamnitchi [1] and Ian Foster [1,2]

[1] Department of Computer Science, The University of Chicago
1100 E. 58th Street, Chicago, IL 60637, USA
{anda, foster}@cs.uchicago.edu
[2] Mathematics and Computer Science Division, Argonne National Laboratory
Argonne, IL 60439, USA

Abstract. Computational grids provide mechanisms for sharing and accessing large and heterogeneous collections of remote resources such as computers, online instruments, storage space, data, and applications. Resources are identified based on a set of desired attributes. Resource attributes have various degrees of dynamism, from mostly static attributes, like operating system version, to highly dynamic ones, like network bandwidth or CPU load.

In this paper we propose a peer-to-peer architecture for resource discovery in a large and dynamic collection of resources. We evaluate a set of request-forwarding algorithms in a fully decentralized architecture, designed to accommodate heterogeneity (in both sharing policies and resource types) and dynamism. For this, we build a testbed that models two usage characteristics: (1) resource distribution on peers, that varies in the number and the frequency of shared resources; and (2) various requests patterns for resources. We analyzed our resource discovery mechanisms on up to 5000 peers, where each peer provides information about at least one resource. We learned that a decentralized approach is not only desirable from administrative reasons, but it is also supported by promising performance results. Our results also allow us to characterize the correlation between resource discovery performance and sharing characteristics.

1 Introduction

Opportunistic sharing of Internet connected computers is a low cost method for achieving computational power. Recently, this trend was supported by research in the domain of computational grids [5]: collections of shared, geographically distributed hardware and software resources made available to groups of remote users.

In computational grids resources can be computers, storage space, sensors (e.g., telescopes), software applications, and data, all connected through the Internet and a middleware software layer that provides basic services for security, monitoring, accessing information about components, etc. Resources are owned by various administrative organizations and shared under locally defined policies that specify what is shared, who is allowed to share and under what conditions. A set of individuals and/or institutions defined by such sharing rules is called a Virtual Organization (VO)[6].

A basic service in grids is resource discovery: given a description of resources desired, a resource discovery mechanism returns a set of (contact addresses of) resources that match the description. Resource discovery in a grid is made challenging by the potentially large number of resources and users (perhaps millions) and considerable heterogeneity in resource types and user requests. Resource discovery is further complicated by the natural tendency for VOs to evolve over time, with, for example, institutions joining and leaving (along with their resources and users), the number of resources shared by an institution varying, and resource characteristics such as availability and CPU load changing.

These characteristics create significant difficulties for traditional centralized and hierarchical resource discovery services. Hence, we investigate a flat, fully decentralized architecture, developing a candidate architecture design and studying the characteristics of this design via detailed simulation studies. Our architecture is distinguished by its peer-to-peer flavor: entities that participate in resource discovery are equally important for the system's correct and efficient functioning.

There are many common characteristics of grid environments and current peer-to-peer systems: dynamism, wide-area scale, and heterogeneity are perhaps the most significant. Recently, decentralized file-sharing systems, such as Gnutella and Freenet, have been extensively analyzed [2, 10], but these results are of little relevance for us because of several important differences with our problem:

1. Anonymity is a major objective of file-sharing systems like Gnutella and Freenet and, consequently, design decisions were made to achieve it. In our environment, anonymity is not only unnecessary but may also be undesirable, for example, for accountability, performance tuning, or replication decisions.
2. The dynamics of the Gnutella network are perhaps different from the dynamics of a Virtual Organization.
3. Resource sharing in a grid will often be based on different policies, such as community contributions and/or payment, that will hopefully avoid phenomena such as Gnutella's free riding behavior [1].
4. User request patterns may be different. While in Gnutella a user is unlikely to request the same file many times, in grids it is quite usual that a user will use the same kind of resource multiple times.
5. In file-sharing systems, the answer has to perfectly match the request. In the case of resource discovery, matches may be approximate (e.g., a 800 MHz processor is likely to be acceptable if we are asking for 500 MHz processor).
6. Properties used to refer to resources may be mutable.

Hence, we cannot use performance analysis of the large-scale Gnutella network [10] for estimating the performance of a similar solution for our problem. It is our objective in this paper to also present a framework for our architecture evaluation and a preliminary set of performance results. Our results show that a flat, decentralized, self-configuring architecture is a promising solution for dealing with large, variable, and heterogeneous collections of resources. These results are even more significant since we did not put effort into improving performance.

The rest of this paper is as follows. We discuss related work in Section 2. Section 3 presents our design decisions. We describe in Section 4 the emulated grid that we have built as a testbed for evaluating various design alternatives and we present our measurements in Section 5. We conclude in Section 6 with lessons learned and future research plans.

2   Locating Resources in Wide-Area Systems

Two classes of related work are relevant for our study: resource discovery in dynamic, self-organizing networks; and resource discovery in wide-area systems. The former category has benefited from huge attention recently due to the popularity of peer-to-peer (P2P) file-sharing systems. Such systems identify resources (files) through their names and use a variety of strategies to locate a specified named file, including aggressive flooding (Gnutella [15]), combination of informed request forwarding and automatic file replication (Freenet [2]), and intelligent positioning of data into search-optimized, reliable, and flexible structures for efficient and scalable retrieval (as in CAN [9], Chord [12], and Tapestry [14]).

The most successful wide-area service for locating resources based on names is DNS. Its hierarchical organization and caching strategies take advantage of the rather static information managed.

All of the above-mentioned systems use names as their search criteria. However, in our context, requests specify sets of desired attributes and values: for example, the name and version of the operating system and the CPU load. From this perspective, Web search engines are resource discovery mechanisms more similar to what we need for grids: given a set of criteria (search keys), they return the addresses of relevant resources (web pages). However, Web search engines do not deal well with dynamic information.

Nonetheless, using unique names as global identifiers is an appealing idea: one can position information, based on global IDs, into search-optimized structures (as in search trees or, more scalably and reliably, Plaxton networks [7]) for faster search. Globe [13] is one system that assigns location-independent names to resources as a means for retrieving mobile resources (e.g., mobile services) in wide-area systems. However, while we could imagine defining a mapping from attribute-value pairs to names (e.g., by assigning a distinct name to each meaningful combination of attribute-value pairs) and then maintaining a mapping between names and the physical resources that have those attributes, the volatility of attribute values would make the utility of this mapping uncertain. Moreover, unlike in name-based search systems, matching resource descriptions and requests can benefit from a certain degree of approximation: for example, a computer with a CPU load of 10% is most likely appropriate for matching a request for a computer with a CPU load of at most 20%.

While aware of the potential existence of clever methods for organizing grid resource information in search-efficient structures, we believe that using name-based search is not feasible for resource discovery grids. Among the distributed resource sharing systems that do not use global names for resource discovery is Condor's Matchmaker [8]: resource descriptions and requests are sent to a central authority that performs the matching. The centralized architecture is efficient for the local area network for which Condor was initially designed, but it assumes the willingness of an organization to operate the central server.

Another relevant experience is provided by Globus's MDS [3]: initially centralized, this service moved to a decentralized structure as its pool of resources and users grew. In MDS-2, a Grid is assumed to consist of multiple information sources that can register with index servers via a registration protocol. Index servers, or users, can use an enquiry protocol to query directory servers to discover entities and to obtain more detailed descriptions of resources from their information sources. Left unspecified is the techniques used to associate entities into directories and to construct an efficient, scalable network of directory servers. Our research is complementary to MDS, proposing and evaluating mechanisms that can be used to organize these directories (the equivalent of what we call *nodes* or *peers* in this paper) in flat, dynamic networks.

3   Resource Discovery Problem Restated: a Peer-to-Peer Approach

A grid is a collection of resources shared by different organizations or/and individuals. Many organizations will have strictly specified sharing policies, like time intervals when their resources are available for non-internal users or the types of projects to which their resources may contribute. Attempting to enforce uniform rules over the grid would drastically limit participation. Moreover, the pool of resources shared by an organization may vary over time, subject to local computing load and sharing policies. Therefore, a natural solution is to allow every organization to control access to information about its local, shared resources.

We assume that every participant in the VO (organization or individual) has one or more servers that store and provide access to local resource information. We call these servers *nodes* or *peers*. A node may provide information about one resource (e.g., itself) or multiple resources (e.g., all resources shared by an organization).

From the perspective of resource discovery, the grid is a collection of geographically distributed nodes that may join and leave at any time and without notice (for example, as a result of system or communication failures). Although we assume the sets of resources published by nodes are disjoint, there may be multiple resources with identical descriptions, for example, multiple copies of the same data or identical machines.

These observations and assumptions are direct consequences of the problem characteristics. We present our design decisions in the following.

3.1 Framework

The basic framework is as follows. We assume users send their requests to some known (typically local) node. The node responds with the matching resource descriptions if it has them locally, otherwise it forwards the requests to another node. Intermediate nodes forward a request until its time-to-live (TTL) expires or matching resources are found, whichever occurs first. If a node has information matching a forwarded request, it sends the information directly to the node that initiated the forwarding (rather than via intermediate nodes), which in turn will send it to its user.

Within this framework, a particular resource discovery algorithm is defined by two mechanisms: the membership protocol that provides each node with (typically partial) membership information about other nodes and a request-forwarding strategy used to determine to which nodes requests should be forwarded. We focus in this paper on the latter, describing and evaluating four different request-forwarding strategies, described below. We are not particularly concerned here with the characteristics of the membership protocol, but note simply that we use a soft-state membership protocol as is common in peer-to-peer systems. A node joins the grid by contacting a member node. Contact addresses of member nodes can be learned through out-of-band information. A node contacted by joining members responds with its membership information. Membership lists are updated by periodic "I'm alive" messages exchanged between *neighbors*—nodes that know each other. Membership information can also be enriched over time: upon the receipt of a message from a previously unknown node, a node adds the new address to its membership list.

The request-forwarding strategy decides to which node (among the locally known ones) a request is to be forwarded. In addition to contact addresses, nodes can store other information about their peers, such as information about requests previously answered. The tradeoff between the amount of information about neighbors and search performance generates a large set of alternatives, from random forwarding (no information about the resources provided by other nodes) to one-hop forwarding, when nodes know exactly which node has the requested resource. Because information is dynamic, nodes do not cache the information itself (i.e., the attribute values), but the address(es) where relevant information was previously found.

3.2 Request Forwarding

Nodes forward the requests they cannot answer to a peer selected from the locally known nodes. We evaluated four request-forwarding algorithms:

FRQ1. Random: chooses randomly the node to which a request is forwarded. No extra information is stored on nodes.

FRQ2. Experience-based + random: nodes learn from experience by recording the requests answered by other nodes. A request is forwarded to the peer that answered similar requests previously. If no relevant experience exists, the request is forwarded to a randomly chosen node.

FRQ3. Best-neighbor algorithm records the number of answers received from each peer (without recording the type of request answered). A request is forwarded to the peer who answered the largest number of requests.

FRQ4. Experience-based + best-neighbor: identical with FRQ2, except that, when no relevant experience exists, the request is forwarded to the best neighbor.

The following section presents the emulated grid that serves as a testbed for the evaluation of these four request-forwarding algorithms in different grids.

4 An Emulated Grid for Resource Discovery

We opted for building and using an emulated grid to understand whether a fully decentralized, flat design approach for resource discovery is appropriate in terms of response time, response quality, and scalability. Because our focus is on large scale simulations (thousands of nodes), we preferred to build an emulated grid instead of using a general purpose, usually unscalable, discrete event simulator. Unlike other grid simulators [11], we designed this framework with the sole purpose of analyzing resource discovery strategies.

In our framework, each node is implemented as a process that communicates with other nodes via TCP. Each node maintains two types of information: a) information about a number of resources (its contribution to the VO) and b) information about other nodes in the system (including, but not restricted to membership information). The amount of resource information hosted by nodes varies: some have information about a large number of resources; others, only one resource. In our preliminary experiments, we assume the amount of information about other nodes that can be stored locally is unlimited.

The performance of the resource discovery mechanism depends on usage and environment characteristics like scale, resource distributions, and user request patterns. We evaluated our request-forwarding strategies for a number of nodes from 1000 to 5000. We studied our architecture using requests matching a set of 10000 distinct resources, some with identical descriptions. Request similarity is difficult to quantify and model. We simplified this problem by considering only simple requests (requests for one resource) and perfect matching. While this setup is not realistic, it helps us understand the effects of each of the parameters we consider. We shall extend our experiments with more realistic scenarios when analyzing the requirements of the query language.

In the remaining of this section we give details on how we model resource distributions on nodes and user requests.

4.1 Resource Distributions

When analyzing resource distributions, we have to consider two issues. The first is the distribution of resources on nodes: some nodes share a large number of resources, others just one. We modeled three resource distributions, of different degrees of fairness, as presented in Figure 1. Because of space limitations, we present in this paper only the results measured in environments with unbalanced and balanced resource distributions.

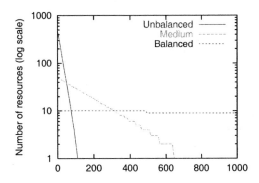

Fig. 1. Geometric distribution of resources on 1000 nodes varies from highly unbalanced (few nodes provide a large number of resources, while most nodes provide only one) to fair (all nodes share the same number of resources).

The second aspect we need to model is resource frequency: we need to distinguish between common resources (ones that are numerous and widely available) and rare (even unique) resources. Assuming R resources of D distinct types, we consider all resources in a grid are equally common (with the same frequency R/D) and we compare resource discovery performance in grids with different values for R/D. This is a simpler model than permitting the frequency to vary over individual resources and tracking requests for common and rare resources.

4.2 User Requests

While usage patterns can be decisive in making design decisions, we tackle the problem of not having real user request logs, a problem inherent in systems during the design phase. We experimented with two request distributions, random and geometric, in which requests were chosen to match existing resources.

In our experiments, the number of distinct requests in the random distribution is approximately twice as large as that in an equally-sized geometric distribution (and hence, on average, the same request is repeated twice as much in the geometric distribution than in the random distribution).

In each of our experiments we randomly chose a set of 10 nodes to which we sent independently generated sets of 200 requests. The same sets of requests, sent to the same nodes, respectively, are repeated to compare various request-forwarding algorithms.

4.3   Starting Topology

The connection graph defined by membership information strongly influences the resource discovery performance: the more nodes known to the local node, the more informed its request-forwarding decision can be. We described the membership protocol previously but we did not detail the starting topology: the graph whose vertices are nodes in the grid and whose edges connect pairs of nodes that know each other, as it looks before requests are processed.

We generated the starting topology using the Tiers network generator[4]. In the experiments presented here we consider that all nodes had joined the grid before the first request was generated. We assume no failures. The connection graph changes over time, influenced by design and usage factors (location of requested resources in graph, request-forwarding algorithm, number and diversity of user requests), therefore the starting topology is important mostly to avoid unrealistically optimistic starting configurations, e.g., a star topology.

5   Experimental Results

We used the testbed presented above to evaluate the performance of four request-forwarding algorithms in grids with different resource distributions. We are interested in understanding response time per request and success rate. Currently we measure response time as the number of hops traversed for answering a request. Because in our experiments requests only refer to existing resources, success rate less than 1 is due to dropped requests because of dead ends or exceeded TTL.

We present in this section the evaluation of the four request forwarding algorithms under different sharing and usage conditions. First, we consider an environment with common resources (100 resources of each type) and measure the average number of hops per request for the four forwarding algorithms. Second, we compare these results with the same experiments in an environment with less common resources (10 of each type). In these two sets of results, user requests are generated to follow a geometric distribution. To understand the influence of user request pattern on resource discovery performance, we compare performance when requests follow a geometric and, respectively, a random distribution in environments with different levels of resource frequency.

Because of the randomness encapsulated in our testbed and in our request-forwarding algorithms, we repeated our experiments multiple times. The results shown in this section are the average values of measurements obtained in multiple runs.

Note that only the experience-based forwarding algorithms take advantage of the time and space-locality of user requests. Given our assumption of infinite storage space for logs, the response time for the experience-based algorithms is a lower bound for these particular algorithms. However, these optimistic results are, at least partially, counterbalanced by our measurements including the system's warm up (while nodes learn about other nodes' resources).

Figure 2 presents the average number of hops per request for various degrees of sharing fairness, when there are on average 100 resources of each type in the system. The random forwarding algorithm (labeled FRQ1 in Figure 2) has the advantage that no additional storage space is required on nodes to record history, but it is also expected to be the least efficient. This intuition is confirmed by the unbalanced resource distribution (Figure 2 left), but is infirmed in the case of the most balanced distribution, as seen in Figure 2 right. In all distributions, the experience-based + random algorithm (labeled FRQ2) performs the best, while its more expensive version (FRQ4) proves to be equally or less efficient. Best neighbor algorithm (FRQ3), which is less expensive in terms of storage space (since it records only the number of requests answered by each node, not the requests themselves), performs well only in the unbalanced distribution; in all the other cases, because of the uniformly small number of distinct resources per node, it gives false hints on locating resources. Its influence is the reason for FRQ4 performing poorer than FRQ2, most clearly seen in the balanced distribution.

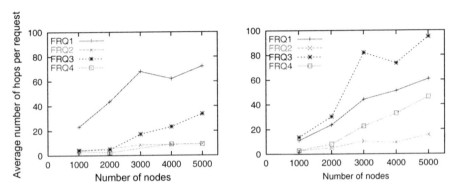

Fig. 2. Average number of hops per request as a function of the number of nodes in the grid, for two environments with different resource distributions. (Left: unbalanced. Right: balanced). The number of resources considered is 10000. Resource frequency (the number of resources of the same type) is constant:100.

Figure 3 compares resource discovery performance for grids with different resource frequencies: when there are on average 100 ($R/D = 100$) and respectively 10 ($R/D = 10$) resources of each type. For the grid with less common resources, the average number of hops is large (in the order of 100s), so we present the percentage of answered requests within a time-to-live of 100. Observe that in this environment performance decreases faster with the number of nodes; the lower 4 lines in each graph in Figure 3 represent the results measured in the environment with less common resources. Not surprisingly, the four forwarding algorithms perform comparatively almost the same, independent of resource frequency.

The influence of different user request patterns is presented in Figure 4. We measured average number of hops per request for the best performing forwarding algorithm (experience-based + random) in the two environments with different

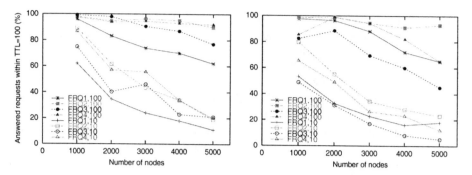

Fig. 3. Percentage of answered requests within time-to-live 100 in two environments. Left: unbalanced resource distribution. Right: balanced resource distribution. For each resource distribution we considered different resource frequencies: $R/D = 100$ (the upper 4 plots in each graph) and 10, respectively.

resource frequencies. Again, the influence of user request patterns is stronger in the environment with less common resources: the number of hops per request is more than 4 times larger when requests follow a random distribution, compared to at most 2 in the environment with common resources.

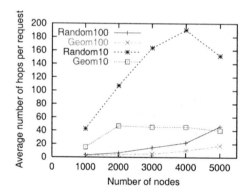

Fig. 4. The influence of different user requests patterns (random and geometric distributions) on resource discovery performance in environments with different resource frequencies (100 and 10, respectively) and unbalanced resource distribution. The request-forwarding algorithm used was experience-based+random (FRQ2).

6 Conclusions and Future Work

We argue in this paper that resource discovery in grid environments requires a decentralized, flat architecture. The inherent problems with such architectures are the tradeoffs between communication costs and performance. To better understand these tradeoffs and to evaluate different strategies for resource discovery, we built a simple grid emulator and modeled some relevant parameters: the pattern of user requests and the distribution of resource information in the grid. Results obtained for collections of up to 5000 nodes that host descriptions of a total of 10000 resources are presented. Our results suggest that a decentralized resource discovery strategy may be a feasible solution: if a request can be forwarded in 20 msec. (assuming 10 msec. latency in a metropolitan area network and 10 msec. necessary for request processing), then a path of 20 hops takes less than half a second.

It is interesting to observe the relation between discovery performance and environment characteristics: our experiments show that the best performing algorithm (and the most expensive, in terms of storage space) performs well independent of the type of resource distribution. The best-neighbor algorithm performs well for an unbalanced resource distribution. The least expensive forwarding algorithm—random—performs satisfactorily in all cases and is at its best when resources are equally distributed over nodes. The relative performance of the forwarding algorithms considered is independent of the average resource frequency.

Three of the four request-forwarding algorithms evaluated in this paper attempt to improve search performance by using past experience. What differentiates these algorithms is the type of information they choose to remember about the past. The algorithm that remembers the neighbor that helped the most in the past has a good guess only when few nodes have a lot to share while others share close to nothing. However, in an environment where all nodes contribute equally, this algorithm tends to perform worse than random.

The simple strategies evaluated, while promising, leave room for improvements. One limitation of our framework is the uneven spread of information: only nodes contacted by users learn. An obvious improvement is to also keep the other nodes informed, by exchanging history information (for example, along with membership information). Another simple improvement is to attach history information to request messages and hence to avoid visiting already visited nodes.

Our results suffer from limitations due to the computational expensive experiments. More accurate measurements require a larger set of (ideally larger) experiments: larger number of requests, larger number of runs per experiment, larger number of nodes. We plan to enrich our understanding of the problem through careful analytical evaluations.

The most interesting outcomes of this work are still to come. Future work includes three directions: 1) further development of the emulated grid to include capabilities for processing realistic requests and simulating data dynamism; 2) design and evaluation of different membership protocols and new request-forwarding strategies; and 3) reliability evaluation. Our final objective is to propose a coherent suite of resource discovery mechanisms and an expressive query language that are well suited to a large, heterogeneous community of grid members.

Acknowledgments

We are grateful to David Beazley for his generosity in sharing computational resources. This research was supported by the National Science Foundation under contract ITR-0086044.

References

1. ADAR, E., AND HUBERMAN, B. Free riding on gnutella. *First Monday 5*, 10 (2000).
2. CLARKE, I., SANDBERG, O., WILEY, B., AND HONG, T. Freenet: A distributed anonymous information storage and retrieval system. In *Workshop on Design Issues in Anonymity and Unobservability* (2000).
3. CZAJKOWSKI, K., FITZGERALD, S., FOSTER, I., AND KESSELMAN, C. Grid information services for distributed resource sharing. In *10th IEEE Symposium on High Performance Distributed Computing* (2001).
4. DOAR, M. A better model for generating test networks. In *IEEE Global Internet* (1996), pp. 86–93.
5. FOSTER, I., AND KESSELMAN, C., Eds. *The Grid: Blueprint for a New Computing Infrastructure.* Morgan Kaufmann, 1999.
6. FOSTER, I., KESSELMAN, C., AND TUECKE, S. The anatomy of the grid: Enabling scalable virtual organizations. *International Journal on Supercomputing Applications* (2001).
7. PLAXTON, C. G., RAJARAMAN, R., AND RICHA, A. W. Accessing nearby copies of replicated objects in a distributed environment. In *ACM Symposium on Parallel Algorithms and Architectures* (1997).
8. RAMAN, R., LIVNY, M., AND SOLOMON, M. Matchmaking: Distributed resource management for high throughput computing. In *7th IEEE International Symposium on High Performance Distributed Computing* (1998).
9. RATNASAMY, S., FRANCIS, P., HANDLEY, M., KARP, R., AND SHENKER, S. A scalable content addressable network. In *ACM SIGCOMM* (2001).
10. RIPEANU, M. Peer-to-peer architecture case study: Gnutella network. In *International Conference on Peer-to-peer Computing* (2001).
11. SONG, H. J., LIU, X., JAKOBSEN, D., BHAGWAN, R., ZHANG, X., TAURA, K., AND CHIEN, A. A. The microgrid: a scientific tool for modeling computational grids. In *Supercomputing* (2000).
12. STOICA, I., MORRIS, R., KARGER, D., KAASHOEK, M., AND BALAKRISHNAN, H. Chord: A scalable peer-to-peer lookup service for internet applications. In *ACM SIGCOMM* (2001).
13. VAN STEEN, M., HOMBURG, P., AND TANENBAUM, A. Globe: A wide-area distributed system. *IEEE Concurrency* (1999), 70–78.
14. ZHAO, B., KUBIATOWICZ, J., AND JOSEPH, A. Tapestry: An infrastructure for fault-resilient wide-area location and routing. Tech. Rep. UCB//CSD-01-1141, U. C. Berkeley, 2001.
15. Gnutella protocol specification. http://www.clip2.com/articles.html.

An Adaptive Service Grid Architecture Using Dynamic Replica Management

Byoung-Dai Lee and Jon B. Weissman

Department of Computer Science and Engineering, University of Minnesota, Minneapolis,
55455-0192, MN, USA
{blee, jon}@cs.umn.edu

Abstract. As the Internet is evolving away from providing simple connectivity towards providing more sophisticated services, it is difficult to provide efficient delivery of high-demand services to end-users due to the dynamic sharing of the network and connected servers. To address this problem, we present the service grid architecture that incorporates dynamic replication and deletion of services. We have completed a prototype implementation of the architecture in Legion. The preliminary results show that our architecture can adapt to dynamically changing client demand in a timely manner. The results also demonstrate that our architecture utilizes system resources more efficiently than static replication system.

1 Introduction

The popularity of the Internet has grown enormously since its early deployment in the 1970's. To support newly emerging applications such as e-commerce and distributed high-performance computing for science and engineering, the Internet is evolving away from providing only simple connectivity towards providing more sophisticated services. As a result, diverse network services ranging from content-delivery provided by Web servers to high-performance computational servers such as in NetSolve [8] are currently deployed across the Internet. However, due to the dynamic sharing of the network and connected servers, it is difficult to provide efficient delivery of high-demand services to end-users.

The Service Grid [7] is an infrastructure for generic service delivery that has been designed to address several bottlenecks of the current Internet. Most notably, lack of reliability, transparency, and efficiency in service delivery. Our solution is to perform **dynamic** replication and deletion of services in response to user demand and system outages. Replication is the process by which one or more copies of a service are made. Although the idea of replication is not new, it presents several interesting challenges in the context of network services. For example, both server loads and network closeness should be taken into account when selecting a site to host a newly created service replica. The main features of our architecture are as follows.

- *adaptive* : the Service Grid adapts to dynamic changes in client demand in a timely manner. When demand is high, a new service replica may be dynamically created.

When demand is low, system resource utilization is increased by deleting the underutilized replicas from the system.

- *scalable* : information collection and replica management is distributed

- *transparent* : clients do not need to consider the degree of service replication, where replicas are located in the network, and which replica is best for them, etc.

In this paper, we limit our discussion to the Service Grid replication mechanism and focus on computationally-intensive high-performance services. We have completed a prototype implementation of our architecture in Legion [1], a wide-area object-based distributed computing system developed at the University of Virginia. The preliminary results show that our architecture can adapt to dynamically changing client demand in a timely manner. The results also demonstrate that our architecture utilizes system resources more efficiently than static replication system.

The paper is organized as follows: Section 2 gives related work. In the next section, we describe the proposed service grid architecture. Section 4 presents various algorithms for dynamic replica management while section 5 shows experimental results. Finally, we conclude in section 6.

2 Related Work

Many research groups [2][4][5][6][12][13][14] have developed algorithms and architectures for replica selection among statically replicated servers. Research into dynamic replication has been mostly limited to the Web environment. In Fluid replication [3], clients monitor their performance while interacting with the service. When performance becomes poor, a replica is created automatically. To select a replica site, they employ a distance-based discovery mechanism. In contrast, our solution for replica creation considers the characteristic of the service in addition to communication. RaDaR [11] proposes a web hosting architecture that supports dynamic migration and replication of web pages. In their architecture, if utilization is above a threshold, the system decides to migrate the web page near the host where most of the requests are coming from. CgR [9] proposes replication for enhancing the current Web infrastructure. In their work, one primary server forms the root of a logical tree of replicated servers, which serve as part of the primary server's namespace. Using a client-side proxy, the client can access either the primary server or replicated servers. The Bio-Networking Architecture [10] is inspired by biological metaphors of population growth in nature and provides a highly distributed replication mechanism.

3 Architecture

Our architecture consists of three core components: Replication Manager (RM), Group Manager (GM), and Site Manager (SM) (Fig. 1) RM is the decision-maker for global replica selection, creation and deletion, and tracks the location and state of all the replicas. Clients belong to a particular GM, established at configuration time.

When a client wants to access the service, it first contacts the GM assigned to it to receive binding information for a replica that can provide the best performance. Once receiving the binding information, the client can directly access the service replica without intervention by the GM.

Every site in the Service Grid runs a SM, whose primary job is to interact with the GM to determine the network performance between replicas and client groups. We believe that all hosts at one site are likely to see the same network performance when communicating with any hosts at a remote site. Therefore, the SM can reduce the overhead associated with collecting network performance since only one probe between sites is necessary to characterize the network performance between any pair of machines hosting a replica and a client respectively.

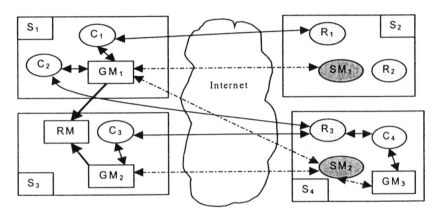

Fig. 1. Service Grid Architecture: Three replicas (R_1, R_2, R_3) are running at two different sites (S_2, S_4). R_1 is dedicated to GM_1 and R_3 is shared across GM_1, GM_2 and GM_3. Since we chose GM_2 as the primary GM for R_3, only GM_2 needs to contact RM to update status information of R_3. Client (C_i) belongs to a group (GM_j), and may run on machines located outside the Service Grid perimeter.

The GM maintains a cache of local replicas allocated to it by the RM over time. This replica pool is available to the clients within the GM. Each replica maintains a list of GMs that are currently using the replica and reports its load status to them periodically so that the GMs can have up-to-date information on the replica status. Among all GMs that are sharing a replica, a primary GM is responsible for propagating the information to the RM so that the RM will also have an up-to-date global view of the system. With this protocol, the GM offloads much of the traffic that would otherwise reach RM[1], promoting scalability. In addition to information collection and replica selection, the GM is also responsible for decision-making about when to acquire replicas and when to release replicas based on perceived performance and replica utilization.

Replica creation and deletion are initiated by the GMs in a distributed fashion. When the RM receives a replica acquisition request from the GMs, it decides whether to return an existing replica or to create a new replica based on the replica utilization

---

[1] Replicating the RM for very large Service Grid is the subject of future work

by other groups. When a GM sends a replica release request and there is no other GM that is using the released replica, the RM puts that replica in an idle replica pool.

In addition to serving clients requests, a service replica periodically reports its status information to the GMs that are using it. However, the periodic status report may consume unnecessary network resources if the replica is not accessed frequently. To address this problem, the replica dynamically changes the window size for periodic status reporting. For example, if a replica is dedicated to a GM, this GM will require much less frequent update. By selecting a larger window size, the network traffic between the GM and the replica can be reduced. On the other hand, if a replica is shared across many GMs, each GM cannot estimate the status of the replica accurately because it lacks global information. In this case, the replica sends its status more frequently so that each GM can have up-to-date information about the replica.

4 Replica Management

Both GM and RM make replica management decisions to improve the performance that end-users will experience and to increase system resource utilization. To meet these requirements, algorithms for replica management must respond effectively to dynamically changing status of both client demand and replica utilization. For example, if a GM tries to acquire new replicas due to a transient short-term increase in client demand, then valuable system resources may be wasted.

The following sub-sections describe algorithms for both GM and RM replica management.

4.1 Replica Management in the GM

The GM runs these algorithms for replica management: replica selection, replica acquisition, and replica release. The challenge in designing algorithms for replica acquisition and replica release is that these algorithms should combine the goal of providing good performance to end-users with the goal of utilizing system resources efficiently. The GM runs both the replica acquisition and replica release algorithms periodically based on a configurable time parameter.

4.1.1 Replica Selection
Replica selection is the process by which the GM selects a replica among its local cache of replicas that is predicted to provide the best performance for the requesting client. If the cache is empty, then replica acquisition is required. Replica selection in the GM is based on response time prediction. With up-to-date status information about replicas in its local cache, the GM can predict the response time of the service accurately.

```
ReplicaAcquisition (R_curr, R_prev, P, Q)
{
    /*
    Suppose current time is t
    R_curr : average response time of local replicas over current time window
    R_prev: average response time of local replicas over previous time window
    T_threshold: maximum threshold of average response time
    P: the number of consecutive time windows such that
        R(t-1) ≥ R(t-2) ≥ ... ≥ R(t-P) and R(i) ≥ T_threshold, where
        R(i) : average response time at time window i ----------- (1)
    Q: the number of consecutive time windows such that
        R(i) ≥ T_threshold, t-1 ≥ i ≥ t-Q -------------------------------- (2)
    p, q: variables for storing the number of time windows that satisfy (1) and (2)
    */
    if (R_curr ≥ T_threshold) {
        if (R_curr ≥ R_prev)
            p++;
        else
            p = 0;
        q++;
    } else
        p = q = 0;

    if (p ≥ P or q ≥ Q)
        send "replica acquisition" request to the RM
}
```

Fig. 2. Replica Acquisition Algorithm

Response time (T_{resp}) consists of three components: service time (T_s), waiting time (T_w) and communication time (T_c) and can be formulated as $T_{resp} = T_s + T_w + T_c$. The GM will select a replica that achieves a predicted minimum T_{resp} from its cached pool. Service time denotes the time necessary for completing the service at the replica. Waiting time is the time that the request will wait in the replica's waiting queue before being served by the replica and is computed by multiplying T_s by the replica queue length. The service time and the queue length in the replica are periodically updated by the replicas. Communication time is the time for sending the request to the replica and receiving the results from the replica. By periodically probing SMs associated with local replicas, the GM can maintain current network performance between replicas and a client site.

4.1.2 Replica Acquisition

When a service is overloaded or the network is congested, end-users will suffer increased response time. By dynamically acquiring additional replicas from the RM, the GM can provide better performance to its end-users. The acquired replica may be a replica that already exists or a newly created one. This decision is made by the RM based on the degree of sharing for the existing replica and system resource utilization.

```
ReplicaRelease (U_threshold, P, Q, M)
{
    /*
    Suppose current time is t
    NumR: the number of currently cached replicas within this group
    U_threshold : minimum utilization
    P: the number of consecutive time windows such that
        U(t-1) ≤ U(t-2) ≤ ... ≤ U(t-P) and U(i) ≤ U_threshold, where
        U(i) : utilization of a replica at time window i ---------- (1)
    Q: the number of consecutive time windows such that
        U(i) ≤ U_threshold, t-1 ≥ i ≥ t-Q ------------------------------ (2)
    M: minimum number of replicas to retain within the group
    p, q: variables for storing the number of time windows that satisfy (1) and (2)
    */
    if (M ≥ NumR) return;
    replica_bins = empty /* contains candidate replicas for release */
    for (each local replica)  {
        U_curr <- utilization of the replica over current time window
        U_prev <- utilization of the replica over previous time window

        if (U_threshold ≥ U_curr)  {
            if (U_prev ≥ U_curr)  {
            p++;
            else
                p = 0;
            q++;
        } else
            p = q = 0;

        if (p ≥ P or q ≥ Q)
            insert the replica into replica_bins
    }
    find a replica in replica_bins whose utilization is the smallest and return the replica
}
```

Fig. 3. Replica Release Algorithm

Periodically, the GM computes the average performance over a recent time window. We define performance of a replica over a time window as the average response time of clients in the group that used the replica over the time period. With the performance of each replica in the cache, the average performance of the GM is calculated by averaging the performance of each replica.

Since the calculated performance includes both server load and network performance, we believe that it is a good indicator that represents performance that clients would experience. Once the average performance is computed, the GM next applies the replica acquisition algorithm to decide if it needs to acquire an additional replica from the RM.

The algorithm is based on a response time threshold ($T_{threshold}$) and two parameters, P and Q ($Q>P$), that control the degree of aggressiveness of replication (Fig. 2). Each GM is free to select these parameters differently. In particular, the threshold will be client- and service-specific. With P, the GM can avoid acquiring unnecessary replicas due to temporary network congestion or transient increase of client demand. P requires that response time be monotonically increasing above the threshold for P consecutive time epochs. If the test on P fails, we apply the Q test which is less restrictive. Q requires that the response time be simply above the threshold for Q consecutive time epochs. Smaller values of P and Q lead to more aggressive replication. P allows an immediate response to rapidly growing demand, while Q permits some performance fluctuation and is more conservative. Counters for P and Q are reset when the measured response time goes below threshold to help eliminate the risk of a transient response.

4.1.3   Replica Release

If the GM caches more replicas than it needs to meet its current threshold, some replicas may be idle and system resources would in turn be wasted. The GM will release unnecessary replicas back to the RM as long as clients requests can be serviced within the response time threshold.

As a utilization metric, the number of requests that the replica has served within this group over the time window is used. This is the local utilization. The replica may be actively used by other groups. As in replica acquisition, the GM should not respond to a transient decrease in client demand. We apply the same principle within the release algorithm as in replica acquisition. The difference is that the algorithm should be applied against each local replica. Fig 3. shows the replica release algorithm.

As in the replica acquisition algorithm, there are three configurable parameters: $U_{threshold}$, P and Q. If there are multiple underutilized replicas, the GM selects the least frequently used replica and releases it. Release does not mean that the replica is deleted. Deletion is a decision that is ultimately up to the RM, analogous to replica creation. A replica that has been released by all GM is idle, and is a possible candidate for deletion by the RM. In the current version of release algorithm, it will release at most one replica each time it is run (at each time interval). In addition, the GM indicates the minimum number of replicas it wishes to keep cached (M) irrespective of their utilization.

4.2 Replica Management in RM

The RM must perform the following replica management tasks: replica acquisition and replica release. Replica acquisition first examines the pool of available replicas not currently used by the group making the request. The RM determines whether an existing replica can provide predicted performance below the group's threshold while not compromising the performing of other groups sharing the replica. If this criteria cannot be met. The RM will create a new replica. Replica release simply indicates to the RM that the replica has been removed from the GMs cache. The RM notifies the replica of this change which allows the replica to eliminate any status updates to this GM saving network resources. In addition, the RM periodically checks the status of idle replicas (replicas released by all GMs). The RM is configured to maintain a minimum pool of idle replicas in the system. When this limit is exceeded, the RM will delete the replica that has been idle for the longest period of time.

5 Experiments

We have built a Service Grid prototype using the Legion system, a wide-area object-based distributed computing infrastructure [1]. In our Service Grid prototype, a service replica is implemented by a Legion object and accessed via remote method invocation. In this paper, we present results for a matrix multiplication service. In the prototype, the replica acquisition/release algorithms are run every 2 minutes, the service replica transmits its status every 10 seconds if it is dedicated to a single GM, otherwise it transmits its status every 1 second to each GM that is using it.

We present data for a subset of our larger testbed, which includes 11 hosts across three different sites, University of Minnesota, University of Virginia, and University of California at Berkeley. Clients are deployed across three sites (two of which are Service Grid sites), University of Minnesota (UMN), University of Texas at San Antonio (UTSA), and University of Virginia (UVA). In our experiments, UMN has 8 clients, UVA has 8 clients and UTSA has 5 clients. We generated a synthetic workload of client requests to the matrix multiplication service that is shaped to contain both demand growth and decline (Fig. 4).

Workload

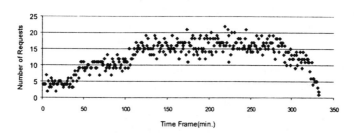

Fig. 4. Stair-shaped workload: Each point at t on x-axis in the graph represents the number of total client requests generated between t and t-1 minute

5.1 Response Time Prediction

Accurate prediction of response time is critical to replica management. The experimental results show that the response time prediction can be done with high accuracy for this service, often within 10 % (Fig. 5). However, prediction can drift when the rate of request generation exceeds the rate of information exchange. We are implementing an adaptive mechanism for controlling the interval for information collection.

Response Time Prediction

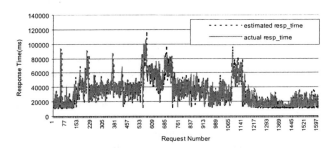

Response Time Prediction Accuracy

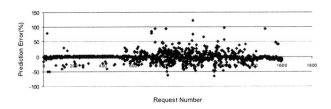

Fig. 5. Accuracy of response time prediction

5.2 Performance Comparison

To compare performance of our replica management scheme, we selected several parameter values from experimentation (Table 1). When a GM is created, it acquires an initial replica from the RM and always maintains at least one replica in its local cache (i.e. $M = 1$).

Table 1. Configurable parameters for GM

Parameters	UMN	UVA	UTSA
Maximum threshold (ms)	65000	85000	55000
P (replica acquisition)	3	3	2
Q (replica acquisition)	7	7	5
Minimum utilization	5	5	3
P (replica release)	4	4	4
Q (replica release)	9	9	9

We compare performance against pure static replication (2 and 8 replicas), and hybrid static/dynamic replication. In the hybrid approach, two replicas are statically replicated on UMN and UVA and each GM starts with these two replicas. In dynamic and hybrid schemes when client demand increases, the GM acquires additional replicas, and when client demand decreases, the GM releases underutilized replicas until the number of local replicas is at most two. Replica acquisition may return existing replica or may result in the creation of a new replica depending on the current system state.

Fig. 7-8 show the response time measured at the client sites under the different schemes. Static replication with 8 replicas achieves the lowest response time as it uses a large number of replicas. However, it suffers from very low utilization (Fig. 6).

Both dynamic and hybrid schemes are able to achieve performance below threshold (the performance objective) at a lower cost (higher utilization). Interestingly, they have the effect of "shortening" the impact of the workload peak. It appears that 4 static replicas would likely achieve the best overall performance given this workload, but in general this cannot be predicted apriori. In addition, suppose that only enough resources for two replicas were available at the time this service was initially deployed. A static scheme cannot exploit newly available resources were they become available later. Dynamic replication schemes make much more efficient use of system resources because they replicate only when necessary and release resources when demand declines. The hybrid scheme achieves a good balance of low response time and good utilization and appears to be a promising approach.

Average Replica Utilization

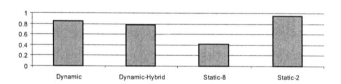

Fig. 6. Comparative utilization for different replica management policies

Average Response Time

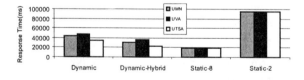

Fig. 7. Comparative performance for different replica acquisition policies

Static-8

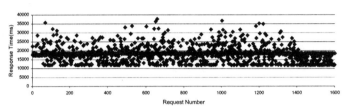

Dynamic-Hybrid

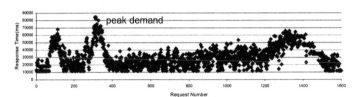

Dynamic

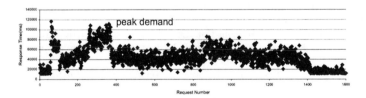

Static-2

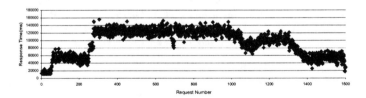

Fig. 8. Measured response time under 4 replica acquisition strategies

6 Conclusions

We described a new architecture for the efficient delivery of high-demand network services, the Service Grid. To achieve scalable, reliable, and adaptive performance, the Service Grid performs dynamic service replication and deletion in response to changing client demand. It implements an algorithmic framework for dynamic replica management that controls the degree of aggressiveness in creating and removing replicas. A Service Grid prototype was built using the Legion system and preliminary results for a computationally-intensive service indicate that dynamic replica management can be done to meet end-user performance goals at a much lower cost than fully static replication. Future work includes investigating the sensitivity of both response time and utilization to the parameters of the replica management algorithm.

7 References

1. A.S. Grimshaw and W.A. Wulf, "The Legion Vision of a Worldwide Virtual Computer", *Communications of the ACM*, Vol. 40(1), 1997
2. A. Vahdat et al., "Active Names: Flexible Location and Transport of Wide-area Resources", *Proceedings of the USENIX Symposium on Internet Technologies and Systems*, 1999
3. B. Noble et al., "Fluid Replication", Proceedings of the Network Storage Symposium, 1999
4. C. Yoshikawa et al., "Using Smart Clients to Build Scalable Services", *Proceedings of the USENIX Technical Conference*, January 1997
5. Ellen W. Zegura et al., "Application-Layer Anycasting: A Server Selection Architecture and Use in a Replicated Web Service", *IEEE/ACM Transactions on Networking*, Vol. 8(4), August 2000
6. Jaspal Subholk et al., "Automatic Node Selection for High Performance Application on Networks", *Proceedings of the 7th ACM SIGPLAN Symposium on Principles and Practice of Parallel Programming*, May 1999
7. Jon B. Weissman and Byoung-Dai Lee, "The Service Grid: Supporting Scalable Heterogeneous Services in Wide-Area Networks", *Proceedings of Symposium on Applications and the Internet*, January 2001
8. H. Casanova and J. Dongarra, "NetSolve: A Network Server for Solving Computational Science Problems", University of Tennessee TR CS-95-313, 1995
9. M. Baentsch et al., "Enhancing the Web Infrastructure- From Caching to Replication", *IEEE Internet Computing*, Vol. 1(2), March 1997
10. Michael Wang et al., "The Bio-Networking Architecture: A Biologically Inspired Approach to the Design of Scalable, Adaptive and Survivable/Available network Applications", *Proceedings of Symposium on Application and the Internet*, January 2001
11. M. Rabinovich et al., "A Dynamic Object Replication and Migration protocol for an Internet Hosting Service", *IEEE International Conference on Distributed Computing Systems*, May 1999
12. R.L. Carter and M.E. Crovella, "Server Selection using Dynamic Path Characterization in Wide-Area Networks", *Proceedings of IEEE Infocom '97*, April 1997
13. Sandra G. Dykes et al., "An Empirical Evaluation of Client-side Server Selection Algorithm", *Proceedings of IEEE Infocom '00*, March 2000
14. Y. Amir et al., "WALRUS – A Low Latency, High Throughput Web Service Using Internet-wide Replication", *Proceedings of the 19th International Conference on distributed Computing Systems Workshop*, June 1999

Identifying Dynamic Replication Strategies for a High-Performance Data Grid

Kavitha Ranganathan and Ian Foster

Department of Computer Science, The University of Chicago
1100 E 58ᵗʰ Street, Chicago, IL 60637
krangana@cs.uchicago.edu, foster@mcs.anl.gov

Abstract. Dynamic replication can be used to reduce bandwidth consumption and access latency in high performance "data grids" where users require remote access to large files. Different replication strategies can be defined depending on when, where, and how replicas are created and destroyed. We describe a simulation framework that we have developed to enable comparative studies of alternative dynamic replication strategies. We present preliminary results obtained with this simulator, in which we evaluate the performance of five different replication strategies for three different kinds of access patterns. The data in this scenario is read-only and so there are no consistency issues involved. The simulation results show that significant savings in latency and bandwidth can be obtained if the access patterns contain a small degree of geographical locality.

1   Introduction

A data grid connects a collection of geographically distributed computer and storage resources [6] that may be located in different parts of a country or even in different countries, and enables users to share data and other resources. Research projects such as GriPhyN [11], PPDG, and the Eu Data Grid aim to build scientific data grids that enable scientists sitting at various universities and research labs to collaborate with one another and share data sets and computational power.

Physics experiments such as CMS, ATLAS, LIGO and SDSS [11] will churn out large amounts of scientific data (in some cases, the scale of petabytes/year). This data needs to be used by thousands of scientists around the world. The sheer volume of the data and computation involved poses new problems that deal with data access, processing and distribution.

There are two aspects to a grid: sharing of data and sharing of resources. A scientist located at a small university may need to run a time consuming processing job on a huge data set. She may choose to get the data from where it exists to the local computing resource and run the job there. Alternatively it may be better to transfer the job to where the data exists or, both the job specification and the data may be sent to a third location that will perform the computation and return the results to the scientist. We focus here only on the data distribution aspect of a grid.

The data grid envisioned by the GriPhyN project is hierarchical in nature and is organized in tiers. The source where the data is produced is denoted as Tier 0 (e.g. CERN). Next are the Tier 1 national centers, the Tier 2 regional centers (RC), the Tier 3 workgroups and finally Tier 4, which consists of thousands of desktops.

1.1 Replication

When a user generates a request for a file, large amounts of bandwidth could be consumed to transfer the file from the server to the client. Furthermore the latency involved could be significant considering the size of the files involved. Our study investigates the usefulness of creating replicas to distribute data sets among the various scientists in the grid. The main aims of using replication are to reduce access latency and bandwidth consumption. Replication can also help in load balancing and can improve reliability by creating multiple copies of the same data. Static replication can be used to achieve some of the above-mentioned gains but has the drawback that it cannot adapt to changes in user behavior. In our scenario, where the data amounts to petabytes, and the user community is in the order of thousands around the world, static replication does not sound feasible. Such a system needs dynamic replication strategies, where replica creation, deletion and management are done automatically and strategies have the ability to adapt to changes in user behavior. Our study examines different dynamic replication strategies for a grid. There are many related questions of resource discovery (so that the request goes to the nearest replica) and furthermore how to distribute these requests among replicas to archive best results. In this study however we shall concentrate on the replica placement issue.

The three fundamental questions any replica placement strategy has to answer are: When should replicas be created? Which files should be replicated? Where should replicas be placed? The answers to these questions lead us to different replication strategies.

We use simulation to evaluate the performance of each different strategy. Since most datasets in the scientific data grid scenario are read-only, we do not consider the overhead of updates. This paper describes a grid simulator framework and also reports the preliminary results obtained using our simulator.

The rest of the paper is organized as follows. Section 2 describes the specific grid scenario that we use for our simulations. Section 3 discusses the simulator we built to conduct our experiments. Section 4 describes the replication and caching strategies that we evaluate. Section 5 presents the results of the experiments and we interpret the results of the experiments in Section 6. We end the paper with our conclusions and future directions in Section 7.

2   Grid Scenario

The particular data grid setup that we are studying in this paper is described below.

There are four tiers in the grid with all data being produced at the top most tier (the root). Tier 2 consists of the regional centers around the country; in the scenario considered in the experiments reported here, we have four of them. The next tier is composed of work groups at universities or research labs. The final tier (individual workstations) consists of the sources from which the requests arrive. There are a total of 85 nodes in the grid with 64 of them generating requests.

The storage capacity at each tier is given in Table 1. In our experiments, we assume that all network links are 320 Mbytes/sec in bandwidth [13]. In reality network bandwidths vary widely across tiers. The total data generated at the source is assumed to be 2.2 petabytes. The data is stored in files of uniform size of two gigabytes each.

Table 1. System parameters. Network performance and node capacity of a node at each tier in the hierarchy as described in [13].

Tier	Network Bandwidth to Next Tier (MB/s)	Storage Capacity (TB)
1	320	2200
2	320	1000
3	320	120

All requests for files are generated from the leaf nodes. Request patterns for the files can exhibit various locality properties, including:

Temporal Locality: Recently accessed files are likely to be accessed again.

Geographical locality (Client locality): Files recently accessed by a client are likely to be accessed by nearby clients.

Spatial Locality (File Locality): Files near a recently accessed file are likely to be accessed.

In our definition of spatial locality we have to specify what "near" means. This definition involves a study of the nature of the data in the files and how we can relate files to each other. Since this paper deals with a general data grid we defer the study of relationships of data until we model a specific grid.

We yet do not know to what extent file access patterns will exhibit the locality properties described above and whether there will be any locality. We can only make educated guesses at this point. The worst-case scenario is when the access patterns do not exhibit any locality at all, generating random access patterns can simulate this situation.

3   Methodology of Study

To identify a suitable replication strategy for a high performance data grid we decided to use a simulator. Since none of the tools currently available exactly fitted our needs, we built a simulator to model a data grid and data transfers in it. Our simulator uses

PARSEC [15], a discrete event simulation tool to model events like file requests and data transfers.

3.1 The Simulator

The simulator consists of three parts. The basic core simulates the various nodes in the different tiers of the data grid, the links between them, and the file transfers from one tier to another. Various replication strategies are built on top of this core and compose the next layer. The final component is the driver entity of the program, which triggers file requests. The driver entity reads an input file, specifying the access patterns to be simulated.

3.2 How the Simulation Works

Topology specification: Starting a simulation involves first specifying the topology of the grid, including the number of nodes at each tier, how they are connected to each other, the bandwidth of each link, and the location of the files across various nodes.

Starting the simulation: Access patterns are read from a file, with each line representing one access and specifying at what time which node needs a particular file. The driver reads the data and triggers the corresponding node. When a node receives a "File needed by me" trigger it needs to locate and request the "nearest" replica of that file.

Locating nearest replica: There are various proposed methods for locating the nearest replica; some of these can involve complex algorithms to identify the closest copy. Location of the best replica is however a related but different topic than what we are trying to answer. This paper concentrates on designing and isolating the best replica placement strategy for a grid. However, to show the effectiveness of any dynamic replication strategy a node needs to be able to identify the nearest replica. We solve this problem by using the 'least number of hops' heuristic. The nearest replica is one, which is the least number of steps away from the node. In the case of a tie between two or more replicas, one of them is selected randomly.

File Transfer: Once the server gets the request for a file, it sends it off to the client. The tree structure of the grid means that there is only one shortest path that the messages and files can travel to get to the destination. When a file is being transferred through a link, the link is busy and cannot transport any other file for the duration of the transfer. The delay incurred in transferring a file depends on the size of the file, the bandwidth of the link and the number of pending requests. A node is busy for the duration it transfers its file to the network and any incoming data has to wait for the current transaction to finish.

Record Keeping: Each node keeps a record of how much time it took for each file that it requested to be transported to it. This time record forms a basis to compare various replication strategies. The same series of file request are run through different strategies and the one that has a lower average response time is considered better than the others. The various replication strategies are described in the next section.

Scaling: The amount of data in the system is in the order of petabytes. To enable simulation of such large data values, a scale of 1:10,000 was used. That is, the number of files in the system was reduced by a factor of 10,000. Accordingly the storage capacity at each tier was also reduced. Table 2 below illustrates this fact.

Table 2. Grid parameters before and after scaling

	Actual Size	After Scaling
Number of files	1,000,000	100
Storage at Tier 1	2200 Terabytes	220 Gigabytes
Tier 2	1000 Terabytes	100 Gigabytes
Tier 3	120 Terabytes	12 Gigabytes

The link bandwidths and file sizes remained the same. The reason we use a scaling factor is to make the simulation of such a system feasible on a single machine. The meta-data for a million files would be very memory intensive. Since we need to scale the number of files, the storage capacity at each tier needs to be scaled accordingly. This is because the performance of replication strategies is directly dependent on the percentage of files that can be stored at each node. Scaling both the number of files in the system and the capacity at each node achieves this. We do not scale the file sizes also as that would have an increasing effect on the percentage of files that can be stored at each node. Since the file sizes are not scaled, the bandwidths also remain unscaled so that the transport latency is modeled correctly. Individual workstations are assumed to be able to cache one file of size 2 Gigabytes.

Access Patterns: Since the physics data grid is not yet functional there are no actual file access patterns available as of now, and we must work with artificial traces. We derive three such traces. The simulation was first run on random access patterns. This being the worst-case scenario, more realistic access patterns that contained varying amounts of temporal and geographical locality were also generated The three different kinds of traces are described below:

P-random: Random access patterns. No locality in patterns.

P1: Data that contained a small degree of temporal locality

P2: Data containing a small degree of geographical and temporal locality

The index used to measure the amount of locality in the patterns is denoted by 'q', where $0<q<1$. If $q = 0$, it means that requests are completely random and there is no locality. At the other end of the spectrum, when $q =1$ it means all requests are for the same file. We used $q = 0.05$ to generate data with a small degree of temporal/geographical locality, using geometric distribution for file popularity.

3.3 Performance Evaluation

We compare different replication strategies by measuring the average response time and the total bandwidth consumed.

Response Time: This is the time that elapses from when a node sends a request for a file until it receives the complete file. If a local copy of the file exists, the response time is assumed to be zero. The average of all response times for the length of the simulation is calculated.

Bandwidth Consumption: This includes the bandwidth consumed for data transfers occurred when a node requests a file and when a server creates a replica at another node.

4 Replication/Caching Strategies

We implemented and evaluated six different strategies. This work and our results both demonstrate what the simulator is capable of doing, and also help us understand the dynamics of a grid system.

In this paper we distinguish between caching and replication. Replication is assumed to be a server side phenomenon. A server decides when and where to create a copy of one of its files. It may do this randomly or by recording client behavior or by some other means. But the decision to make a copy (replica) and send it to some other node is taken solely by the server. Caching is defined as a client side phenomenon. A client requests a file and stores a copy of the file locally for future use. Any other nearby node can also request that cached copy. The different strategies are discussed below.

Strategy 1: No Replication or Caching: The base case against which we compare the various strategies is when no replication takes place. The entire data set is available at the root of the hierarchy when the simulation starts. We then run the set of access patterns and calculate the average response time and bandwidth consumed when there is no replication involved

Strategy 2: Best Client: Each node maintains a detailed history for each file that it contains [12] indicating the number of requests for that file and the nodes that each request came from. The replication strategy then works as follows: At a given time interval each node checks to see if the number of requests for any of its file has exceeded a threshold. If so, the best client for that file is identified. The best client is the one that has generated the most requests for that file. The node then creates a replica of that file at the best client. Thus all files that exceed the threshold of the number of requests are replicated elsewhere. Once a replica is created, the 'request details' for the file at the server node are cleared. After this, the recording process begins again

The file replacement algorithm at each node is discussed later and is the same for all of the replication strategies to facilitate a common ground for comparing them.

Strategy 3: Cascading Replication: The best analogy for this strategy is a three-tiered fountain. The water originates at the top. When it fills the top ledge it overflows to the next level. When this level also overflows the water reaches down to the lowest part.

The data in this strategy flows in a similar way. Once the threshold for a file is exceeded at the root, a replica is created at the next level, but on the path to the best client. Hence the new site for the replica is an ancestor of the best client. Once the threshold for the file is exceeded at Level 2 it is then replicated at the next lower tier and so on. A popular file may ultimately be replicated at the client itself.

The advantage of this strategy is that storage space at all tiers is used. Another advantage is that if the access patterns do not exhibit a high degree of temporal locality, geographical locality is exploited by this strategy. By not replicating at the very source of requests but at a higher level the data is brought closer to other nodes in the same sub-tree.

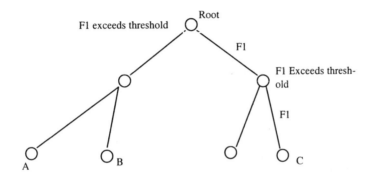

Fig.1.*Cascading Replication.* At the root the number of requests for F1 exceed the threshold and a copy is sent to the next layer. Eventually the threshold is exceeded at the next layer and a copy is sent to Client C.

Strategy 4: Plain Caching: The client that requests a file stores a copy locally. Since these files are large (2 Gigabytes each) and a client has enough space to store only one file at a time, the files get replaced quickly.

Strategy 5: Caching plus Cascading Replication: This combines strategy three and four. The client caches files locally. The server periodically identifies the popular files and propagates them down the hierarchy. Note that the clients are always located at the leaves of the tree but any node in the hierarchy can be a server. Specifically, a Client can act as a Server to its siblings. (Siblings are nodes that have the same parent).

Strategy 6: Fast Spread: In this method a replica of the file is stored at each node along its path to the client [14]. That is, when a client requests a file, a copy is stored at each tier on the way. This leads to a faster spread of data. The generic file replacement strategy used for all the cases is discussed below.

File Replacement Strategy: The storage spaces at all levels eventually fill up. An efficient file replacement strategy is needed so that popular files are retained and not displaced as and when new files arrive. Initially we decided to expunge the least popular file from the list. But this might delete a relatively new file that has just come in and not yet been requested that might become popular in the future. Thus there needs to be a measure of time and hence the age of each file in that cache. The replacement strategy we employed takes care of both these aspects and is a combination of least popular and the age of the file. If more than one file are equally unpopular, the oldest file is deleted

We clear the popularity logs at a given time interval in order to capture the dynamics of the access patterns. Over time users may shift from using one group of files to another group etc. We can thus expect that the effectiveness of the strategy will depend on how well the time interval is tuned to the access behavior. Another parameter that has to be tuned for each scenario is the threshold. Only if the number of requests exceeds this threshold is the file replicated. We can imagine refining the algorithm so that the "time_to_check" interval and threshold automatically change according to user behavior. However, this is left for future work.

5   Experimental Results

We present the results for five strategies, no replication, plain Caching, Best Client, Caching+Cascading, and Fast Spread. We do not discuss pure Cascading as its results can be found in strategy 5, Cascading+Caching. The experiments were run on the three access patterns defined earlier: P-random, P1, and P2 and each simulation was run for a thousand requests.

Random patterns are the worst-case scenario and it seems sensible to assume the patterns will exhibit some amount of geographical and temporal locality, as scientists tend to work in groups on projects. That said we proceed to discuss the results obtained from the experiments.

When P-random data was used, all strategies except for Best-Client and Cascading show significant improvement in the access latency as compared to the case of no replication. Best-Client does not seem to work well for random access patterns, as the average response time is four times more than when no replication/caching policy is used. Again, in terms of bandwidth savings, Best Client utilizes almost the same amount of bandwidth as the base case of no replication. In the case of P1 access patterns (patterns with a small amount of temporal locality) all strategies except for Best-Client yield positive savings in both access latency and bandwidth consumption. Only in the case of P2 (patterns with both temporal and geographical locality) does Best-Client show any savings. Even in this case the bandwidth savings by using Best-Client are marginal (10% savings as compared to the base case of no replication/caching) although the latency savings are significant (40% when compared to the base case). However Best Client consistently performs much worse than Plain Caching.

We next discuss the results obtained by the other three strategies as Best-Client does not seem a good candidate for a replication strategy for a grid. The two graphs below contain results for Cascading+Caching, Fast Spread, and Plain Caching. The first two strategies are compared, with Plain Caching being the standard of comparison. Thus the graphs illustrate the savings achieved by Fast Spread and Cascading, beyond those achieved by only caching the files.

As Fig.3 indicates, Cascading does not work well when the access patterns contain no locality. For random data, the response time is far better when Plain Caching is used rather than Cascading. Fast spread works much better than Plain Caching for random data. There is almost a 50% reduction in response times in the case of Fast Spread.

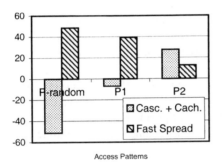
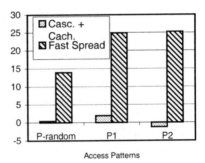

Fig.3. Percentage savings in response time (*left*) and bandwidth consumption (*right*) as compared to Plain Caching for all three kinds of access patterns

In the case of P1 patterns, the advantage of Fast-Spread over Caching decreases and Cascading works almost as well as Caching. Once the data contains more locality (as is the case with P2) Cascading has a significant improvement in performance, its average response time is almost 30% less than that for Plain Caching. Fast Spread however has less than 15% improvement over Caching for patterns that contain geographical locality. These results are interpreted further in Section 6.

We now discuss the amount of bandwidth savings for the different cases. As shown in Fig.3, Cascading does not differ significantly from Caching in terms of bandwidth consumption. The difference between the two strategies falls with the range of plus or minus 2% for all the access patterns. Fast Spread on the other hand leads to large savings in bandwidth usage, up to 25% when the access patterns contain locality.

6   Discussions

Among the methods of replication that we consider in the paper, Best-Client performs the worst. In many cases the overheads it creates are more than the advantages of the strategy and it performs worse than the base case of no replication.

Considering the remaining candidates Plain Caching, Cascading + Caching and Fast Spread there is no sure best strategy for all scenarios. Fast Spread consistently performs better than Caching both in terms of response time and bandwidth savings.

In spite of the overhead Fast Spread has, in terms of excessive creation of replicas its advantages over Caching are plainly evident. The bandwidth savings of Fast Spread are up to 25% more than that of Caching [refer to Fig.3]. The disadvantage is that it has high storage requirements. The entire storage space at each tier is fully utilized by Fast-Spread.

Cascading on the other hand utilizes less then 50% of the storage space at each tier since it involves a judicious creation of replicas. The bandwidth requirements of Cascading however are greater than that for Fast Spread. This is because every replica that is created has to be sent separately to the new location as opposed to Fast Spread where a copy is created in the process of transferring the requested file.

Cascading, moreover does not work well when the access patterns are totally random. In fact it does not even work as well as Caching for random user patterns. This can be attributed to the fact that the overhead in creating these extra copies of files is not offset by the advantage of moving them closer to the users. The copied files are not asked for often enough to justify the increased data movement. However, when the patterns contain a small amount of locality, the performance of Cascading improves significantly. It even performs better than Fast Spread for P2 patterns, with an average response time almost 18% better than that for Fast-Spread. There are however no significant bandwidth savings in using Cascading over Caching when we assume only a small amount of geographical locality.

These results lead us to conclude that if grid users exhibit total randomness in accessing data then the strategy that would work best is Fast Spread. If however there are sufficient amount of geographical locality in the access patterns, Cascading as a replication policy would work better than the others. With more or less the same amount of bandwidth utilization as Caching, Cascading lowers response times significantly, while judiciously using storage space.

The above results also indicate that depending on what is more important in the grid scenario, lower response times or lesser bandwidth consumption, a tradeoff between Cascading and Fast Spread can be made. If the chief aim is to elicit faster responses from the system, Cascading might work better. On the other hand if conserving bandwidth is of top priority, Fast Spread is a better grid replication strategy.

7 Conclusions and Future Work

We have presented and evaluated dynamic replication strategies for managing large data sets in a high performance data grid. Replication enables faster access to files, decreases bandwidth consumption, and distributes server load. In contrast to static replication, dynamic replication automatically creates and deletes replicas according to changing access patterns, and thus ensures that the benefits of replication continue even if user behavior changes.

We discussed the components of the simulator we built and explained how we used the simulator to study the performance of different replication strategies within a grid environment We generated three different kinds of access patterns, random, temporal, and geographical and showed how the bandwidth savings and latency differ with access patterns. Two strategies performed the best in our tests: Cascading and Fast Spread. While Fast Spread worked well for random request patterns, Cascading worked better when there was a small amount of locality. We analyzed why we thought these were the best strategies and the pros and cons of each method.

In future work, we want to use the simulator to test the performance of some more advanced replication strategies. We also have plans to extend the simulator so that we can plug in different algorithms for selecting the best replica.

In our work so far, the replication strategies we discussed exploit both temporal and geographical locality of the request patterns. What we put off for later is considering the spatial locality of the requests. Once we better understand the relationship among various files in a scientific data set, some amount of pre-fetching is possible.

Another area for further research is to study the movement of code towards data. We have assumed here that clients ask for files and locally run the data through their code to analyze the data. Thus we have only considered moving data towards code. Another option is to move code towards where data resides and communicate only the result of the computation back to the client. This is a feasible option considering that in the data grid scenario the data may be tens of thousands of times larger than either the code or the result.

A data grid enables thousands of scientists sitting at various universities and research centers to collaborate and share their data and resources. The sheer volume of the data and computation calls for sophisticated data management and resource allocation. This paper is one step into better understanding the dynamics of such a system and the issues involved in increasing the overall efficiency of a grid by intelligent replica creation and movement.

Acknowledgements

This research was supported by the National Science Foundation's "GriPhyN" project under contract ITR-0086044.

References

1. Acharya, S., Zdonik, S.B.: An efficient scheme for dynamic data replication: Technical report CS-93-94-43, Brown University
2. Baentsc, M., et al.: Quantifying the overall impact of caching and replication in the web. University of Kaiserslautern February (1997)
3. Bestavros, A., Cunha, C.: Server-initiated document dissemination for the WWW. IEEE Data Engineering Bulletin, Vol. 19 (1996) 3–11
4. Bestavros, A.: Demand-based document dissemination to reduce traffic and balance load in distributed information systems. IEEE symposium on Parallel and Distributed Processing, San Antonio, TX (1995)
5. Bhatacharjee, S., Calvert, K.L., Zegura, E.: Self-organizing wide-area network caches. Georgia Institute of Technology GIT-CC-97/31(1997)

6. Chervenak, A., Foster, I., Kesselman, C., Salisbury, C., Tuecke, S.: The Data Grid: Towards an Architecture for the Distributed Management and Analysis of Large Scientific Data Sets. J. Network and Computer Applications (2000)

7. Chuang, J.C.I., Sirbu, M.A.: Distributed Network Storage with Quality-of-Service Guarantees. Proc. INET'99 (1999)

8. Fan, L., Cao, P., Almeida, J., Broder, A.Z.: Summary cache: a scalable wide-area web cache sharing protocol. ACM SIGCOMM (1998)

9. Foster, I., Kesselman, C. (eds.): The Grid: Blueprint for a New Computing Infrastructure. Morgan Kaufmann (1999)

10. Foster, I., Kesselman, C., Tuecke, S.: The Anatomy of the Grid: Enabling Scalable Virtual Organizations. Intl. J. Supercomputer Applications, (to appear).

11. GriPhyN: The Grid Physics Network Project http://www.griphyn.org

12. Gwertzman, J., Seltzer, M.: The case for geographical push-caching. 5th Annual Workshop on Hot Operating Systems (1995)

13. Holtman, K.: HEPGRID2001: A Benchmark for Virtual Data Grid Schedulers. http://kholtman.home.cern.ch/kholtman/tmp/benchv3.ps

14. Michel, S., Nguyen, K., Rosenstein, A., Zhang, L., Floyd, L., Jacobson, V.: Adaptive Web Caching: Towards a New Global Caching Architecture. Proceedings of the 3rd International WWW Caching Workshop (1998)

15. Parsec home page http://pcl.cs.ucla.edu/projects/parsec

16. Rabinovich, M., Aggarwal, A.: RaDaR: A scalable architecture for a global Web hosting service. The 8th Int. World Wide Web Conf, May (1999)

17. Samar, A., Stockinger, H.: Grid Data Management Pilot (GDMP): A Tool for Wide Area Replication. IASTED International Conference on Applied Informatics, Innsbruck, Austria (2001)

18. Wolfson, O., Jajodia, S., Huang, Y.: An Adaptive Data Replication algorithm. ACM transactions on Database Systems (1997)

Ensemble Scheduling: Resource Co-Allocation on the Computational Grid

Jon B. Weissman and Pramod Srinivasan

Department of Computer Science and Engineering, University of Minnesota, Twin cities
jon@cs.umn.edu

Abstract. This paper investigates a novel scheduling paradigm, ensemble scheduling, that can be used to schedule mixed workloads consisting of single- and multi-resource applications in Grid environments. Ensemble scheduling exploits the pattern of prior resource requests for ensemble (multi-resource) applications to dynamically partition the workload across the system resources. We show via simulation that an ensemble-aware scheduler can provide better performance both for ensemble applications and the more common single resource applications in Grid environment.

1 Introduction

Computational Grids offer an attractive platform for resource-intensive parallel scientific applications. The Grid has the potential to enable applications that require resources contained in one or more remote sites. For example, applications may require coupling of multiple supercomputers for very large-scale simulations [1], access to remote instruments [5], or access to remote data sources [2], all spanning resources in multiple sites. The applications of interest in this paper require *temporal* coupling between the distributed resources because the application components interact directly during the course of the execution. We term the resources required by these applications as *resource ensembles* and the applications as *ensemble applications*. In contrast, embarrassingly parallel applications such as parameter studies and monte-carlo simulations while often scalable to multi-site resources, do not require simultaneous resource availability: resources can be freely added as the computation proceeds.

Grid infrastructure projects such as Legion [6] and Globus [4] are developing software that allow remote resources to be accessed and coupled together. However, ensuring that the resources required by applications are available simultaneously is a difficult problem. This problem has been termed resource co-allocation. Much of the research into this problem has focused on implementation mechanisms based on resource reservation. The primary issues are how to specify and guarantee a reservation for a single ensemble application across different sites with different administrative policies controlling resources. Increasingly, resource schedulers including the Maui scheduler and Portable Batch Scheduler (PBS) are planning reservation support.

It is clear that reservations and co-allocation support will become a standard part of production Grids, and ensemble applications will become more commonplace. We also believe that as Grids mature, they will play a role similar to today's production parallel supercomputers serving a variety of high end scientific applications including a **mixture** of traditional parallel application (e.g. single MPP-style applications) and ensemble applications. Production Grids will likely become rapidly over-subscribed much like production parallel supercomputers [3]. Consequently, efficient scheduling of Grid resources across this mixed workload becomes crucial to achieving high performance for **both** application classes. Prior work established that individual multi-resource application could be efficiently scheduled in Grid environments [9].

In this paper, we investigate how both types of applications can be efficiently scheduled together. We develop a new class of scheduling algorithms that exploit two specific properties of ensemble applications: (1) they often require specific resources (e.g. a particular telescope or a remote data source or several MPPs), and (2) they will repeat (e.g. the ensemble of resources requested by an application will repeat). The latter property is based on the view that ensemble applications will be run repeatedly over time. These properties suggest that ensemble applications will make predictable **and** repeatable requests to the system.

We compared the performance of *ensemble-aware* scheduling to simple scheduling policies such as random and shortest queue for a wide-range of simulated workloads. We found that it always outperforms random scheduling and that it outperforms shortest queue for a large number of characteristic workloads. In many instances, ensemble-aware scheduling leads to better performance for **both** single resource applications and ensemble applications. We present the application and scheduling models and a summary of our performance results.

2 Ensemble Scheduling

2.1 Application Model

Ensemble applications require resources in multiple sites. For simplicity, we assume that an ensemble application requires a single resource in one or more sites. In contrast, *regular* applications require resources in a single site only. We model the underlying computational Grid as a connected network of resources with dynamically varying available capacity. Resources are represented as having a type, capacity, and active queue, and a waiting queue (Fig. 1). The type indicates the class of the resource and its attributes. For example, MPP-O2K represents an Origin 2000 MPP. The capacity is the size of a resource in units that are meaningful to the type of resources. For example, it could be the number of processors within a MPP resource, the number of simultaneous connections allowed to a remote data server, etc. Applications request some number of resource units. As applications are allocated against the capacity, the available capacity *ac* decreases (perhaps to 0). The active queue is the set of applications that are currently using the resource (and how much they are using) and the waiting queue is the set of applications waiting to use some amount of the resource. Applications are modeled completely by their resource requirements. Each resource is utilized by an application component running at the site where the resource is contained. Each application component communicates and synchronized periodically during the execution.

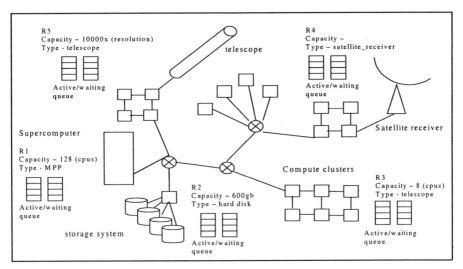

Fig. 1. Grid Model.

For each desired resource, the application specifies the *min_amt* and *desired_amt* of the resource. The *min_amt* is the minimum amount required to run the application, and the *desired_amt* is the amount that if allocated, is predicted to be the best for the application. There is no benefit to allocating an amount of resources that exceeds the *desired_amt*. If the application were allocated its *desired_amt* for each requested resource, then it would attain its ideal execution time, *ideal_time*. This can be captured by an application-specific cost function f that determines execution time as a function of allocated resources, where a_i is the allocated amount for resource R_i, for example,

$$f(a_1=desired\_amt_1, a_2=desired\_amt_2, ...) = ideal\_time$$

The application also indicates the time frame that the resource is needed: *start_resource_time_i* and *end_resource_time_i* for each requested resource R_i (offset from the application's beginning execution time). In this paper, we have adopted a co-allocation model for resources in which: *start_resource_time = 0* with the resource allocation held for the duration of the application (*end_resource >=_time ideal_time*). In production environments, an application may not always be able to obtain its *desired_amt*. If an allocated resource amount, $a_i < desired\_amti$, then the execution time must be penalized.

This captured by the function f. An example of f is the following:

$$f(...) = max_i(desired\_amt_i / a_i) * ideal\_time$$

This particular f is constructed by assuming:

- All resources are held for the entire duration of the application

• Resource sharing has a linear penalty per resource

It applies to both regular applications (single resource) and ensemble applications (multiple resources). It proportionally penalizes the execution time by a linear term in the event that the desired amount is not available. Linear sharing models have been proposed to model a variety of resource types such as CPUs and networks. The scheduling model does not depend in any way on this formulation of f. Different penalty function can easily be used.

When an application is assigned to a resource and $min\_amt < ac$, the application is placed on the *active_queue* of the resource to start execution, and the available capacity ac of the resource is decremented by a_i. If an application is assigned to a resource, but its $min\_amt > ac$, then the application must be queued on the *wait_queue* until additional resources are released by active applications upon their completion. Applications are allocated against the resource in a FCFS discipline. An ensemble application does not begin executing until **all** requested resources are available simultaneously with at least min_amt capacity. Applications enter the Grid with their resource requirements (Fig. 2).

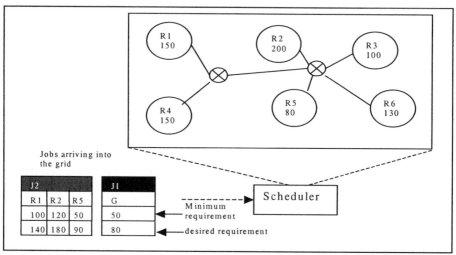

Fig. 2. Application Resource Requirements. J_1 is a regular application and J_2 is an ensemble application.

2.2 Workload Model

The workload consists of a mixture of regular and ensemble applications. Regular applications are characterized by a single resource request and ensemble applications by multiple resource requests. Regular applications may request an amount of a specific resource (e.g. they must run on R_j) or a resource class (e.g. they must run on any MPP-O2K). Similarly, an ensemble application can request a specific resource or a resource class for each required resource. We believe that ensemble applications will have four key properties:

- The # of distinct resources they request will typically be small (e.g. 2 to 5)
- The # of distinct resources ensembles requested will also small
- Ensemble applications will be on the high-end of resource consumption
- Ensemble applications will repeat

The first property reflects current practice in which the number of distinct resources (e.g. MPPs) used within ensemble applications is small (<5) [7]. The second property reflects a belief that while ensemble applications will be more common in production Grids, they will still be in the minority as compared with single resource applications. The third property reflects a prediction that ensemble applications (particularly supercomputing coupling) are likely to be resource-intensive. For example, an application that wishes to use 3 MPPs probably requires close to all available processors within each MPP (otherwise a single MPP could be used). The first three properties are not crucial to scheduling algorithm, but they influence how the system workload is generated. The final property is critical to the scheduling algorithm and is based on our belief that in production Grids, ensemble applications will be run repeatedly. Because the effort in building ensemble applications will be large, this effort is justified for applications that are expected to be repeatedly. In fact, application repetition is also a property of many single resource MPP applications [3][8]. However, we believe it will be the rule, not the exception, for ensemble applications. Application repetition arises in several ways including: the application will be run on different data sets or requires interaction with remote devices or instruments that are providing periodic data.

Ensemble applications require co-allocation of all required resources. Two model of co-allocation are possible: *reservations* and *earliest-possible-time*. Reservations are needed if the application requires access to resources at very specific times (e.g. a telescope is providing data every 2 hours). Earliest-possible-time determines the earliest time that all desired resources will be free based on a prediction of the wait time for each resource. This information is known in our model since the time a resource will be held is simply the application execution time (which is provided by *f*). In this paper, we have experimented with *earliest-possible-time* with reservations left for future work. Ensemble scheduling is compatible with either co-allocation model.

Generating the application mix is controlled by a parameter which specifies the percentage of ensemble vs. regular applications. Ensemble applications are generated by following the four properties above. In particular, a small set of resource ensembles each with 2 to 5 resources is pre-generated (this satisfies properties 1 and 2). An ensemble application is generated by selecting one of these pre-generated ensembles with uniform probability (this satisfies property 4). The amount of desired resources for regular and ensemble applications are generated differently. Some analysis of supercomputing workloads indicated that jobs (i.e. regular applications) were much more likely to request a smaller number of processors (i.e. resources) [3]. A exponential pdf is used to model this relationship (Fig. 3, where the amount of requested resources is [1..MaxR]). Following property 3, we generated an inverted distribution for ensemble applications since we believe that they are more likely to request a resource amount near the full capacity of the resources.

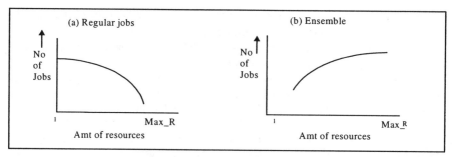

Fig. 3. Workload Generation. PDF is (a) is $4x^{1/2}$ and b) $1/4x^{1/2}$. Y-axis is the number of ensemble applications generated with a specific number of resources requested.

2.3 Scheduling Model

Regular and ensemble applications arrive to the system with their resource requirements. A scheduling algorithm is used to assign the incoming application stream to the available Grid resources. Applications are scheduled using a FCFS discipline on all resources. In this initial study, ensemble applications are generated to request a specific set of resources based on the belief that most ensemble applications are designed to access specific resources (e.g. R_1 and R_2). Therefore, scheduling them is straightforward. In future work, we plan to relax this model to allow certain application components within an ensemble application the freedom to specify a resource class (e.g. any MPP-O2K). In contrast, we assume that a fraction of regular applications may be freely run on any resource in the system. In this initial study, we set this fraction at 100%.

For a given synthetic workload containing a mix of regular and ensemble applications, we have compared three global scheduling approaches. Since ensemble applications use a fixed specific set of resources, they are simply queued on the resources they have requested. For regular applications, we have implemented the following algorithms:

shortest_queue

    pick resource with shortest waiting queue such that *min_amt >= max_capacity*

random

    pick a random resource such that *min_amt >= max_capacity*

ensemble_aware

    pick a resource that has participated in the fewest ensembles to date such that *min_amt >= max_capacity*

The first two algorithms require no explanation. The *ensemble_aware* algorithm tracks the resources that have been used to schedule prior ensemble applications in the past (when an ensemble application arrives to the system and is put on a set of resources, we increment a counter on each of those resources). The *ensemble_aware* algorithm will push regular applications away from resources used by ensemble applications. The intuition behind this algorithm is that by pushing regular application away from resources that ensemble application are likely to want in the future, we should be able to improve the performance of ensemble application. In addition, because the components of ensemble applications will likely require a large amount of individual resources and will likely have a longer duration, it may also benefit regular application to avoid these resources. This is where we would expect *shortest_queue* to perform worse than *ensemble_aware* because *shortest_queue* cannot distinguish between the type of application component that is queued in on a resource. However, by restricting regular applications to execute on a subset of resources, this may also have a negative impact on regular applications. The question we seek to answer is: when can ensemble scheduling be expected to outperform traditional policies and vice-versa?

3 Results

Using simulation, we established the performance range of *ensemble_aware* scheduling as compared with traditional policies: *shortest_queue* and *random*. Ensemble and regular applications are generated with an exponential arrival distribution with requested resource amounts based on the exponential pdf of Fig. 3. The Grid is simulated to contain N resources, R_1, ..., R_N and a capacity is computed for each using a uniform distribution [1 .. MaxR]. The application duration (i.e. the ideal execution time) for each application class is also taken as a uniform distribution. The duration of ensemble applications is scaled by a parameter (duration ratio) to capture their increased resource demand (from 1 to 20). The results establish that for a wide-range of parameter settings, *ensemble_aware* scheduling outperforms these traditional policies for regular applications (Fig. 4), particularly if the % of ensemble applications is small, between 5% and 20% (we expect this to be the more common case). For *shortest_queue*, as the % of ensemble applications increase, the performance becomes similar. The reason is that as the % of ensemble applications increases, the queue length on ensemble resources begins to grow, and *shortest_queue* will naturally begin to avoid these resources. As the duration of ensemble applications approaches that of regular applications, the performance of *ensemble_aware* scheduling falls off. If the durations are similar, then regular application could run on ensemble resources with little additional penalty, but stacking them on a subset of non-ensemble resources causes ensemble scheduling performance to worsen.

However, *ensemble_aware* scheduling is always better for ensemble applications. As the % of resources that can be used for ensemble applications increases, the performance benefit of *ensemble_aware* scheduling increases (Fig. 5). However, *ensemble_aware* scheduling performs best when the duration of ensemble applications is similar to that of regular applications (Fig. 6). The reason is that as the duration of ensemble applications becomes much greater than regular applications, putting regular applications on ensemble resources does not impact the ensemble applications as much. Random scheduling also proved to be considerable worse than either *shortest_queue* or *ensemble_aware* (Fig. 7) and is plotted separately (note the change in y-scale). Collectively, these results suggest that a hybrid policy that is sensitive to application workload may have merit: when the duration of ensemble applications is similar to regular applications, use *shortest_queue*, but when the duration of ensemble applications is a factor of 10 or more greater, then use *ensemble_aware* scheduling.

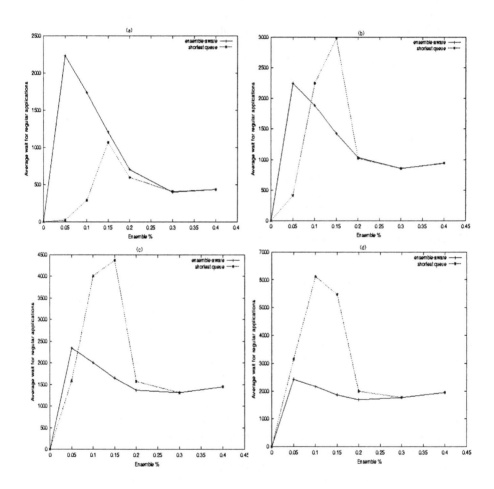

Fig. 4. Performance of Regular Applications. Duration ratio of ensemble to regular applications is (a) 5, (b) 10, (c) 15, and (d) 20. Duration ratios between the largest applications relative to the average size application were between 6 and 20 on the real workloads we examined [3].

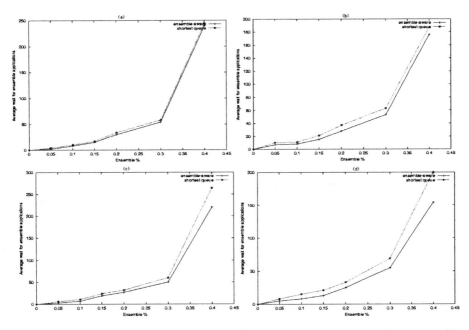

Fig. 5. Performance of Ensemble Applications. Percentage of resource available to ensemble

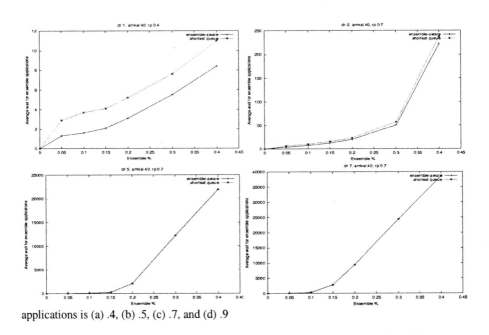

applications is (a) .4, (b) .5, (c) .7, and (d) .9

Fig. 6. Sensitivity of Ensemble Applications Performance to Duration Ratio. Duration ratio is 1, 2, 5, and 7, % of resource availability to ensemble applications is 0.7

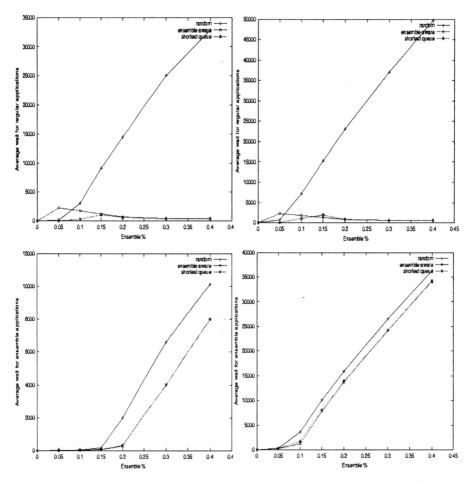

Fig. 7. Performance of Random Scheduling. Top two graphs are for regular applications, bottom two graphs for ensemble applications. Impact on regular applications is greatest. In all cases, random scheduling is worst.

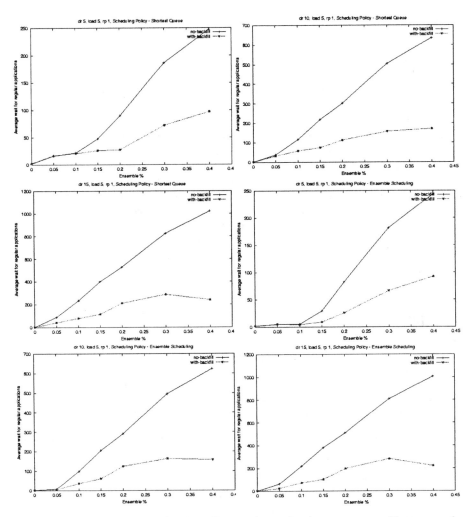

Fig. 8. Backfilling Regular Applications. Top graphs are for shortest queue and bottom are for ensemble_aware scheduling policies. Duration ratio is 5, 10, and 15 for each

None of the scheduling policies presented exploit or require execution information about the application (this was used for simulation purposes only). A final question we considered was whether the use of information such as in a backfilling scheduler would improve performance for regular jobs? Since regular applications could sit behind longer running ensemble applications, they would seem to be perfect candidates for backfilling. We allowed regular applications to be placed on a resource and backfilled if they did not delay the applications already on the queue. The results indicate that backfilling can significantly boost performance for regular applications under either scheduling policy particularly as the % of ensemble applications increases (Fig. 8).

4 Summary

We have presented a novel scheduling technique for scheduling mixed workloads consisting of single- and multi-resource ensemble applications in Grid environments. Ensemble-aware scheduling was shown to promote better performance for both regular and ensemble applications over a wide parameter range. In the vast majority of cases, it performed better or equal to *shortest_queue*. However, when the durations were similar, *shortest_queue* outperformed *ensemble_aware* scheduling for regular applications since the latter restricted the set of available resources to use. This suggests that a hybrid scheduling policy that could adaptively switch between the two policies could be useful. Similarly, such a policy could be configured to bias towards either regular or ensemble applications. We also determined that the use of backfilling improved performance for regular applications under both scheduling policies. Future work includes applying backfilling to ensemble applications as well. Finally, our scheduling model considered only the earliest-possible-time co-allocation strategy. Incorporating reservations into our model and analyzing the resulting performance of the scheduling models is the subject of future work.

5 Bibliography

1. S. Brunett et al., "Implementing Distributed Synthetic Forces Simulations in Metacomputing Environments", *Proceedings of HCW '98*.
2. M. Faerman et al., "Adaptive Performance Prediction for Distributed Data-Intensive Applications", *Proceedings of SC99*, November 1999.
3. D. Feitelson, Parallel Workload Archive, http://www.cs.huji.ac.il/labs/parallel/workload/logs.htm, 1999.
4. I. Foster and C. Kesselman, "Globus: A Metacomputing Infrastructure Toolkit", *international Journal of Supercomputing Applications*, 11(2), 1997.
5. *The Grid Blueprint for a New Computing Infrastructure,* (I. Foster and C. Kesselman, editors), Morgan Kaufmann Publishers, 1998.
6. A.S. Grimshaw and W.A. Wulf, "The Legion Vision of a Worldwide Virtual Computer", *Communications of the ACM,* Vol. 40(1), 1997.
7. P. Messina, "Distributed Supercomputing Applications", in *The Grid Blueprint for a New Computing Infrastructure,* (I. Foster and C. Kesselman, editors), Morgan Kaufmann Publishers, 1998.
8. W. Smith, I. Foster, and V. Taylor, "Predicting Application Run Times Using Historical Information", in *Job Scheduling Strategies for Parallel Processors*, D. Feitelson and L. Rudolph (eds.), Springer-Verlag, 1998, Lect. Notes Computer Science, vol. 1459.
9. J. Weissman, "Scheduling Multi-Component Applications in Heterogeneous Wide-Area Networks", *Proceedings of HCW '99*.

JobQueue: A Computational Grid-Wide Queuing System*

Dimitrios Katramatos[1], Marty Humphrey[1], Andrew Grimshaw[1], and
Steve Chapin[2]

[1] Department of Computer Science, University of Virginia
Charlottesville, VA 22903, USA
{dk3x, humphrey, grimshaw}@cs.virginia.edu
http://www.cs.virginia.edu
[2] Department of Electrical Engineering and Computer Science, Syracuse University
Syracuse, NY 13244, USA
chapin@ecs.syr.edu
http://www.ecs.syr.edu

Abstract. In a Computational Grid, it is not easy to maintain grid-wide control over the number of executing jobs, as well as a global view of the status of submitted jobs, due to the heterogeneity in resource type, availability, and access policies. This paper describes the design and implementation of JobQueue, which is a Computational Grid-wide queuing system, or metaqueuing system, implemented in Legion. JobQueue is unique because of its ability to span multiple administrative domains. It can also be reconfigured dynamically along a number of dimensions and in the general case does not require special privileges to create, facilitating new flexibility for Grid users.

1 Introduction

Computational Grids can combine thousands of hosts from hundreds of administrative domains, connected by transnational and worldwide networks. A Computational Grid functions similarly to an electric power grid: it couples geographically distributed resources and offers consistent and inexpensive access to these resources irrespective of their physical location or access point [1]. In essence, a Computational Grid allows resources to be used as a single virtual and extremely powerful resource. From the perspective of the computational scientist, Computational Grids can provide the high-performance computing infrastructure necessary for dealing with modern challenging problems.

In the computational science community, sharing of resources is common. All computing systems have certain limits and exceeding these limits leads to low throughput - everybody waits while little or no work is being done. The use

---

* This work was partially supported by Logicon (for the DoD HPCMOD/PET program) DAHC 94-96-C-0008, NSF-NGS EIA-9974968, NSF-NPACI ASC-96-10920, and a grant from NASA-IPG.

of queuing techniques for jobs alleviates this problem. Queuing software uses certain criteria to ensure fair and efficient utilization of the computing resources it supervises. In the same sense, Computational Grids may offer tremendous computational power at much lower costs than conventional systems, but they too have capacity limits.

The ability to *throttle* the level of concurrent resource usage and otherwise schedule resources from a system-wide perspective is an important requirement of emerging Computational Grids such as NASA's Information Power Grid [7]. Without controlling the number of grid-wide simultaneously-executing jobs, there is no way to predict how long any particular job will execute because resources can become oversubscribed. Controlling resource usage from a global perspective is a particularly challenging aspect of a Computational Grid because of the existence of multiple administrative domains and the volume and complexity of heterogeneous resources.

A system-wide view of jobs includes the ability to determine if a particular job is waiting, executing, or has finished, when it was submitted, when it started/completed execution, and how long it has been running. It is also necessary and/or desirable to have the capability to kill jobs, restart them, and migrate them. Operating Systems and conventional queuing systems such as PBS [2], GRD [9], and LSF [8] offer a subset of these capabilities; however, providing such functionality for a Computational Grid requires solutions to a set of different, more complex problems.

Conventional queuing systems are used for controlling jobs within some administrative domain, e.g. a company, an organization, a research facility, etc. Within this domain the queuing system centralizes control and regulates the flow of jobs. A Computational Grid can span many administrative domains, each one with its own security restrictions, with its set of filesystems, and most importantly with or without it own queuing system. Consequently, a queuing system for a Grid must be able to deal with the individualities of all grid domains. One needs to imagine a grid-wide queuing system as being a step higher in the hierarchy: it accepts job submissions and sees to it that these jobs get executed, either by directly assigning them to resources or by handing them off to lower level resource managers. Furthermore, it monitors, directly or indirectly, execution progress. Consider a grid consisting of a large number of sites with subsets of them controlled by PBS, LSF, GRD, etc. and subsets without centralized control. A grid-wide queuing system will have to "talk" to each site's queuing manager to run and monitor a job there, however it will have to play the role of a local manager for sites without a local manager. Thus, a grid-wide queuing system needs to be able to utilize a whole range of different interfaces of "subordinate" queues and also offer regular queuing functionality. There has been a recent idea for a uniform command line interface for job submissions [10]. This idea can be easily realized when a grid-wide queuing system is present. When there is indeed an agreement on a uniform interface, grid-wide queues could be modified to "speak" the new language or more realistically be augmented with a translating module (see Fig. 1).

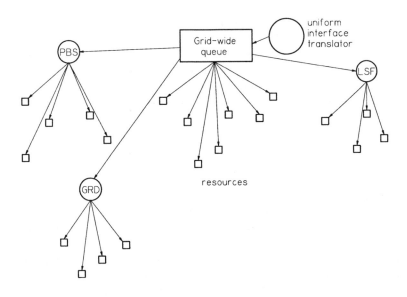

Fig. 1. Grid-wide queuing system hierarchy with uniform interface.

This paper describes the design and initial implementation of a job queuing system for the Legion object-based grid computing system [4]. The main component of the queuing system is a new object focused on job administration, the *JobQueue*. The JobQueue is a metaqueuing system that offers a job-throttling mechanism, a priority-based waiting queue, job control, and job monitoring features. In essence, the JobQueue is a high-level overseer that assures that the number of jobs simultaneously executing will never exceed the specified limits. It mediates between a user and the system's resources to accept job submissions, maintain order and fairness while at the same time provide the capability of prioritizing jobs, monitor job progress throughout execution, and provide job control and recovery capabilities.

2 Requirements

The JobQueue is not just another implementation of the typical functionality found in conventional queuing systems, although it does generally provide equivalent capabilities. There are three key requirements: the JobQueue must be able to span multiple administrative domains, it must have arbitrary scope, and cannot require special privileges for its operation.

2.1 Disjoint Administrative Domains

The JobQueue is a mechanism by which to overcome the boundaries of the domains participating in the grid system and regulate the "flow" of jobs grid-wide.

Whether or not the individual resources are themselves directly controlled by a queuing system such as PBS or LSF, the JobQueue facilitates a global control of resource usage. When a JobQueue spans multiple administrative domains, the resource providers can optionally decide an appropriate policy to implement in the JobQueue with regard to underlying resource usage. Without such a policy, the JobQueue implements a fair-share usage policy across all resources.

2.2   Arbitrary Scope

A JobQueue can be dynamically configured for particular users, particular resources, particular access control, or particular applications. Resources can be dynamically added to or removed from the resource pool of the grid system. This is to be expected in a wide-area distributed system; at any given time resource providers may limit or increase resource availability, malfunctions may happen, etc. It is desirable to have a system that can adapt to such changes. The JobQueue incorporates a feedback mechanism that essentially allows resources to ask to be given work when they're lightly loaded. Limitations to resource availability can be imposed by removing links to specific resources and thus preventing lower-level schedulers to select them. Known resource failures can also be handled the same way; if, however, the system attempts to utilize a failed resource and subsequently the job fails to execute, the JobQueue can later restart the failed job on a different resource.

2.3   No Special Privileges Requirement

Another unique feature of the JobQueue is that it can be started and set up by an ordinary user, provided that certain restrictions are in place. A possible scenario for this mode of operation is that a user wants to share a resource with some specific other users and also wants to restrict simultaneous access to a certain number of users at a time. Consider for example the case of a software package with a certain number of licenses. Conceivably, this user, as the owner of the resource, could utilize some other standard queuing system to impose these restrictions. This means he/she would have to go through the trouble of installing such a queuing system on a certain machine, on which he/she should have administrative rights. However, with the JobQueue this procedure is almost trivial, and no privileged access to a machine is required. The user can dynamically create a JobQueue instance and configure it to control the resource of interest and allow only a given number of simultaneous users. Requests to use the resource can be funneled to the private JobQueue from the "system" JobQueue, or can be sent directly to the private JobQueue. With the same ease, this instance can be destroyed when no more sharing is desired. Issues with regard to "non-system" JobQueues are further discussed in the next section.

3 Design Issues of a Metaqueuing System

The basic desired functionality of a metaqueuing system is to be able to enqueue job execution requests, initiate execution, maintain a pre-set number of grid-wide simultaneously executing jobs, and sporadically monitor progress and kill jobs. For this, the metaqueuing system can use the mechanisms a grid computing environment provides for utilizing resources spanning several different administrative domains. These mechanisms enable, for example, the execution of programs on any participating host system and the forwarding of data between participating filesystems. Additional useful functionality includes the capability to spot hung jobs and to restart jobs that have failed to execute for certain reasons. The remainder of this section discusses several issues in the design of such a queuing system.

3.1 Decentralized Control and Resource Coordination

With widely distributed resources it would be bad practice to centralize control and have one system component regulate the flow of jobs through the entire system. However, if multiple metaqueuing systems exist, it may become difficult to coordinate resource usage between the instances. There are many ways in which to distribute resource responsibility (see Fig. 2):

- each metaqueue maintains a list of resources it can schedule jobs on; resources can be added/removed dynamically to/from this list,
- each metaqueue is restricted to request lower-level services from system components that are already assigned to specific system areas and utilize resources only in those areas (Fig. 2 shows the Legion resource management infrastructure, Legion RMI, providing this functionality),
- instead of simply partitioning resources between a number of metaqueues, a hierarchy of instances can be used; each metaqueue instance can regulate resources directly or funnel requests to lower level metaqueue instances.

The first and second approaches provide control and monitoring within a partition of the grid system. The third approach is more complex but has the advantage of providing full grid-wide control and monitoring while allowing finer control of jobs, adapted to resource idiosyncrasies. In all cases however, the actual partitioning of the system's resources is a matter of policy; there can be partitioning according to physical location of resources, resource type, random, or some other policy. In an Computational Grid, it is inevitable that multiple metaqueuing systems must exist. The unresolved issues with any configuration is both how to direct user requests to the "best" metaqueue and how to ensure that the metaqueues collectively implement a well-defined policy. As the number of metaqueues increases, the actual policy implemented will be increasingly difficult to determine and/or verify.

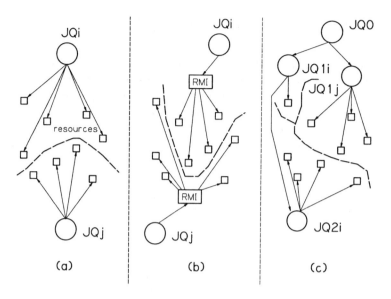

Fig. 2. Decentralized control and resource coordination: (a) direct partition, (b) indirect partition through Legion RMI, (c) hierarchy of JobQueues.

3.2 Privileged/Unprivileged Creation and Configuration

Certainly, allowing any user to create, setup, and use a metaqueue without any restrictions is not a good idea, as this would make any control over resource usage impossible. It seems prudent to make these operations privileged and available only to resource providers and administrators. A user is granted access to a metaqueuing system through the grid computing system's regular access control mechanisms. If a metaqueuing system can be created/setup by a user, then it should operate in "private" mode where several restrictions are set in place, allowing the particular user to utilize only specific resources and to only manage his/her own jobs. The particular issue is that allowing user- or group-specific queues offers new flexibility and control, but allowing too many metaqueues to be multiplexed over the same resources effectively eliminates the desired goal of control from the perspective of the resources themselves. Coordinating resource usage becomes very complex in this case as it is hard to control the number of jobs submitted by all users that run simultaneously in the overall system or even in one of its areas.

3.3 Predictability

Related to the previous issue is the predictability of the metaqueuing system. That is, after a job is submitted, how long will it be before it starts execution? In a priority-based queuing environment this time period depends on several factors. If higher priority jobs get submitted all the time chances are that lower-priority jobs will face starvation. When all priorities are equal the scheduling is first-come first-served. Even so, the waiting period depends on the number of available running slots; if all slots are taken and thus the maximum number of jobs allowed to execute simultaneously has been reached, the next job will have to wait until one of the executing ones finishes.

It is possible to predict when a job will get started if at submission time additional data are given to the metaqueuing system. If for example the upper limit of execution time is known for the jobs already executing and for those waiting ahead of a specific job, the waiting time can be easily estimated. Another approach is by using advanced reservations. That is, a user can specify when a job is desired to run, and the Computational Grid-wide queuing system will try to make the necessary arrangements for it, if possible. Naturally, this scheme requires that the underlying infrastructure support advance reservations. In a Computational Grid, it should also be assumed that resources can be accessed via Grid means and via local means. Does predictability in a metaqueue require (temporarily) denying access via local means? It is unclear whether resource providers can justify this to their local users.

4   Implementation in Legion

Legion [4] is an object-oriented Grid Computing system developed at the University of Virginia. It is intended to connect many thousands or even millions of computers ranging from PCs to massively parallel supercomputers. Legion offers the necessary resource management infrastructure (Legion RMI) [3] for managing this vast amount of resources uniting machines of thousands of administrative domains into a single coherent system while at the same time supports site autonomy.

4.1   Job-handling in Legion

Legion supports two kinds of programs [5]:

- Legion-aware, which run as objects, and
- general, non Legion-aware.

In both cases programs need to get registered with the Legion system. The registration process creates managing objects and instructs the system which binaries to use for creating and executing program instances. However, a Legion-compatible program runs as a Legion object whereas for non-Legion programs—practically anything that executes on a regular operating system, even scripts—a different, more complex procedure needs to be followed. In essence, a special object is created to act as a proxy between the Legion system and the program binary. This is necessary as a generic binary lacks the special functionality needed to execute as a Legion object. With the use of proxy objects and a set of system tools it is possible to run almost any kind of program—without making any changes to the program code—on any suitable resource participating in the computational grid.

4.2 New Functionality

The raw program execution mechanism of Legion covers the basic service of executing programs. However, using the mechanism independently, without a queuing system, creates the set of problems discussed in section 1, i.e.:

- there is no way of controlling the total number of jobs executing simultaneously grid-wide, as any user can start any number of running sessions at anytime,
- there is no global job handling and monitoring capability

The JobQueue provides the additional functionality needed to overcome these problems. While the procedure for registering executables with the Legion system remains exactly the same, in the new queuing system the run operation is broken down to three phases: (1) job submission, (2) job preparation, execution, and monitoring, and (3) job clean-up.

The main component of the queuing system, the JobQueue object, is responsible for the second phase. The first and third phases are done with the use of special software tools. When a job is submitted to the JobQueue, the object stores all necessary information for handling this job and returns a handle, a "ticket", which one can use for future references to the job. After submission, the JobQueue takes care of preparing, starting, and monitoring progress of this job.

Breaking down the run operation in the above mentioned phases and assigning the main portion of the operation to an administrative object makes possible to control the number of jobs that execute simultaneously in the Legion system. A submitted job will enter the second phase only when the number of total simultaneously executing jobs monitored by the JobQueue is less than the number of total jobs allowed, as specified by the Legion system administrator, i.e. when a running slot is available. If none is available, the job will have to wait - along with other submitted jobs - in a waiting queue. The order of waiting jobs in this queue is determined by priority number assigned to jobs by their owners and/or the administrator.

4.3 Internal JobQueue Operations

While a job is handled by the JobQueue, a user can communicate with the queue object and perform certain operations like inquiring about the job's status, changing its priority (only while waiting and within certain limits), killing it, or restarting it. The basic operation of the queuing system starts with job submission. All necessary information for executing a job are stored in a data structure, a job data block, and submitted to the queue object. The queue object creates a unique ticket for the job (which is returned to the user as a response to the submission), as well as a record to store the data block, the ticket, and other job-related information. This record gets stored in a priority queue structure, and waits for its turn to be dequeued and used for executing the job. At this point two things are possible: either the job will get successfully started and its job record will get moved to the list of running jobs, or it will fail to start, in which case the job record will get moved to the list of failed jobs. The run operation is non-blocking; once the job finishes execution, the queue object receives notice that execution is over by means of a callback, in the same manner that a CPU is notified of an event with an interrupt. Once a job has finished its record gets moved to either the list of done jobs, if execution was successful, or the list of failed jobs otherwise (see Fig. 3).

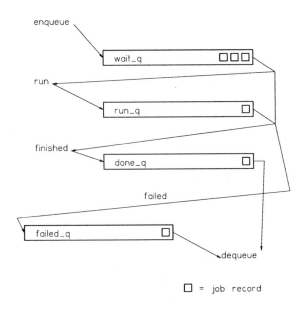

Fig. 3. Diagram of internal queue object operations.

The queue object will attempt to run a job whose record is waiting at the head of the priority queue when there is an available run slot. The initial attempt is always after a job submission. If this attempt fails, the queue object will attempt again after another job submission or in the following cases:

− when a job is done,
− when a job fails,
− when the number of allowed jobs gets increased.

Note that the job that will run in any case is always the one waiting at the head of the queue and not the one submitted, unless they're the same. The basic operation cycle ends with an inquiry about the job by the user, in which case the queue object responds with the job's status. If the job is done or has failed, the corresponding record gets marked for deletion, and later on gets deleted, at which point the job exits the queuing system.

The JobQueue object also performs two periodical independent operations, using timer alarms. The first one involves checking for job records marked for deletion and deleting them if a certain amount of time has passed. The second one is much more complex as it is the main job monitoring operation. During this operation the queue object:

- pings running jobs to verify they're alive,
- updates job statistics,
- kills jobs that have exceeded their maximum allocated running time, and
- restarts jobs that have exceeded their maximum restart time period.

The ping operation is non-blocking in the same manner as the run operation described above. A problematic job is bound not to respond to a ping, thus the queue object should never block and wait when pinging jobs. Instead, proxy objects report status to the queue object. A running job is the child of a proxy object and is being watched over by its parent. The proxy object will notify the queue object when the child's execution terminates for whatever reason. Thus, the pinging operation is intended to watch over the proxy objects themselves, since a failed proxy object causes faulty job monitoring. The queue object attempts to kill jobs that do not respond to pings for a certain amount of time and moves their corresponding records to the list of failed jobs.

Whenever the queue object performs an operation on a job, it "pretends" to be the owner of the job by switching its own method parameters, its "credentials", to the ones of the actual job owner, then switching back again. In this way the queue object invokes methods on other system objects on behalf of the job owner. Thus, any security privileges and restrictions that the owner may have remain in effect.

4.4 Implementation

The initial implementation of the queuing system has as its main focus the throttling, handling, and monitoring of jobs. It does not yet address the control centralization and resource coordination issues. The invocation of JobQueue object methods is controlled by means of an access control list (ACL). Certain methods are accessible only by the object owner. As the administrator is typically the owner of the (all) queue object (objects) it is not normally possible for regular users to affect the queuing system operations in any way other than they are allowed to (while not directly restricted, we have not experimented with users creating their own JobQueues). Additionally, when a tool operation affects a specific job in some manner (e.g. when killing a job), the tool includes in its communication to the queue object the identity of the user who made the request. The queue object always enforces the rule that certain operations can be requested only by the user who is the actual job owner, or the administrator.

For example, it will prevent user A from killing a job belonging to user B, unless A is the administrator.

We are currently investigating the user of the JobQueue across NPACInet, which is a Legion network in daily operation across NPACI resources of CalTech, Virginia, SDSC, Michigan, Texas, etc. [6] We are working with a select number of users to evaluate the effectiveness of the API and core mechanisms. Initial experiments have examined reliability issues with good results, e.g. handling of over 10,000 job submissions (several different jobs, each with a number of instances) presented no problems. Even after system failures the JobQueue "remembered" its previous status and continued to handle running and submitted jobs.

5 Conclusions

The significant problem a metaqueuing system has to solve is the throttling of grid-wide simultaneously executing jobs. Without control over the number of jobs the response time of the system becomes totally unpredictable. The JobQueue, a metaqueuing system for the Legion grid computing system, provides this important functionality, as well as global job handling and monitoring. In its current implementation the JobQueue is intended to be an administrative system object and perform job control with a single instance. Future work will focus on offering solutions to the issues of non-centralization of control and resource coordination in the presence of multiple instances, privileged vs. unprivileged creation of metaqueuing systems, and predictability of metaqueuing systems.

References

1. Grid Computing Info Center
   (*http://www.gridcomputing.com*)
2. A. Bayucan, R.L. Henderson, C. Lesiak, N. Mann, T. Proett, and D. Tweten. "Portable Batch System: External Reference Specification." Technical Report, MRJ Technology Solutions, November 1999.
3. Steve J. Chapin, Dimitrios Katramatos, John Karpovich, Andrew Grimshaw. "Resource management in Legion." *Future Generation Computer Systems*, vol. 15 (1999), pages 583–594.
4. A. Grimshaw and W. Wulf. "The Legion Vision of a Worldwide Computer." *Communications of the ACM.* pages 39–45, January 1997.
5. A. Natrajan, M. Humphrey, and A. Grimshaw. "Capacity and Capability Computing using Legion." In *Proceedings of the 2001 International Conference on Computational Science*, San Francisco, CA, May 2001.
6. A. Natrajan, A. Fox, M. Humphrey, A. Grimshaw, M. Crowley, N. Wilkins-Diere. "Protein Folding on the Grid: Experiences using CHARMM under Legion on NPACI Resources." In *Proceedings of the 10th International Symposium on High Performance Distributed Computing (HPDC)*, San Francisco, California, August 7-9, 2001.
7. Bill Johnston, Dennis Gannon, and Bill Nitzberg. "Grids as Production Computing Environments." In *Proceedings of the Eighth IEEE Symposium on High Performance Distributed Computing*, 1999.

8. LSF Reference Guide, Version 4.0.1, June 2000.
   (*ftp://ftp.platform.com/docs/lsf/4.0/html/ref_4.0.1/index.html*)
9. Global Resource Director.
   (*http://www.arl.hpc.mil/docs/grd/grd.html*)
10. Joe Werne and Michael Gourlay. "Uniform Command-line Interfaces for Job Submissions and Data Archiving." Presentation given at GGF-2, July 15-18, 2001, Vienna, Virginia USA.

A Scheduling Model for Grid Computing Systems

Anuraag Sarangi   Alok Shriram   Avinash Shankar

Computer Science and Engineering,
Sri Venkateswara College of Engineering,
Post Bag No.3, Pennalur,
Sriperumbudur – 602105,
Tamil Nadu, India.
{urs_anuraag@hotmail.com, alster_s@hotmail.com,
avinashsvce@hotmail.com}

Abstract. Application-level scheduling in Grid Computing systems is an extensively researched field. The past decade has seen many different techniques and algorithms emerge to tackle this research problem. In this paper we present results of our preliminary studies of an innovative approach to scheduling. This algorithm utilizes a collective, event-based and decentralized (gridCoED) strategy on a metacomputing level to allocate jobs to a set of nodes in a grid environment. We present the design of the model and appropriate simulation results. We also highlight some of the salient features of our model that makes it suitable for application-level scheduling in grid computing systems.

1. Introduction

Over the decade of grid computing development, application-level scheduling has always been an area of intense research. Many approaches have been tried and tested throughout these years. However, achieving an optimal scheme for scheduling has proved all the more difficult. It is so because of the numerous factors that go into consideration while developing such a scheme, especially issues of heterogeneous resource management and administrative policy considerations. In this paper, we propose a scheme for efficient job scheduling over a set of nodes[1] on a metacomputing level; a highly collective, event-based, decentralized (gridCoED) scheme. This paper is a further study of the scheme, as applied in a metacomputing environment, that was proposed by the authors [16,18] for a general distributed computing environment earlier. The primary objective of this research is to develop and study a scheduling model that reduces the mean response time of a job from its initial genesis to its termination.

---

[1] In this paper, a node refers to a processor, workstation, or a computing machine in a grid environment and the terms are used interchangeably. Also, the terms, jobs and processes are used interchangeably to indicate computation-intensive applications.

2. Background and Related Work

Over the years, many scheduling infrastructures have been studied like the FCFS, Backfill, and EqualUtil strategies[5]. Below we present some of the general architectures that have been realized. The particular aspect presented below forms the basis of the gridCoED scheme. These scheduling infrastructures rely on a *centralized*, *hierarchical*, or *decentralized* architecture.

Centralized scheduling involves assigning one node in the system as the scheduler. This node will maintain universal awareness[9] of all status information of all the other nodes in the system and map jobs to suitable nodes. However, it presents scalability problems and single point-of-failure issues.

Hierarchical scheduling makes use of a layered structure of job scheduling wherein different levels of schedulers execute scheduling policies (which maybe different from each other) over their own relevant plane, i.e. they utilize meta-schedulers that schedule other coarse-grained jobs over a set of schedulers, and so on. These levels of meta-scheduling may thus keep extending. These are quite popular scheduling algorithms, and many have evolved along the lines of cluster based scheduling [3,4,13,14,17]. Their biggest advantage is that they can incorporate different local scheduling policies as well as higher levels of scheduling policies. However, they may also suffer from the same fault-tolerant issues as the centralized architecture given above.

Decentralized scheduling does not take any particular structure. Here, the nodes directly communicate with each other (or with a common job pool server) to share their loads. Many different attempts have been made in the past to develop an optimal scheduling scheme of this type [5]. Our scheme (gridCoED) is also an attempt in this area. This type of an architecture presents many advantages to the user including reduced global system status information, reduced communication bottleneck, better scalability, no single point-of-failure, etc. These issues, as applicable to gridCoED, will be dealt with in greater detail later.

There are many specific examples of related work in scheduling that have been undertaken in the past. Priority based scheduling, for example, provides sub-optimal solutions for a set of homogeneous nodes which are allocated a set of prioritized jobs. Examples of these types of algorithms include [7]. Cluster based algorithms, which map task clusters onto the same node to reduce communication time, have also gained popularity in research circles; examples include [3,4,13,14,17]. We can also utilize the idle time of nodes to duplicate jobs, i.e., duplication based scheduling, as demonstrated in [1,15].

Some of the well-known grid scheduling models are part of projects such as Apples, and Nimrod/G. The Apples model is used largely for parallel applications. Each scheduler considers its process application resource requests and then matches it with the predicted load and availability of the system resources. The scheduler, or agent, as they are referred to keep track of various resource status by using what is known as a Network Weather Service. The Nimrod/G system uses a resource management and scheduling scheme for large-scale resource management. Here, resource allocation is accomplished by taking in parameterized requests. This scheme targets primarily scientific applications. Master-Worker [6] scheduling is another popular model used in grid computing systems. However, it suffers from many drawbacks including the one given below.

Most of the above algorithms neglect the need for a solution to the single point-of-failure problem. They assume replication and shadow servers to be a sufficient solution to the problem. In our algorithm, fault tolerance to this problem is inherently built-in. In fact, it is to provide for this fault-tolerance that gridCoED has to suffice with a sub-optimal solution. This will be later explored in detail in the paper.

The basis of gridCoED lies in a dual sender-receiver-initiated(sr) methodology. It is a more sophisticated grid version of the standard sender-initiated or receiver-initiated schemes (for example, the drafting algorithm studied in [8] and applied in [12] in relation to process migration) used in general distributed computing systems. Eager's schemes [2] are sender-initiated, i.e. the loaded machines probe others in the system asking for permission to offload their processes on them. Standard receiver-initiated schemes rely on the idea of an idle workstation that probes others in the system asking for work. The drafting algorithm in [8,12] relies on pre-emptive process migration to off-load processes to machines which are in the Low state. The main difference between drafting and gridCoED lies in their fundamental features. Drafting is a purely receiver-initiated model while gridCoED relies on direct sender-receiver participation. In drafting, the processors in Low state (relatively idle workstations) probe the ones in High state asking for work. gridCoED does not focus on the search for idle machines. It relies only on better performance machines (with discrete load parameters, and not relative states (Low, Normal, High) which can cause fluctuations and improper load sharing for machines on the border line of the relative states) at particular instances of time. Another feature of drafting that reduces its effective efficiency when compared with gridCoED is that the load value of the sender is extended (piggybacking) by every broadcasting message in the system. This involves more network traffic and thereby more congestion. gridCoED reduces the broadcasting requirements to a minimum and ensures greater efficiency. All machines keep track of global system status in drafting, which is not the case in gridCoED. Moreover, the sophistication in our model allows for many new salient features to become inherent in the architecture of the scheme. These features are explored later in the paper under Section 6.

The following section brings out the intricate details of the gridCoED scheme while providing the underlying concept behind the idea. Section 4 provides the preliminary simulation results and analysis for this study. Section 5 gives further discussion about the results from the simulation. Section 6 provides the salient features of gridCoED. Section 7 lists some open problems involved and gives some concluding remarks for our present and future work in this subject.

3. gridCoED Design

For our model, we consider jobs (or processes) as applications that need to be run on a node. These jobs may consist of parallel computation-intensive tasks, in which case these tasks are the ones that are mapped onto a node (machine). However, for this model, once a task, or a job, is started on a machine, it runs to completion, i.e. there is no preemptive migration of tasks. The gridCoED model coherently combines both the selection strategy and the scheduling strategy of a scheduling model [5].

A crucial requisite behind this scheme is that the load of a machine in the grid network must be known and updated as needed. The machine load [20], we define as, machine load = CPU utilization in percentage. We propose to keep a list of loads for every machine. Now each machine creates a table for itself (we call it the *gridtable*) that rates the machines according to their machine loads and includes the IP addresses of the machines that rank lower than it on the load table in ascending order of the load (CPU utilization) on each machine at that particular instance in time. This amounts to the status information required in this scheme. Since gridCoED is a purely distributed and decentralized strategy, no global system information for universal awareness [9] is maintained. This is actually an advantage of the strategy, as we shall see later.

The criterion for the transfer of a job in the gridCoED scheme is determined by a threshold. Here, if the machine load L exceeds or equals the threshold level T, i.e., L >= T, then the machine needs to offload jobs to other machines until the load again reduces below the threshold (L < T) after offloading or completing the execution of some of its other jobs. Since we have considered a non-preemptive mode of operation if L >= T, then only new jobs generating on that node will be offloaded to other remote nodes. The situation L < T will arise only when the node completes some of its already-running jobs.

When the situation arises that L >= T, then selection of jobs to transfer is done according to which new jobs originate in the source machine. Again, these new jobs come under another threshold, S. According to this threshold, the overall workload requirements should exceed the threshold S for the job to be termed as "significant" and be selected for transfer to a remote processor. The threshold is provided to eliminate "insignificant" processes, like background processes, to be continually transferred in the system and consequentially cause unnecessary congestion in the network.

The gridCoED scheme is event-based. There are in particular, two prominent events that the scheme is based on. Event A takes place when a job originates in the system (i.e. anywhere in the network of machines). Event B takes place when a job terminates in the system (either in its source machine, or in a target machine). We factor into account the fact that during the course of the execution of a job (or task) in a workstation the load does not *significantly* increase or decrease, i.e. fluctuate. We presume a very generic, decentralized topology; the only criterion being that each workstation has access over the network to all other workstations. gridCoED is a fully decentralized scheme. Therefore, there is no central scheduling "authority" in the system. Each machine handles its own scheduling requirements, as we shall see below. We consider each event individually, although they appear to be somewhat similar.

Event A

Suppose a new job originates at a terminal. We call this the source machine. If the load is below the threshold value T, then the process is executed locally. Otherwise, if the job workload requirements exceed the threshold S, then the search for a target machine begins. A global variable called *gridnewproc* (carrying the IP address of the source machine) is broadcast over the network to all terminals. Each machine then checks if the IP address of the source machine is in its *gridtable*. If so, then according to which machine is able to ask for the job the fastest, i.e., the fastest response, gets the entire job (or a particular task) migrated to it. This particular machine is thus the target machine from the potential target machines that reply to the job transfer request. Thus, the workstations in the system collectively look out for each other. Only the lesser-loaded machines need to reply. Rest can ignore *gridnewproc* since they are already more heavily loaded than the source machine (and therefore, do not have its IP address on their *gridtable*). Then the update procedure begins. The target

Fig. 1. Load tables as new process enters at Processor A.

Fig. 2. Load tables after new process is pulled in by Processor B.

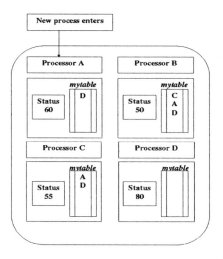
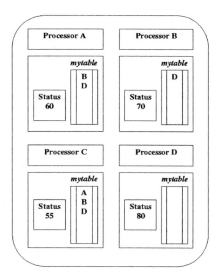

machine recalculates its own status (load) after the job starts execution. It then checks its *gridtable* to see if this new load invalidates any of its table entries (i.e., if its load has become greater than any of the loads of the other machines listed in its *gridtable*). If so, it then removes the machine entries from its own table, and sends its status to the removed machines for them to update their own *gridtable*. The whole procedure above thus allows for the job to be moved to a better performance, lesser-loaded node.

Event B

In the case when a job leaves the system, i.e. when it terminates execution and sends back the results to the source machine, the target machine broadcasts a message *gridoldproc* which contains its own IP address and its new recalculated load after the job has left. All the machines then check this new message for its validity in their tables and update accordingly. If they find that the target machine's load has changed such that their own load becomes greater than the target machine's, then they eliminate the target machine's entry in their *gridtable* and send their load information to it. The target machine then updates its *gridtable* accordingly.

Both events are applicable to all workstations in the system. Therefore, many of the workstations could be in various sequences of these events simultaneously. Of course, this requires very efficient synchronization techniques. Given in figures 4 and 5 is an illustration of a hypothetical scenario when a system with four machines is subjected to gridCoED scheduling.

More Events

Two more events need to be highlighted in this scheme. As mentioned above, we do want this scheme to be dynamic. Therefore, we have to consider the cases where a node enters or leaves the system. While entering the system, a machine has to calculate its load and then broadcast it over the network. After it receives other machines' loads, it creates its own *gridtable* and joins the system. In the early stages, it may very well serve as the best system (since it is not been heavily loaded yet) and thus be able to draw out many jobs from other more loaded machines.

While leaving the system, it is mandatory for the machine to complete all its allocated jobs. It broadcasts a *gridleaving* signal to indicate that it cannot accept any more new jobs. Therefore, it never responds to any more "calls for help". It waits for all jobs that it is executing to complete, waits for its own remotely executing jobs to return results; and then broadcasts a *gridquit* signal to let all relevant machines remove it from their load tables. Latency is reduced in the gridCoED model since we give the new job directly to the machine that responds the fastest. Therefore, there is no delay involved in waiting for all possible machines to reply. Hence we present a nearly optimal choice of target machines to the source machine.

4. Simulation Environment

Here we present the study of our simulation that we conducted as further analysis of gridCoED. For comparison purposes, we employ Eager et al. s' [2] Algorithm 3 as illustrated above. The motivation behind this simulation was to study the performance of gridCoED as compared to a well-established technique, like that of Eager's. We establish the mean response time of both the schemes as our distinctive parameter to measure. In this simulation, for Eager's model, the source machine probes k potential target machines and based on their loads, it decides on the target machine to transfer the process to. We have also combined a certain aspect of Mitzenmacher's [10] scheme, i.e., in our simulation $k = 2$. This is because Mitzenmacher argued that selection between two randomly chosen remote processors provides good efficiency in load balancing, as was mentioned in Section 2 above.

In the process of the simulation we have considered an eight processors system. We consider non-preemptive processes, i.e. they have to be executed to completion once started on a remote processor. We have simulated conditions like varying transmission times and varying process sizes in a multitasking environment in our model. Both the network transmission times and the process sizes are generated by a random number generator with the distribution functions as shown in the Tables 1 and 2. The inter-process arrival time is not a Poisson distribution but rather, it is a discrete distribution as shown in Table 3. Here we have considered the case of $p=8$ process generators, all the machines can generate processes in the system. A simplifying assumption that we make is that no processes are generated simultaneously in the system. Thus, the inter-arrival times listed are indicative of the times when the process enters the whole system.

Another assumption about the loading is that the increase in load will be proportional to the process size. The process size is also indicative of process execution time when the process is run on an unloaded ideal benchmark machine. Thus, at any instance of time, due to multiprocessing requirements, the new execution time of a process that is about to start executing on a remote processor is given by, New_exec_time = ideal_exec_time + (ideal_exec_time * %CPU utilization of target machine at that time)

5. Simulation Results and Analysis

Each of the algorithms was simulated according to their basic design. For simulation purposes, in the gridCoED scheme, only the best target machine responded for each source machine's request. Eager's Algorithm 3 stayed unaltered, with $k = 2$. When the manual simulation was done (with 24 iterations; tables 4 and 5 show the simulation results; all time units are in seconds), and the graph of overall response times as compared with the process sizes was drawn between the two schemes and the ideal execution times, the trends were observed as in Figure 6. As the number of loads in the system began to increase (we consider a multitasking environment) the gridCoED scheme performed slightly better providing faster overall response times. From the results here we get a slight performance improvement of about 0.4% (with respect to the mean response time; refer table 6) in favor of gridCoED. Thus, we see that the gridCoED scheme performs just as well as Eager's scheme, as applied in a metacomputing environment.

$$P_{opt} = [_{i=1}\Sigma^n(i)\{\text{where load on i} <= \text{load on x}\}] / [_{i=1}\Sigma^n(i)] . \qquad (1)$$

Here,   P: probability for an optimal solution
        i: any processor in the system
        n: total number of processors in the system
        x: source processor

Therefore, as the value of n goes on increasing the probability of an optimal allocation decreases. Therefore, the performance level of Eager's scheme will reduce.

Table 1. Random Inter-Arrival Time distribution (The above table illustrates the random distribution function for the Inter-Arrival time between processes. Random Numbers are generated and on the basis of the random numbers the inter-arrival time of the process is fixed)

Inter-arrival time (sec)	Probability	Cumulative Probability	Random No. Distribution
2.5	.200	.200	1-200
5.0	.200	.400	201-400
7.5	.200	.600	401-600
10.0	.200	.800	601-800
12.5	.200	1.000	801-000

Table 2. Random Process Execution Time / Process Size distribution (This table is used to assign the execution time to the process. As mentioned earlier, a simplifying assumption is made that the execution time is also indicative of the process size)

Execution time (sec) / Process Size	Probability	Cumulative Probability	Random digit Assignment
40	.200	.200	1-200
50	.200	.400	201-400
60	.200	.600	401-600
70	.200	.800	601-800
80	.200	1.000	801-000

Table 3. Random Transmission Time distribution (This table is used to assign the transmission time in a random manner)

Trans-Mission time (sec)	Probability	Cumulative Probability	Random Digit Assignment
.1	.250	.250	1-250
.2	.250	.500	251-500
.3	.250	.750	501-750
.4	.250	1.000	751-000

Table 4. Eager's simulation results with n = 2 responding target machines.

Sl. No.	Gen Proc	Proc Size	I-A Time	Start Time	Ttime S-T	Proc Trans Time	Proc St	Proc End	Ttime T-S	End Time	Overall Resp Time	Ma-ch1	Ma-ch2
1	2	70	Null	0	0.3	2.1	2.4	73.8	0.3	74.1	74.1	5	0
2	7	40	12.5	12.5	0.3	1.2	14	58	0.2	58.2	45.7	4	5
3	7	50	7.5	20	0.4	2	22.4	74.4	0.4	74.8	54.8	1	4
4	6	60	10	30	0.1	0.6	30.7	96.1	0.1	96.2	66.2	0	4
5	0	50	5	35	0.4	2	37.4	90.4	0.4	90.8	55.8	5	2
6	4	70	7.5	42.5	0.1	0.7	43.3	118.9	0.1	119	76.5	3	7
7	1	50	12.5	55	0.1	0.5	55.6	110.1	0.1	110.2	55.2	5	2
8	5	50	5	60	0.1	0.5	60.6	116.6	0.1	116.7	56.7	7	6
9	6	80	5	65	0.4	3.2	68.6	155.8	0.4	156.2	91.2	3	1
10	4	40	5	70	0.2	0.8	71	115	0.2	115.2	45.2	0	6
11	7	60	2.5	72.5	0.4	2.4	75.3	140.1	0.4	140.5	68	0	6
12	5	50	7.5	80	0.2	1	81.2	136.2	0.2	136.4	56.4	4	0
13	4	50	10	90	0.4	2	92.4	145.4	0.4	145.8	55.8	2	0
14	7	80	2.5	92.5	0.3	2.4	95.2	186.4	0.3	186.7	94.2	6	3
15	4	60	5	97.5	0.2	1.2	98.9	167.3	0.2	167.5	70	1	0
16	7	50	5	102.5	0.2	1	103.7	160.7	0.1	160.8	58.3	1	3
17	6	70	10	112.5	0.3	2.1	114.9	192.6	0.3	192.9	80.4	0	2
18	7	80	2.5	115	0.1	0.8	115.9	203.9	0.1	204	89	4	2
19	6	80	5	120	0.4	3.2	123.6	215.6	0.4	216	96	3	4
20	0	80	12.5	132.5	0.4	3.2	136.1	228.1	0.4	228.5	96	3	2
21	3	50	7.5	140	0.1	0.5	140.6	198.6	0.1	198.7	58.7	7	1
22	3	50	7.5	147.5	0.1	0.5	148.1	204.6	0.1	204.7	57.2	2	5
23	6	80	2.5	150	0.4	3.2	153.6	247.2	0.4	247.6	97.6	3	1
24	3	50	2.5	152.5	0.2	1	153.7	212.7	0.2	212.9	60.4	6	2

Table 5. gridCoED simulation results.

Sl. No.	Gen Proc	Proc Size	I-A Time	Start Time	Ttime S-T	Proc Trans Time	Proc St	Proc End	Ttime T-S	End Time	Overall Resp Time
1	2	70	Null	0	0.3	2.1	2.4	73.8	0.3	74.1	74.1
2	7	40	12.5	12.5	0.3	1.2	14	55.6	0.2	55.8	43.3
3	7	50	7.5	20	0.4	2	22.4	75.4	0.4	75.8	55.8
4	6	60	10	30	0.1	0.6	30.7	95.5	0.1	95.6	65.6
5	0	50	5	35	0.4	2	37.4	91.4	0.4	91.8	56.8
6	4	70	7.5	42.5	0.1	0.7	43.3	119.6	0.1	119.7	77.2
7	1	50	12.5	55	0.1	0.5	55.6	110.6	0.1	110.7	55.7
8	5	50	5	60	0.1	0.5	60.6	115.1	0.1	115.2	55.2
9	6	80	5	65	0.4	3.2	68.6	157.4	0.4	157.8	92.8
10	4	40	5	70	0.2	0.8	71	115.8	0.2	116	46
11	7	60	2.5	72.5	0.4	2.4	75.3	141.9	0.4	142.3	69.8
12	5	50	7.5	80	0.2	1	81.2	138.2	0.2	138.4	58.4
13	4	50	10	90	0.4	2	92.4	149.4	0.4	149.8	59.8
14	7	80	2.5	92.5	0.3	2.4	95.2	181.6	0.3	181.9	89.4
15	4	60	5	97.5	0.2	1.2	98.9	164.9	0.2	165.1	67.6
16	7	50	5	102.5	0.2	1	103.7	160.7	0.1	160.8	58.3
17	6	70	10	112.5	0.3	2.1	114.9	196.1	0.3	196.4	83.9
18	7	80	2.5	115	0.1	0.8	115.9	203.9	0.1	204	89
19	6	80	5	120	0.4	3.2	123.6	211.6	0.4	212	92
20	0	80	5	132.5	0.4	3.2	136.1	225.7	0.4	226.1	93.6
21	3	50	7.5	140	0.1	0.5	140.6	197.1	0.1	197.2	57.2
22	3	50	7.5	17.5	0.1	0.5	148.1	205.1	0.1	205.2	57.7
23	6	80	2.5	0	0.4	3.2	153.6	242.4	0.4	242.8	92.8
24	3	50	2.5	152.5	0.2	1	153.7	211.7	0.2	211.9	59.4

Table 6. Mean Response Times in seconds for comparison purposes.

Ideal	60.42
gridCoED	68.81
Eager's	69.14

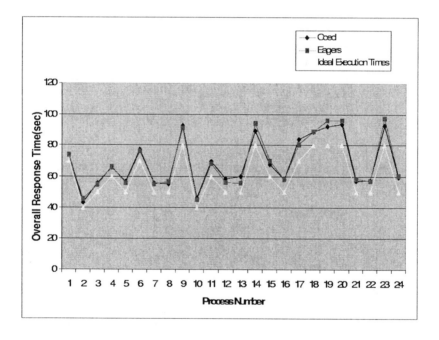

Fig. 3. Performance graph for comparison.

On the other hand, gridCoED does not suffer from the same disadvantages due to scalability as Eager's scheme as shown here. As long as consistent and up-to-date tables are maintained as specified, the algorithm outperforms Eager's in more ways than one. The only hindrance to gridCoED seems to be that the broadcasting of messages could pose a problem in highly loaded system environments. However, they will not have a significant impact when the system is lightly or moderately loaded.

6. Features

We consider below some of the salient features involved in gridCoED. This will help us to better understand the significance of the algorithm.

Single point-of-failure - the attractiveness of the algorithm is in the fact that any node (i.e. machine) that fails in the system need not participate in the scheme until it is "resurrected" again. The algorithm still guarantees a better performance machine, if available, to a significant process that enters into the system. Also, by incorporating some redundancy into a very large-scale system, i.e. by sending a process to two nodes for execution rather than just one, we are also able to provide for better fault-tolerance. In case one of the nodes fails, then the other node will send the required results back to the source machine.

Global system status - The gridCoED model relies on a highly distributed algorithm. Not all machines have global information on the status (or load) of the rest of the machines. Instead, in this model, each machine keeps track of a limited number of statuses of the other machines and acts accordingly.

Scalability - we propose that gridCoED be modeled in a hierarchical organization of interconnected networks of workstations. This scheme can then be used at every level of the hierarchy. However, there is no central root node in the model, thus differentiating this arrangement from a purely hierarchical model.

Security - features in the scheme allow only authorized access to the network by the grid users. Since, a grid system might consist of many different networks with different administration domains, we keep track of the access rights of users (along with a global ID) and their programs and map them to the domains where they may be authorized to execute their programs.

Applicability to metacomputing – gridCoED is applicable to grid computing systems since it involves scheduling over a decentralized metacomputing environment, where local schedulers may have their own scheduling policies. Thus, gridCoED provides for seamless and flexible scheduling in its implementation.

7. Conclusions and Future Prospects

We have presented our study of the gridCoED scheme along with some comparison results from related works. Eager et al. [2] quote in their paper, "We show that extremely simple adaptive load sharing policies, which collect very small amounts of system state information and which use this information in very simple ways, yield dramatic performance improvements." We argue that our scheme is optimal in view of this perspective provided by Eager.

When we take a closer look at Eager's ideas of an optimal scheme, we see that gridCoED methodology fits the criteria very well. It is a simple scheme relying on very small broadcast packages sent out to the machines in the network. It optimizes on the fact that the better target machines in a population will be selected and the process will be executed there. It reduces the overall transmission costs in the network by using the tables to handle process allocation and cutting down on broadcast messages. It also improves on the stability by maintaining current tables. These advantages clearly point out that our scheme is definitely in par with Eager's views of an ideal load balancing strategy.

gridCoED model performs satisfactorily, but it could of course be modified to perform even better with various other types of system parameters. A few of the problems that are under current research are provided below:

- We would like to exploit greater parallelism from gridCoED in a dynamic metacomputing environment, and provide more extensive simulation results.
- The issue of preemptive process migration[11,19] should be incorporated into our overall system; and how it will affect the tables in the machines is to be seen.

We feel that gridCoED provides the flexibility, efficiency, and fault-tolerance required for a good scheduling model in a grid computing environment.

References

1. I. Ahmed and Y. K. Kwok, "A new approach to scheduling parallel programs using task duplication", *Proceedings of the International Conference on Parallel Processing*, Vol. 2. (1994) 47-51
2. Eager et al. "Adaptive Load Sharing in Homogenous Distributed Systems", *IEEE Transactions on Software Engineering*, Vol. 12. (1986) 662-675
3. H. El-Rewini and T.G. Lewis, "Scheduling parallel programs onto arbitrary target architectures", *Journal of Parallel and Distributed Computing*, Vol. 9, No. 2. (1990) 138-153
4. A. Gerasoulis and T. Yang, "A comparison of clustering heuristics for scheduling directed acyclic graphs onto multiprocessors", *Journal of Parallel and Distributed Computing*, Vol. 16, No. 4. (1992) 276-291
5. Volker Hamscher, Uwe Schwiegelshohn, Achim Streit, and Ramin Yahyapour, "Evaluation of Job-Scheduling Strategies for Grid Computing", *Proceedings of the First IEEE/ACM International Workshop on Grid Computing – GRID 2000.* (2000) 191-202
6. Elisa Heymann, Miquel A. Senar, Emilio Luque, and Miron Livny, "Adaptive Scheduling for Master-Worker Applications on the Computational Grid", *Proceedings of the First IEEE/ACM International Workshop on Grid Computing – GRID 2000.* (2000) 214-227
7. J. J. Hwang, Y.C. Chow, F.D. Anger, C.Y. Lee, "Scheduling precedence graphs in systems with inter processor communication times", *SIAM Journal of Computing*, Vol.18, No. 2. (1989) 244-257
8. R. Lüling, B. Monien, F. Ramme, "Load Balancing in Large Networks: A Comparative Study", 3rd IEEE Symposium on Parallel and Distributed Processing (1991)

9. Muthucumaru Maheswaran and Klaus Krauter, "A Parameter-Based Approach to Resource Discovery in Grid Computing Systems", *Proceedings of the First IEEE/ACM International Workshop on Grid Computing – GRID 2000.* (2000) 181-190

10. Michael Mitzenmacher, "How Useful is Old Information?" *IEEE Transactions on Parallel and Distributed Systems*, Vol.11, No. 1. (2000) 6-20

11. J. Mullender, "Process Management in a Distributed Operating System", *Lecture Notes in Computer Sciences-Experiences with Distributed Systems.* J. Nehmer (Editor). Vol.309, International Workshop Kaiserslautern. (1987)

12. L. M. Ni, C. W. Xu, T. B. Gendreau, "Drafting Algorithm – A Dynamic Process Migration Protocol for Distributed Systems", IEEE 5th Int. Conf. on Distributed Computing Systems. (1985) 539-546

13. S. S. Pande, D. P. Agrawal and J. Mauney, "A new threshold scheduling strategy for Sisal programs on distributed memory systems", *Journal of Parallel and Distributed Computing*, Vol. 21, No. 2. (1994) 223-236

14. S. S. Pande, D. P. Agrawal and J. Mauney, "A scalable scheduling method for functional paralleleism on distributed memory multiprocessors", *IEEE Transactions of Parallel and Distributed Systems,* Vol. 6, No. 4. (1995) 388-399

15. Samantha Ranaweera and Dharma P. Agrawal, "A Task Duplication Based Scheduling Algorithm for Heterogeneous Systems", *Proceedings of the 14th International Parallel and Distributed Processing Symposium (IPDPS'00)* (2000)

16. Anuraag Sarangi and Alok Shriram, "Process Allocation Using ICHU Model", paper presented as a poster in *International Conference on High Performance Computing (HiPC'00)*, Bangalore, India. (2000)

17. V. Sarkar, "Partitioning and scheduling programs for execution on multiprocessors", MIT Press, Cambridge, MA. (1989)

18. Alok Shriram, Anuraag Sarangi, Avinash S. "ICHU Model for Processor Allocation in Distributed Operating Systems", submitted to ACM SIGOPS *Operating System Review.*

19. Johnathan M. Smith and Gerald Q. Maguire, Jr., "Process Migration: Effects on Scientific Computation", ACM SIGPLAN Notices 23930. (1988) 102-106

20. Andrew S. Tanenbaum, *Modern Operating Systems.* Prentice-Hall N.J, U.S. 1992

Exposed versus Encapsulated Approaches to Grid Service Architecture

Micah Beck, Terry Moore and James S. Plank

Computer Science Department
University of Tennessee
Knoxville, TN 37996
{mbeck, tmoore, plank}@cs.utk.edu

Abstract. The dichotomy between the exposed and encapsulated approaches to computer systems architectures is well known in contexts such as the processor design (RISC vs. CISC) and layered network service stacks. In this paper we examine how this basic choice of approaches arises in the design of the Internet Backplane Protocol, a network storage service, and as an issue in Grid architecture more generally.

1   Introduction

One plausible interpretation of the progressive transformation of the Metacomputing of the last decade [1] into the "Grid" computing of this one [2] views it as an effort to realize the potential truth in the slogan that "the Network is the Computer," and to make that realization the basis of a public infrastructure for next generation scientific computing. A trio of powerful trends that dominated the 90's fueled this idea. First, the Internet, driven by the advent of the Web, experienced unprecedented growth, becoming an all-pervasive fabric of connectivity that application developers could assume to be present. Second, the rapid build up of advanced research networks offered the possibility of guaranteed quality of service, end-to-end, for Internet applications on a national WAN. Finally, the continued exponential growth in the local provisions of all fundamental computing resources — processing power, communication bandwidth, and storage — suggested a picture of a network-as-computer of staggering aggregate capacity, if only the necessary software infrastructure could be created to bring these elements together.

But if the network is going to be the computer, the natural question is "What kind of computer is it going to be?" Or more directly, "What engineering approach should

---

This work is supported by the National Science Foundation Next Generation Software Program under grant # EIA-9975015 and the Department of Energy Next Generation Internet Program under grant #DE-FC02-99ER25396.

we take in building it?" In this paper we discuss what we believe to be a key architectural choice to be made in this endeavor, namely, the choice between an *encapsulated* and an *exposed* approach to building high-level functionality from low-level Grid resources.

The distinction between these two approaches is elementary. Any complex, shared computing system requires an architecture that will allow it to provide high performance services and yet be able to support new functionality to address previously unanticipated purposes as they arise. A common way to address this requirement is software layering. At the lowest level such systems are made up of physical resources that implement primitive functions with little protection between them. At higher levels, computing resources are represented as objects that can be much larger and more complex than primitive memory words, and operations defined on those objects are similarly much more complex than primitive machine instructions. What links the primitive and high levels is the *aggregation* of primitive memory and instructions to implement high level objects and operations. In an *encapsulated* approach to service architecture the necessary aggregation of low-level resources is hidden from the user at the higher level; in an *exposed* approach, the aggregation is external to the primitive service so that the low-level resource remains visible at higher levels.

This contrast between encapsulated and exposed approaches to resource engineering is widely known. Most notably, it appears in the historical debate between the supporters of *Complex Instruction Set Computers* (*CISC*) and the supporters of *Reduced Instruction Set Computers* (*RISC*) over how to make the best use of extra processor real estate [3]. Similarly, the decision in the late 70's to implement only the most essential and common communication functions at the network (IP) layer, forcing all stronger functionalities to build on that layer, represents a clear choice in favor of a more exposed approach to resource engineering for the Internet [4, 5].

One way to analyze the choice between exposed and encapsulated Grid architectures is to focus on the fact that, since the infrastructure must be shared by a large group of stakeholders, design approaches will tend to divide in terms of the way they structure that sharing. The *Computer Center model*, for example, which informs the current Grid paradigm, was developed in order to allow scarce and extremely valuable resources to be shared by a select community in an environment where security and accountability are major concerns. Consequently the form of sharing it implements is necessarily highly controlled [6] and access to low-level resources tends to be highly encapsulated. By contrast, the *Internet model* was designed to facilitate the sharing of network bandwidth for the purpose universal communication among an international community of indefinite size. It is therefore designed to be as open (i.e. lightly controlled) and easy to use as possible, and so it tends to leave low-level resources relatively exposed. While admission and accounting policies are difficult to implement in this model, the universality, generality, and scalability of the resource sharing it implements for communication bandwidth has obviously proved powerful.

Given the evident success of the Internet model, what seems most striking to us is that, as the research community continues to roll pell-mell toward a network-as-computer infrastructure, precious little research is being done to explore the possibility of taking a more exposed approach to the other basic elements of network

computing, viz. *storage* and *computation*. In this paper we discuss some of the issues
that have arisen during our efforts to investigate and build an exposed service for
network storage. After filling out the contrast between encapsulated and exposed
design philosophies for network services in general, we look in detail at two specific
instances that have arisen during our work on distributed storage: one where the
exposed approach seems to apply in a natural way (implementation of a file
abstraction) and one where its application is less straightforward and more
problematic (implementation of complex data movement operations). Our goal here
is not to settle any question, but to open a conversation about an extremely important
design option for the scientific computing community that is all but completely
neglected at the moment.

2   Encapsulated vs. Exposed Network Services

To the extent that the scientific computing community is already using the network as
a computer, the Internet provides a ubiquitous communication substrate connecting its
components (with routers acting as special-purpose elements invisible in the
architecture), while network servers provide all access to storage and computation.
Illustrations of such servers and services are plentiful: FTP, NFS, and AFS [7]
provide access to storage; Condor [8], NetSolve [9], Ninf [10] provide lightweight
access to processing; HTTP provides access to both; GRAM [11] provides access to
heavyweight computing resources; LDAP provides access to directory services; and
so on. What is notable about these instances, and is equally true of almost all the other
cases we could add to the list, is that they represent relatively *encapsulated* network
services:

> An *encapsulated* network service implements functionality that does not
> closely model the underlying network resource, but which must be
> implemented by aggregating the resource and/or applying significant
> additional logic in its utilization.

The best effort delivery of datagrams at the IP level, on the other hand, represents a
clear example of a relatively *exposed* network service:

> An exposed network service adds enough additional abstraction to the
> underlying network resource to allow it to be utilized at the next higher level,
> but does not aggregate it or add logic beyond what is necessary for the most
> common and indispensable functionality that uses it.

An important difference between the two approaches emerges when we need to
extend the functionality of a given service. Encapsulated services tend to be
implemented by heavyweight servers and have APIs designed at a high semantic
level, interposing themselves between the client and low overhead, transparent access
to the underlying resources As a result, it can be difficult, inefficient, or in some cases
impossible to build new functionality on top of such APIs. Instead, encapsulated
services tend to implement new functionality through "plug in modules" that extend
the functionality of the server, introducing new code that has access to low level
interfaces within the server. These plug-in modules are the server equivalent of

microcode in CISC processors, raising a familiar set of questions about access control and security for the management of such code. Encapsulation also tends to lead to balkanization, with each server supporting a different set of plug-ins.

Extending the functionality of an exposed service makes different demands because exposed services have lighter weight servers and APIs designed at a simpler semantic level. Since these factors are conducive to lower overhead and more transparent access to the underlying resources, it tends to be much easier and more efficient to build new functionality on top of exposed services. Exposed services promote the layering of higher-level functionality on top of their APIs, either in higher-level servers or in client code.

This layering of services, which is analogous to the user-level scheduling of a RISC processor by a compiler, is perhaps most familiar in the construction of a network services stack. In the world of end-to-end packet delivery, it has long been understood that TCP, a protocol with strong semantic properties (e.g., reliability and in-order delivery) can be layered on top of IP, a weak datagram delivery mechanism. By allowing IP services to retain their weak semantics, and thereby *leaving the underlying communication bandwidth exposed for use by the broadest possible range of purposes*, this layering has had the crucial benefit of fostering ubiquitous deployment. At the same time, in spite of the weak properties of IP datagram delivery, stronger properties like reliability and in-order delivery of packets can be achieved through the fundamental mechanism of retransmitting IP packets. Retransmission controlled by a higher layer protocol, combined with protocol state maintained at the endpoints, overcomes non-delivery of packets. All non-transient conditions that interrupt the reliable, in-order flow of packets can then be reduced to non-delivery. We view retransmission as an *aggregation* of weak IP datagram delivery services to implement a stronger TCP connection.

Despite the familiarity of this exposed approach, it may still not be obvious how to apply it to a resource such as storage. After all, almost every technology for the access and/or management of network storage one can think of — FTP, HTTP, NFS, AFS, HPSS, GASS [12], SRB [13], NAS [14], etc. — encapsulates the storage behind abstractions with relatively strong semantic properties. For that reason, our research in this area had to start by creating a protocol, viz. the *Internet Backplane Protocol* (*IBP*), that supported the management of remote storage resources while leaving them as exposed as possible. IBP is a network service that provides an exposed abstraction of shared network storage [15, 16]. Each IBP *depot* (server) provides access to an underlying storage resource to any client that connects to the server. In order to enable sharing, the depot hides details such as disk addresses, and provides a very primitive capability-based mechanism to safeguard the integrity of data stored at the depot. IBP's low level, low overhead model of storage is designed to allow more complex structures, such as asynchronous networking primitives and file and database systems, to be built on top of the IBP API. The IBP depot and client library are now available for several Unix/Linux variants and Windows, and there is a Java client library (http://icl.cs.utk.edu/ibp); the API is documented in detail [17]. With IBP in place the question becomes how easy or difficult it is to layer storage services with strong semantic properties on top of the weak underlying storage resources provided by IBP depots.

3 Extending the Functionality of IBP

A key principle of exposed designs is that the semantics of low level services should be kept as weak as possible. To illustrate how weak the semantics of the IBP storage service is, we examine the primitive unit of IBP storage allocation, the *byte array*. As an abstraction the IBP byte array is at a higher level than the disk block (a fixed size byte array), and is implemented by aggregating disk blocks and using auxiliary data structures and algorithms. Abstracting away the size of the disk block, a byte array amortizes the overhead of allocation across multiple blocks. If we consider storage services at the disk block level to be the equivalent of "scalar" operations within a processor, then byte arrays allow a kind of "vectorization" of operations. Though our aim was to make the IBP storage service as exposed as possible, this level of encapsulation was considered indispensable to hide the most specific underlying characteristics of the access layer (physical medium and OS drivers) and to amortize per-operation overhead across multiple blocks.

Nonetheless, the semantics of the IPB byte array remain very primitive. This fact becomes clear when you realize that the most intuitive and universal abstraction for storage, viz. the *file*, has strong properties (e.g. unbounded size and duration of allocation) that are not generally available from the underlying storage resource and therefore are not modeled by IBP. Since abstractions with such strong and intuitive semantics are essential for ease of use, they must be implemented either in exposed style (by layering new functionality over the primitive service), or in encapsulated style (by adding powerful new operations that make the low-level service itself less primitive). Our experience has been that the former path is relatively easy to follow when implementing a file abstraction for exposed network storage, but that the latter is more straightforward for implementing a mechanism for one-to-many data movement.

3.1 Layering a file abstraction over IBP

In our exposed approach to network storage, the file abstraction must be implemented in a higher layer that aggregates more primitive IBP buffers. In order to apply the principle of aggregation to exposed storage services, it is necessary to maintain state that represents an aggregation of storage allocations, much as sequence numbers and timers are maintained to keep track of the state of a TCP session. Fortunately, in this case we have a traditional, well-understood model that can be followed. In the Unix file system, the data structure used to implement aggregation of underlying disk blocks is the *inode* (*intermediate node*). Under Unix a file is implemented as a tree of disk blocks with data blocks at the leaves. The intermediate nodes of this tree are the inodes, which are themselves stored on disk. The Unix inode implements only aggregation of disk blocks within a single disk volume to create large files; other strong properties are sometimes implemented through aggregation at a lower level (e.g. RAID) or through modifications to the file system or additional software layers that make redundant allocations and maintain additional state (e.g. AFS, HPSS) [7, 18].

Working by analogy with the inode, we have chosen to implement a single generalized data structure, which we call an *external node,* or *exNode*, for management of aggregate allocations that can be used in implementing network storage with many different strong semantic properties. Rather than aggregating blocks on a single disk volume, the exNode aggregates storage allocations on the Internet, and the exposed nature of IBP makes IBP storage allocations especially well adapted to such aggregations. In the present context the key point about the design of the exNode, which we describe in more detail elsewhere [19], is that it has allowed us to create an abstraction of a network file that can be layered over IBP-based storage in a way that is completely consistent with the exposed resource approach. In the case of one-to-many data movement, however, we have chosen to take a more encapsulated approach

3.2   One-to-many data movement using IBP

IBP's "vectorized" storage services work well in exposed mode as long as operations are simple. Likewise, the reliable transfer of data between client and depot, or between a source and destination depot, are a good fit if it is assumed that TCP can be implemented throughout the underlying network. But such is often not the case. The initial IBP API addressed point-to-point data movement with a single call that models the characteristics of transfer using a reliable TCP connection:

```
IBP_copy(source, target, size, offset)
```

The straightforward client API for IBP is not sufficiently exposed to allow for efficient transfer of data between a single source depot and multiple recipients: If one-to-many communication is implemented through repeated one-to-one communication, this communication can be optimized by reusing the source memory buffer rather than repeatedly reading from disk. Similarly, if there is an underlying UDP multicast service available, or if the network includes satellite, high performance or other links not conforming to the usual model of the public Internet, then TCP may not be the transport layer protocol of choice. However, complex signaling, flow control and retransmission may be required in order to implement reliable data transfer taking advantage of other transport layer protocols.

Given the need to manage low-level resources (e.g. memory buffers) when implementing one-to-many data movement, a natural approach is to implement such functionality at a low level. We have extended the current API with a more complex call that allows multiple targets and arbitrary data movement "operations" to be specified. These operations are implemented using low level processes called *data movers* that plug into the depot software architecture between the depot process and the network

```
IBP_copy(DM_op, target_count, source, target[], int size, int
offset)
```

By encapsulating data movement functionality at a level that allows for efficient access to underlying storage resources and can manage data transfer at the level of memory buffers, the software architecture finesses the problem of providing sufficient transparency to allow such functionality to be layered on top of the IBP API. In the process, however, the design has diverged from the philosophy of exposed-resource network services.

The exposed approach to this problem would seek to enable to implementation of complex data movement on top of the IBP API. You can see how this design approach would work by examining the problems that would arise in trying to use the current API and implementation to execute it:

• The current IBP protocol implements each operation as a separate TCP connection to the depot. However, this is easily optimized using persistent connections and multiplexing multiple concurrent operations over a single connection.

• The current IBP API does not model in-memory buffers and so cannot be used to explicitly optimize the movement of data between disk and network. The addition of short-lived memory buffers is an easy extension to the IBP API and would address this problem.

• High performance vectorized (multi-buffer) transfers of data require the immediate execution of each operation as soon as possible after its predecessor operations have completed. Timeouts and other complex strategies must be used to deal with exceptional conditions.

As in any architecture where there is a substantial latency between operation issue and execution, latency will also be a potential problem here. In processor architecture, the solutions to this problem include pipelining with built-in interlocks to implement dependences, and both predicated and speculative execution. An exposed approach to enhancing the data movement functionality of the IBP depot would follow these strategies. The result would be a more complex, but highly general operation-scheduling function that allows stronger operations to be implemented at a higher level.

4   Conclusion

Starting with any initial design, there is always the temptation to extend it by adding new operations and encapsulating their implementation in the bowels of the existing system. This often has the advantage of backward compatibility with the existing service and of providing maximum control in the implementation of the new functionality. We can see this approach being followed in the addition of Data Movers to the IBP storage service: plug-in functionality was added at the low level and a call directly invoking that new functionality was added to the client API.

The exposed resource approach to network services follows in a long tradition of hardware and software architecture. When, as in the case of the exNode, it is feasible to layer new functionality over an existing API, that is usually the preferred approach. However, when implementing new functionality requires that the service be modified to expose new resources and provide more powerful scheduling functions, taking the exposed approach poses several risks:

• The existing service might need to be substantially restructured to support the new functionality at a higher layer.

• The exposed design of the lower layer might be too complex to be easily programmed at the higher layer.

• The performance of the layered implementation may be inadequate due to the overhead of making multiple calls to the lower layer.

- Inadequate analysis of the requirements for access to low level resources may result in an exposed service that cannot support the new functionality at a higher layer.

These risks seemed substantial enough to lead us to take the encapsulated approach in the current implementation of one-to-many data movement using IBP. However, the design of an exposed data movement interface is being studied, and a prototype implementation is planned. The possible benefits of an exposed resource approach to Grid service architecture are too great to leave unexplored.

If the network is going to be the computer, and if exposed approaches to networking and storage can be developed, then the final component is computation. Exposed approaches to computation would require that the processor resource be exposed to the network in a raw form, allowing arbitrary computations to be performed upon data stored in an exposed storage service and transported using exposed networking services. Several different Grid elements in the current ensemble of services, including GRAM and Network Enabled Servers such as NetSolve and Ninf, perform computations for remote clients. In these cases there is a tradeoff between openness and generality: Gram will execute arbitrary code for a known user; NetSolve and Ninf will perform computations on behalf of arbitrary users but will execute only known and trusted code. The development of a network service that strikes a balance between openness and generality, which we call the *Network Functional Unit*, would be the ultimate and most difficult achievement of the exposed approach to Grid service architecture.

5   References

1. L. Smarr and C. E. Catlett, "Metacomputing," *Communications of the ACM*, vol. 35, no. 6, pp. 44-52, 1992.
2. I. Foster and C. Kesselman, "The Grid: Blueprint for a New Computing Infrastructure." San Francisco, CA: Morgan Kaufman Publishers, 1998, pp. 677.
3. J. L. Hennessy and D. A. Patterson, *Computer Architecture: A Quantitative Approach*, 2nd ed. San Francisco, CA.: Morgan Kaufmann Publishers, Inc., 1996.
4. J. H. Saltzer, D. P. Reed, and D. D. Clark, "End-to-End Arguments in System Design," *ACM Transactions on Computer Systems*, vol. 2, no. 4, pp. 277-288, 1984.
5. D. P. Reed, J. H. Saltzer, and D. D. Clark, "Comment on Active Networking and End-to-End Arguments," *IEEE Network*, vol. 12, no. 3, pp. 69-71, 1998.
6. I. Foster, C. Kesselman, and S. Tuecke, "The Anatomy of the Grid: Enabling Scalable Virtual Organizations," *International Journal of SuperComputer Applications*, 2001.
7. J. H. Morris, M. Satyanarayan, M. H. Conner, J. H. Howard, D. S. H. Rosenthal, and F. D. Smith, "Andrew: A Distributed Personal Computing Environment," *Communications of the ACM*, vol. 29, no. 3, pp. 184-201, 1986.

8. J. Pruyne and M. Livny, "A worldwide flock of condors : Load sharing among workstation clusters," *Journal on Future Generations of Computer Systems*, vol. 12, 1996.

9. H. Casanova and J. Dongarra, "Applying NetSolve's Network Enabled Server," *IEEE Computational Science & Engineering*, vol. 5, no. 3, pp. 57-66, 1998.

10. S. Sekiguchi, M. Sato, H. Nakada, S. Matsuoka, and U. Nagashima, "Ninf : Network based Information Library for Globally High Performance Computing," presented at Proc. of Parallel Object-Oriented Methods and Applications (POOMA), Santa Fe, NM, 1996.

11. I. Foster, C. Kesselman, C. Lee, R. Lindell, K. Nahrstedt, and A. Roy, "A Distributed Resource Management Architecture that Supports Advance Reservations and Co-Allocation," presented at Intl Workshop on Quality of Service, 1999.

12. J. Bester, I. Foster, C. Kesselman, J. Tedesco, and S. Tuecke, "GASS: A Data Movement and Access Service for Wide Area Computing Systems," presented at Sixth Workshop on I/O in Parallel and Distributed Systems, May 5, 1999, 1999.

13. C. Baru, R. Moore, A. Rajasekar, and M. Wan, "The SDSC Storage Resource Broker," presented at CASCON'98, Toronto, Canada, 1998.

14. G. Gibson and R. V. Meter, "Network Attached Storage Architecture," *Communications of the ACM*, vol. 43, no. 11, pp. 37-45, 2000.

15. J. Plank, M. Beck, W. Elwasif, T. Moore, M. Swany, and R. Wolski, "The Internet Backplane Protocol: Storage in the Network," presented at NetStore99: The Network Storage Symposium, Seattle, WA, 1999.

16. M. Beck, T. Moore, J. Plank, and M. Swany, "Logistical Networking: Sharing More Than the Wires," in *Active Middleware Services*, vol. 583, *The Kluwer International Series in Engineering and Computer Science*, S. Hariri, C. Lee, and C. Raghavendra, Eds. Boston: Kluwer Academic Publishers, 2000.

17. A. Bassi, M. Beck, J. Plank, and R. Wolski, "Internet Backplane Protocol: API 1.0," Department of Computer Science, University of Tennessee, Knoxville, TN, CS Technical Report, ut-cs-01-455, March 16, 2001 2001. http://www.cs.utk.edu/~library/2001.html.

18. R. W. Watson and R. A. Coyne, "The Parallel I/O Architecture of the High-Performance Storage System (HPSS)," presented at IEEE Mass Storage Systems Symposium, 1995.

19. A. Bassi, M. Beck, and T. Moore, "Mobile Management of Network Files," in *Third Annual International Workshop on Active Middleware Services*. San Franscisco, 2001, to appear.

A Methodology for Account Management in Grid Computing Environments

Thomas J. Hacker[1], Brian D. Athey[2]

[1] University of Michigan, Center for Parallel Computing,
2281 Bonisteel Blvd., Ann Arbor, MI USA 48109

[2] University of Michigan, Cell & Developmental Biology,
1071 Beal Ave., Ann Arbor, MI USA 48109
{hacker,bleu}@umich.edu

Abstract. A national infrastructure of Grid computing environments will provide access for a large pool of users to a large number of distributed computing resources. Providing access for the complete pool of potential users would put an unacceptably large administrative burden on sites that participate in the Grid. Current approaches to solve this problem require an account for each user at a site, or maps all users into one account. This paper proposes an alternative approach to account allocation that provides the benefits of persistent accounts while minimizing the administrative burden on Grid resource providers. A technique for calculating the upper bound on the number of jobs and users offered to the system from the Grid that is based on historical use is presented. Finally, application of this approach to the National Institutes of Health Visible Human Project is described.

1 Introduction and Motivation

When a national scale Grid computing environment [1] becomes fully operational, potentially tens of thousands of users will be actively using resources made available to them by Grid resource providers. To access these resources, each of these users will require some form of a local account. However, requiring each participating site on the Grid to accurately maintain tens of thousands of accounts is neither desirable, nor feasible.

Many sites will likely have a finite set of users that regularly visit the site for resources. If a Grid user utilizes resources at a site infrequently, or only once, the overhead associated with creating, maintaining and deleting an account for the infrequent user would quickly overwhelm systems staff and provide a strong disincentive for resource sites to participate in the Grid.

To address this problem, a mechanism for binding Grid users to "template" accounts for a finite period of time in a local environment is proposed that provides a mechanism for local resource administrators to provide relatively instantaneous access to local resources, persistence for frequent users, and enables close tracking and accounting of Grid user resource utilization. To predict an upper bound on the number of individual jobs and unique users that will utilize the system, a technique based on historical job logs is presented in the last section of this paper.

The temporary account binding mechanism replaces the fundamental systems paradigm of a strong binding between a real user and an account on a system with the model of a temporary binding between an account and a real user. Authentication and authorization that traditionally has been performed on the local system is replaced with distributed authentication and authorization systems, such as Kerberos, X.509[2], and Akenti[15]. To enforce user accountability, local record keeping can be used to track the actions and resource utilization of users. To preserve local administrative control over accounts, the concept of a "binding pool" is introduced, which represents an administrative domain for mapping Grid users to local accounts in a fashion similar to a NIS domain or Kerberos realm.

1.1 Intergrid Account Protocol

Account management protocols are an instance of *intergrid protocols* [17]. The establishment of a common protocol between virtual organizations to create and delete associations between Grid users, Grid computing environments (GCE), and local resource pools is essential for several reasons. First, in the absence of a common account management protocol, each GCE operated by resource providers requires individual attention to add, delete, and manage users. The amount of effort required to manage each GCE operated by a local site increases as additional GCEs are introduced into the mix of resources and services provided by a site. These efforts represent hidden costs that are rarely perceived by end-users, but are all too well known to site administrators. Thus, minimizing the number of accounts required at a local site can have a substantial financial impact. Second, if an account must be established *a priori* for each user that *might* use the site, the local resource site must maintain a large number of "unoccupied" accounts. This requirement introduces several problems. Each account requires a minimum allotment of resources, such as backed-up disk space for file storage, authentication and authorization entities (the Kerberos principals database, for example), and the purchase of additional software licenses. Additionally, a large number of dormant accounts present an additional security risk to the system. Finally, the aggregate loss of resources (i.e. disk space) due to the required minimum allocations for dormant accounts prevents the commitment of these resources to active users. The third motivation for a dynamic account binding mechanism is the growing reliance on global authentication and authorization facilities, with the corresponding decrease in the usefulness of traditional "local" authentication and authorization mechanisms. X.509 has become a global standard for authentication, and is the basis for several projects that are using X.509 for fine-grained authentication and authorization [2, 19, 21].

2   Current Situation and Related Work

The problem of maintaining accounts across a large number of hosts in a local administrative domain has been addressed over the years with a number of solutions.

Project Athena solved the problem by using Kerberos for verifying user identity, and Hesiod for maintaining password files. This central control mechanism worked well on a limited number of platforms and administrative domains. As the class of desktop hosts that required centralized authentication and authorization mechanisms increased, existing solutions were extended to cover the new systems. Kerberos authentication was added to Apple Macintosh [5] and Microsoft Windows platforms. Other authentication and authorization systems were created that addressed the problem well in one host class, but poorly in others. Examples of these include Novell and DCE.

All of these account management schemes were designed to manage a unique match of user to account (binding pool) for a well-defined administrative domain across a variety of platforms. However, when attempts are made to utilize resources across administrative domains or when the number of users exceeds 100,000, the solutions fail to scale elegantly.

Condor solves the account allocation problem by using one UID ("nobody") to execute jobs for users that do not have an account in a Condor flock [3]. The PUNCH system uses a similar scheme, where all users are represented by logical user accounts within a single physical account [4] with the ability to use a set of dynamic account bindings for system calls.

There are disadvantages to these approaches. If there are multiple jobs on the same system from different users, with all of the users assigned to one UID, it is difficult for the system to distinguish between those users since they all share the same UID (i.e. sharing scratch disk space and accountability). Moreover, with a shared UID, persistence features of the system (i.e. shared memory) are essentially unavailable to users.

The scheme described in this paper is fundamentally different than the PUNCH approach in that it creates a 1:1 account binding between a user and an account that is identical to a normal local account. There are several advantages to this scheme over the single UID approach. First, this solution is a compromise between requiring one firmly bound account for every user that may use the system versus provisioning only one UID for all users. Additionally, account templates provides a form of persistence to frequent users, but also allows new users to use the system without excessive account management overhead. This approach allows site administrators to predict and minimize the effects of Grid usage on systems they administer. Thus, the account template approach described in this paper provides a measured form of persistence, identity, and accountability.

Attempts are now being made in the Grid computing milieu to address the cross-domain authentication and authorization problems. Globus[6, 18], for example, is utilizing X.509 based authentication mechanisms to successfully deploy a computational job across a set of supercomputer systems by statically mapping an X.509 identity to a local account. The process used by Legion [20] to bind users to Legion accounts is identical to the process used in UNIX where an administrator must create an identity and password for a new user. The difference between Legion and the protocol described in this paper is that Legion requires *a priori* creation of an account for an individual user for Legion, whereas this protocol does not. Legion will thus encounter the same problems with dormant accounts that have been described.

3   Account Templates

Using account templates for user account allocation takes advantage of the potential "locality" of the Grid user's utilization pattern to support thousands of Grid users while simultaneously providing site administrators an analytical tool for provisioning their systems to limit and meter utilization of their systems by users from the Grid.

The basic idea is to create a pool of "template" accounts that have no permanent association (or "binding") with a user, and to create temporary persistent bindings between template accounts and Grid users. Each template account uses the regular account attributes that are normal for the host system, but the user information refers to a pseudo user, not a real user. For example, on a UNIX host the template account may use a pseudo anonymous user account that only permits X.509 based secure shell (ssh) logins, with proxy process creation by a root level process after authentication.

Authorization and authentication for distributed services, such as file systems, computational resources, and remote instruments is provided by distributed systems such as Akenti [15] and Keynote [19].

3.1   Binding Pools and Account Template States

To provide for integration with existing systems, there must be an administrative domain to facilitate the use of services (i.e. NFS) on systems that were not designed to operate with temporary account bindings. The set of assignments of template accounts to Grid users represents a pool of bindings (a "binding pool"). A binding pool represents a 1:1 match of a user to a template account within a finite administrative domain. To associate a user with one unique account on a host, a set of hosts should subscribe to one and only one binding pool. For example, a Linux cluster consisting of 64 hosts would subscribe to one binding pool, which may also be subscribed to by any other collection of hosts. It may be the case that user to account template assignments are identical across binding pools, but no assumptions should be made, since the binding pools are intentionally separate.

Firmly bound accounts exist in one of two states: active/available, and unavailable. A firmly bound account is active/available when the account is available for a properly authenticated and authorized user. The firmly bound account in unavailable when the account is still on the system, but has been disabled. Due to the more complex nature of temporary account bindings, additional states are necessary. Each template account in a set of template accounts will be in one of the following states and transitions described in figure 1.

4   System Issues with Temporary Binding

Most operating systems have been designed with an implicit assumption that firm binding between a user and an account is inviolate. When this assumption is invalidated, several systems issues must be addressed. These issues include persistence, multi-role/multi-site usage, accounting, and usage metering. This section will examine these issues.

NEW	New local account that has never had any Grid user association.
ACTIVE	Local account with an active online association to a Grid user.
QUIET	Local account with no active online association to a Grid user.
UNAVAILABLE	Local account not available for any associations to a Grid user.
SCRATCH	Assignment of local account to a Grid user has been broken.
ERROR	An error has occurred in the template, and is unavailable for use.

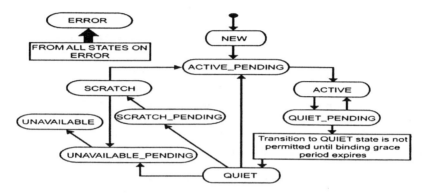

Fig. 1. Account Template States

On UNIX systems, persistent artifacts may be left upon the completion of a process. These artifacts represent persistent state that the operating system maintains on behalf of the user. Examples of this include files held in the file system, shared memory segments, semaphores and message queues. Any account template solution that creates a temporary binding between users and accounts must also have mechanisms to manage these persistent objects. To address these persistence problems, a "grace period" timer is utilized in the state transition from QUIET_PENDING and QUIET states. When a Grid process completes, the binding is not considered breakable until the grace period is expired. This gives the user some guarantee of binding persistence, and allows them to run several consecutive jobs using the bound account template without worrying about losing persistent information that is an artifact of their computation.

If a Grid user is consuming resources in a "usage role" on behalf of a sponsored project, the user's resource consumption should be charged against that project, not another project. To provide for participation in several projects on multiple sites, a mechanism to link resource usage from a "real" account to a project account is necessary. This mechanism is a Resource Consumption Account that sits between "real" user home site accounts and account templates on remote Grid sites. The only access a user can have to Grid resources is through the Resource Consumption Account. Research is currently underway [8] to define mechanisms to successfully deal with this situation.

UNIX based systems use a unique UID as the basis for authorization, and as a key for storing and retrieving resource usage information. With the introduction of high level authorization mechanisms, new extensions to UNIX will be required to map artifacts such as X.509 certificates to the local version of authentication. Host based accounting systems will also need to be extended to store a Grid wide unique identifier, such as an X.500 distinguished name (DN) along with the usual accounting information. In practice, authentication and authorization on hosts for users with template accounts will only work if there is a production quality high-level authorization and authentication system in place at the resource site. Usage metering and accounting will still be done locally on the basis of the template account UID. Work is under way in the Grid community on these mechanisms [8, 7]

5   Determining the Peak Number of Account Templates

For practical considerations, determining an upper bound on the number of template accounts required to satisfy a stream of utilization requests for the Grid is very desirable. Maintaining an arbitrarily large pool of template accounts to satisfy 100% of offered utilization requests would compel a Grid resource provider to incur a large fixed overhead cost, since each template account requires a certain amount of static resources. To calculate a reasonable upper bound on the number of template accounts necessary to satisfy a stream of job requests, we can use the historical resource utilization of the system as a guide for prediction. Given the historical job arrival rate, job time in the system, and probability of a user arriving at the system based upon aggregate use, it is possible to determine an upper bound on the number of template accounts that will provide a predictable grade of service (G.O.S.) to the offered job stream. Consider the following: For a series of weeks from week 1 to a given week c, let N_i is the number of jobs successfully executed during $week_i$, U_i be the complete list of users (with repeats) that submitted a successful job during the week, and S_i represent the average time spent in the system for all the jobs that ran that week.

During the time period of a week, there will be a period during which the number of jobs in the system will reach a maximum. This peak usage is analogous to the "busy hour" in telephone systems in which the maximum is the daily peak reached in the number of outside telephone lines used to service outgoing telephone calls in a private telephone system [13]. Let the maximum number of jobs in the system during the peak period be represented by $J_i max$.

5.1   Characterizing the Job Stream

To model the characteristics of the offered job stream, some underlying observations of the job stream must be established. Jobs in the job stream are initiated by user actions. Paxson [10] determined that user initiated connections (such as Telnet and FTP) demonstrate exponentially distributed interarrivals and independent arrival events, and could be successfully modeled with a Poisson distribution. Since the job stream is also user initiated, it would be reasonable to hypothesize that the job stream could also be modeled with a Poisson distribution. To verify this hypothesis, the interarrival times between requests in the job stream were analyzed. The interarrival times demonstrated an exponential distribution, and the submission of jobs was assumed to be independent, since each represents a unique job submission event by a user. Based upon these characteristics, and examination of the data, it was determined that the arrival rate of the job stream follows a Poisson distribution. The median of the arrival rate can be calculated from the historical job information, or can be estimated based upon some upper limit of execution in the system, such as a queue time limit.

For a given week$_i$, the distribution of arrival rates into the system follows a Poisson distribution with median λ_i. During the "busy period" of peak utilization of the system, the arrival rate of jobs is much higher than the median arrival rate λ_i. Accurately characterizing the arrival rate during the busy period is complex [13,14], but the arrival rate during the busy period can be approximated by taking advantage of the fact that the arrival rate follows a Poisson distribution. If we use an approximation of the median plus two standard deviations, we should be able to generate a value for the arrival rate that is larger than approximately 98% of the values in the Poisson distribution. Thus, we assume that (given that η_i is N_i normalized to units of hours):

$$\lambda_{i\,max} = \lambda_i + 2s = \lambda_i + 2\sqrt{\lambda_i} \equiv \eta_i + 2\sqrt{\eta_i} \qquad (1)$$

The time spent in the system for all jobs was analyzed and determined to be exponentially distributed (this will be useful later). The average time in spent in the system S_i is the arithmetic mean of the time spent in the system for all the jobs in week$_i$, and thus the holding time $1/\mu_i$ is equivalent to S_i.

5.2   Calculating the Peak Number of Jobs

Using Little's Law, the number of simultaneous active sessions during week$_i$ is

$$E_i = \frac{\lambda_{i\,max}}{\mu_i} \qquad (2)$$

Where E_i represents the maximum number of session active during the busy hour of the week.

The job stream offered to the system demonstrates the following characteristics: there are (potentially) an infinite number of sources; job requests arrive at random; job requests are serviced in order of arrival; refused requests are "lost"; and time in the system is exponentially distributed. Given that the system has these characteristics, the Erlang-B distribution can be used to predict the probability that an account binding request will be blocked. Moreover, for a desired blocking grade of service (GOS), the minimum number of account templates required can easily be calculated [12,13,14]. The algorithm developed by [12] can be used to calculate the number of template accounts required to satisfy a desired GOS given E_i.

The historical job logs the for the IBM SP-2 systems at the University of Michigan Center for Parallel Computing and the Advanced Computing Center for Engineering & Science (ACCES) system at the University of Texas at Austin were analyzed to measure the ability of this method to successfully predict the maximum number of account templates required to satisfy an offered job stream. The University of

Michigan logs contain 7,294 jobs over a period of 44 weeks. The University of Texas logs contain 3,160 jobs over a period of 27 weeks. Jobs that were in the system less than 10 minutes were filtered out of the job stream, to remove jobs that did not actually execute in the system. From the logs, the average arrival rate for all of the weeks was calculated using the following equations:

$$\lambda = \frac{\sum_c \lambda_i}{c}, \ \lambda_{max} = \lambda + 2\sqrt{\lambda} \tag{3}$$

Table 1 contains the results of the calculations from (3), along with the calculated average time in the system over all the weeks ($1/\mu$). Using the equation (2), E can be calculated. If we then calculate the peak number of sessions with ½% GOS using the Erlang-B Loss Formula [9, p. 273], E_{max} can finally be determined.

Table 1. Calculated Values for U-M and U-T.

Site	λ (users/hr)	λ_{max} (users/hr)	$1/\mu$ (hours)	E (sessions)	E_{max} sessions
U-M	0.6706	2.308	18.86	43.53	59
U-T	0.5245	1.973	11.588	22.86	36

To measure the ability of this method to utilize information from preceding weeks to predict the peak number of jobs and unique users for a week, the logs from both U-M

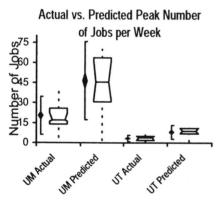

Actual vs. Predicted Peak Number of Jobs per Week

Fig. 2. Peak vs. Predicted Number of Jobs per Week

Table 2. Statistics for Figure 4

Statistic	Median	IQR	95% CI of Median
U-M Actual	17	11.750	16.000
U-M Predicted	45.5	33.000	32.000
U-T Actual	4	3.000	2.000
U-T Predicted	9	4.000	7.000

and U-T were used to successively predict these values. This approach is called the *moving averages approach* in [13] and is used for forecasting demand in telecommunications circuits. After the first few weeks, the technique was fairly successful in predicting appropriate values to satisfy all of the requests for that week measured from the historical logs. Figure 2 shows that the peak number of jobs calculated compared with the actual peak number of jobs measured per week. The predicted peak value of 59 exceeds all of the measured values, and should be able to provide a ½% GOS over all weeks. The ability to calculate the predicted peak number of jobs based upon the average arrival rate and time in the system is useful for allowing system managers to provision the system for a known peak number of jobs.

5.3   Adding a Grace Period to the Binding

The results presented in the previous section is for the scenario in which jobs arrive, are temporarily bound to an account template, and the binding between the user and the template account lasts only as long as the job is in the system. In practice, however, immediately breaking the binding is undesirable for the user and for the system. If a user frequently returns to the system, the aggregate overhead of setting up and tearing down account bindings would be excessive. From the user's point of view, it would be desirable to have a period of time (a "grace period") after the completion of the jobs to be able to collect or analyze the output of the execution. If we introduce a grace period of any significant length to the system, however, some changes must be made to the predictive model to take into account the effects extending the time the account binding is in the system. If we introduce a uniform

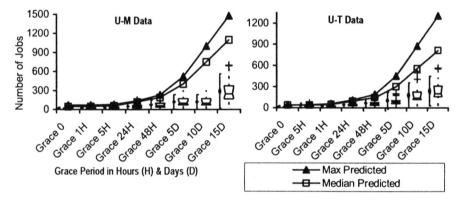

Fig. 3.1- 3.2: Predicted Peak Number of Jobs vs. Actual Peak Number of Jobs

grace period G that is selected by the systems manager, the average holding time for each job $1/\mu$ will be extended to $(1/\mu) + G$, and the corresponding weekly $1/\mu_i$ and aggregate $1/\mu$ will also be extended by G. The arrival rate of the offered jobs to the system λ_i would remain unchanged, and the peak predicted number of jobs would also be scaled appropriately for G. To verify this result, the University of Michigan and University of Texas logs were analyzed to determine the peak number of jobs in the system over all the weeks in the logs for a given grace period G. Figures 3.1 and 3.2 shows the predicted vs. actual peak number of jobs for a set of grace periods from 0 to 15 days for University of Michigan and University of Texas. This analysis demonstrates that the model remains valid when an additional grace period is introduced.

5.4 Predicting the Number of Unique Users in the Job Stream

At the busy period during the week, if the actual peak number of jobs is M, there are M jobs owned by X unique individual users in the system, assuming that the jobs during the busy period start at time t_0 and completes on or after time t_1. For the worst case, one could assume that each job is assigned to a unique individual user, and thus would require M template accounts. In practice, however, the number of jobs attributable to a user is the product of the probability of a job originating from that user in the job stream and M. This is due to the theorem that a Poisson process can be partitioned into a set of independent Poisson processes [9, p. 74]. To apply this theorem, we must determine the probability of the user being the originator of a job in the job stream from the historical logs.

Let p_i = Probability (user$_i$) = (Number of jobs for user$_i$ / Total Number of Jobs). Thus,

$$\lambda_{avg} = p_1 \lambda_{avg} + p_2 \lambda_{avg} + \cdots + p_k \lambda_{avg} \tag{4}$$

$$\lambda_{max} = p_1 \lambda_{max} + p_2 \lambda_{max} + \cdots + p_k \lambda_{max} \tag{5}$$

where k is the number of users in the historical logs. Thus,

$$E_{max} = \frac{1}{\mu} \left[p_1 \lambda_{max} + p_2 \lambda_{max} + \cdots p_k \lambda_{max} \right] \tag{6}$$

$$E_{u1} = \frac{(p_1 \lambda_{max})}{\mu}, E_{u2} = \frac{(p_2 \lambda_{max})}{\mu}, \cdots , E_{uk} = \frac{(p_k \lambda_{max})}{\mu} \tag{7}$$

The predicted number of unique users at the busy period will be the number of terms in (7) that have a values greater than 1.

$$\|U\| \text{ where } U = \{E_{ui} : E_{ui} > 1\} \tag{8}$$

We can then add the grace period G described in the previous section to (7):

$$E_{max} = \left(\frac{1}{\mu} + G \right) \left[p_1 \lambda_{max} + p_2 \lambda_{max} + \cdots + p_k \lambda_{max} \right] \tag{9}$$

The period of time window used in the historical job log to calculate the probability for each user that is used to calculate E_{max} must be at least 2 $(1/\mu + G)$ to capture all possible jobs in the window. For the most accurate results p_i should be based upon an analysis of the job log as far back into the past as is practical. Figures 4.1 and 4.2 shows the predicted peak number of individual users per week vs. the actual peak number of individual users for U-M and U-T. It can be demonstrated that as the grace period G approaches infinity, the maximum number of users calculated from the probability vector approaches the number of individual users that utilized the system. This corresponds to the firm binding case, where over a very long period of time, the number of users that use the system matches the number of users contained within the password file on the system. With the addition of the probability of individual users using the system, system managers can then confidently provision the system for a known peak number of users based upon the historical use information of the system.

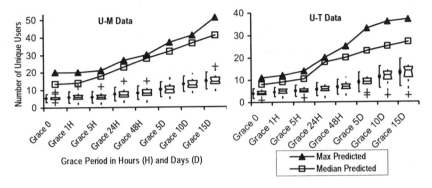

Fig. 4.1-4.2 Predicted Peak Number of Users vs. Actual Peak Number of Users.

5.5   Application: Determine Grace Period and Number of Template Accounts

Now that we can accurately predict an upper bound on the number of template accounts and individual users a Grid resource site would service given the historical logs, GOS, and grace period, we now want to be able to easily calculate the number of template accounts a site would need to support a GOS and grace period selected by the site administrator. The process to do this is as follows: first, calculate average holding time $1/\mu$ by calculating the arithmetic mean of the time in hours in the system for all jobs over a certain filter threshold (to filter out unsuccessful jobs); second, calculate arrival rate λ by dividing the total number of filtered jobs in the log by the number of hours the log covers; third, calculate the user probability vector $\mathbf{p}$ by taking the inverse of the number of times a job comes from a particular user (for example, if user X has 10 jobs, Prob(X) = 1/10). Now, calculate λ_{max} and E using equations (2) and (3).

If you have a package to calculate the Erlang Loss Formula, such as Qsim for Excel [11], or a Java applet [12], you can calculate E_{max}, and the peak number of users by the number of elements of the vector $\mathbf{u} = \mathbf{p}E_{max}$ that are greater than one. This will give you the peak number of users that will utilize the system with a known GOS.

6   Conclusion: Application and Future Work

In this paper, an alternative to existing account allocation techniques was presented that addressed the problems of identity, persistence and accountability present in these systems. The Visible Human Project (VHP) at the University of Michigan sponsored by the National Institutes of Health [16] (NO1-LM-0-3511) plans to serve visible human datasets to learning systems at medical training facilities. The allocation approach described in this paper is critical for supporting thousands of VHP users. For future work, investigation of the effects on this model of self-similar arrival processes described by Paxson [10] from automated processes should be done. Another area for future work is a thorough investigation of the effects of temporary account bindings on Operating Systems design, and investigation of what changes would be required on a UNIX system to support temporary account bindings. Another area of work is the prediction of peak job and users for jointly scheduled production systems, such as the Berkeley Millennium system, Globus, and the U-M/U-T NPACI Grid.

References

1. I. Foster, C. Kesselman (editors), The Grid: Blueprint for a New Computing Infrastructure, Morgan Kauffman Publishers, 1999.
2. R. Housley, W. Ford, W. Polk, D. RFC 2459 "Internet X.509 Public Key Infrastructure Certificate and CRL Profile", January 1999.
3. D. H. J Epema, M. Livny, R. van Dantzig, X. Evers, and J. Pruyne, "A Worldwide Flock of Condors: Load Sharing among Workstation Clusters", Journal on Future Generations of Computer Systems Volume 12, 1996.
4. N. Kapadia and J. Fortes, "PUNCH: An Architecture for Web-Enabled Wide-Area Network-Computing", Cluster Computing: The Journal of Networks, Software Tools and Applications, September 1999.
5. B. Doster, J. Rees, "Third-Party "Authentication for the Institutional File System", University of Michigan CITI Technical Report 92-1.
6. I. Foster, C. Kesselman, C, "Globus: A Metacomputing Infrastructure Toolkit", International Journal of Supercomputing Applications, 11(2): 115-128, 1997.
7. T. Hacker, W. Thigpen, "Distributed Accounting on the Grid", Grid Forum Working Draft.
8. R. Buyya, D. Abramson, J. Giddy, "An Economy Grid Architecture for Service-Oriented Grid Computing", 10th IEEE International Heterogeneous Computing Workshop, April 2001.
9. R. Wolff, Stochastic Modeling and the Theory of Queues. Prentice Hall, 1989.
10. V. Paxson, S. Floyd, "Wide-area Traffic: The Failure of Poisson Modeling", IEEE/ACM Transactions on Networking, pp.226-244, June 1995.
11. 3 Point Technologies, Inc. Qsim Modeling Functions for Excel.
12. S. Qiao, L. Qiao, "A Robust and Efficient Algorithm for Evaluating Erlang B Formula", TR CAS98-03, Department of Computing and Software, McMaster University, 1998.
13. J. Green, The Irwin Handbook of Telecommunications Management. Irwin Professional Publishing, 1996.
14. Intel Support Document #8150:A Traffic Engineering Model for LAN Video Conferencing.
15. M. Thompson, W. Johnston, S. Mudumbai, G. Hoo, K. Jackson, Essiari, "A. Certificate-based Access Control for Widely Distributed Resource",. Proceedings of the Eighth Usenix Security Symposium, Aug. `99.
16. M. J. Ackerman, "The Visible Human Project," J. Biocomm., vol. 18, p 14, 1991.
17. I. Foster, C. Kesselman, S. Tuecke, "The Anatomy of the Grid: Enabling Scalable Virtual Organizations." (to be published in Intl. J. Supercomputer Applications, 2001).
18. R. Butler, D. Engert, I. Foster, C. Kesselman, S. Tuecke, J. Volmer, V. Welch. "A National-Scale Authentication Infrastructure." IEEE Computer, 33(12):60-66, 2000.
19. M. Blaze, J. Feigenbaum, A. Keromytis. "KeyNote Trust-Management System", RFC 2704
20. Legion 1.7 System Administration Manual. The Legion Group, Department of Computer Science, University of Virginia. pp 32-33.
21. W. Doster, M. Watts, D. Hyde. "The KX.509 Protocol", CITI Technical Report 012, February 2001.

Policy Engine: A Framework for Authorization, Accounting Policy Specification and Evaluation in Grids

Babu Sundaram, Barbara M. Chapman

Department of Computer Science, University of Houston, Houston TX 77204, USA
babu,chapman@cs.uh.edu

Abstract. We have developed a policy-based decision framework that provides authorization and cost-based accounting in the EZGrid system, a resource broker for metacomputing. Primarily, this work allows the administrators and the owners to exercise more control over their resources by dictating usage permissions and/or restrictions in a grid environment. This mechanism is independent of the applications and the heterogeneous target domains. The EZGrid resource broker uses the policy engine to evaluate authorization policies of the remote site in the process of making resource choices. Globus Access to Secondary storage (GASS) is used as the back end for staging policy files, if needed, from the remote site to which authorization is required.

1 Introduction

Computational grids [6] are composed of resources from heterogeneous domains that are controlled by varied authorities and administrators. In such an environment, access control is typically enforced through authorization polices that restrict/permit users in gaining access to these resources. Such authorization policies would be varied and specific to each participating autonomous site. For a user who is trying to use resources across the grid, the task of examining, evaluating and managing such usage policies is extremely complicated.

Existing middleware tools like Globus [5] provide tools to authenticate users across the grid by single sign-on mechanism. Also, Globus provides the tools to enable users submit jobs to their "grid resources". However, there is no existing mechanism to gather and store details of a site's general usage policies, user-specific access permissions and thus they cannot be queried during resource selection.

Resource brokers could simplify the task of selecting suitable resources for a user job. This is achieved by automatically identifying the "best" grid resources available to the user and then matching them with the requirements of the job. Such a broker requires detailed knowledge of resource usage permissions so that it would ignore those resources that are not available during the time period considered. Also, knowledge about accounting details at the remote site is required in order to ensure that allowed quotas and usage credits are not exceeded. These tasks require a service that would transparently fetch and evaluate the remote site's policy during the decision-making process.

Tool support to transparently and conveniently implement such policy-based mechanisms is lacking in current grid systems. Methods to express appropriate policies, which would enable the owners to dictate usage policies for their resources, need to be identified. Further, automated frameworks, which would allow the administrators to specify, and help the users to examine and evaluate, such fine-grained authorization policies, need to be designed.

The EZGrid project [3] at the University of Houston aims to simplify the use of computational grids. Built using services of the Globus toolkit, it combines features for viewing static and dynamic information about available resources, manual and automatic selection of resources and submission of jobs. This process takes access and accounting policies into consideration for making optimal resource choices.

This paper provides an overview of the Policy engine framework that we have implemented in EZGrid. After a short description of EZGrid, the second section gives a brief survey of related work. Section 3 explains the complexities involved in policy expression and evaluation over grids. In section 4, we present the details about the internals of the policy engine. Section 5 explains the current status of the system and its role in the EZGrid resource broker. This is followed by comments on future work and open research issues. Finally, we draw some conclusions in Section 7.

1.1 The EZGrid System

EZGrid is an ongoing project at University of Houston that aims to provide brokerage services for multi-site computing. The system mentioned in [3] provides a user interface coupled with a resource brokerage system to equip users to make resource choices in making job submissions over the grid. The major components of this system are the user interface, grid objects, broker kernel and the job manager. Globus toolkit is used to achieve grid middleware services, whenever possible. GSI [2] is used for authentication of users across multiple sites by single sign-on. GRAM [4] is used for allocating resources and submitting job requests to the remote sites. File transfer to/from the remote site and access to secondary storage are obtained through GASS[1].

The broker kernel module automates the resource selection process for the user's job subject to the time and cost constraints specified by the user, history about previous "similar" job submissions, static and dynamic information of resources and access policies at the remote sites. Automation of the resource selection process is based on a minimal set of job specifications provided by the user. Firstly, those resources are identified that are available on the grid and which the user has right of access to. Obviously, the resources that belong to a domain with a policy that would disallow the user to access them at the given time should be discarded. This task requires a service, during decision-making, which would transparently evaluate the remote site's policy. The policy engine provides this service to facilitate the examination of the most recent usage policies at various sites to arrive at the ultimate machine choice.

2 Related Work

Policies enable the administrators to dictate how other users can use their resources. Considerable research has been done to specify and evaluate policies to achieve authorization in distributed systems. Mechanisms are needed to evaluate the policies and match the characteristic of the jobs with appropriate jobs. The most notable among these are the Classified advertisements [9], a product of the Condor technology [7] from the University of Wisconsin, GAA-API[10], a generic API to provide authorization for applications in a uniform fashion, designed at University of Southern California and GSI, a part of the Globus project.

"Classified Advertisements" or Classad have long been used in Condor, a system used for high throughput distributed computing. Classad is a matchmaking scheme used to match a set of requirements (expressed as attributes and values) against a second set of possible requirements. Classad matchmaking is used to match the requirements of the client against the offers of the servers to promote high throughput computing by utilizing idle cycles in a cluster of workstations. Classad is implemented with a set of attributes and logical expressions that evaluate a match. This is done by specifying one's own requirements with references to its own attributes using the notation self.<attribute name> and referring to the attributes of the other Classad with the notation other.<attribute name>. Each party specifies its matching requirements in an expression that evaluates to either true or false. If the requirements of the Classad being matched evaluate to true, the match is successful, otherwise unsuccessful. This was examined as policy language in the work on policy specification in Globus proxies[11].

GAA-API is an authorization model that is extensible across applications and administrative domains. The framework consists of a policy language to express existing access control models and an API to facilitate the application to check for authorization based on a set of policies and credentials. This mechanism is independent of the calling applications and provides authorization service between interacting entities across autonomous security domains.

The Globus grid security infrastructure (GSI) provides a single sign-on mechanism for users while allowing the sites to enforce local access control. In the work of [11], a policy specification mechanism was developed for Globus that used the proxy certificate extensions to include user policies that dictate the valid life time of the proxy, sites to which the proxy can be delegated, sites from which the proxy can be accepted from etc. This allowed the user to specify the usage of the proxy in a fine-grained fashion and disallow the misuse of stolen credentials. Additionally, site administrators can express the authorization policies that are examined by the gatekeeper while accepting job requests from the clients. This work was aimed at achieving more protection against stolen credentials while our work exphaizes authorization and accouting in brokerage systems. Further, in our work, no specific policy expression language is required to achieve policy specification and evaluation across sites.

3   Challenges in Policy Expression and Enforcement in Grids

Grid computing has proven to be a very viable alternative to conventional large scale computing. With owners belonging to varied domains sharing their resources over the grid, it is imperative that ownership and usage policies are strictly honored and enforced. With the current status of grid middleware and tools, administrators and owners do not have enough support to express fine grained usage policies that specify how, when and in what quantity can remote users access their resources. In [11], authors proposed and implemented a mechanism to express user and site policies with the purpose of achieving more protection against stolen credentials and exercising fine grained access control for users. Yet, there is no well defined model to express and examine accounting and authorization policies of a remote site while making a job submission. This is a critical necessity for brokerage systems that examine a user's grid sites for resource choices based on a set of user specifications about the job. In the next section, we explain our implementation of the policy engine that provides a mechanism for policy expression and evaluation in the context of making job submissions over the grid.

4   The Internals of Policy Engine

Policy engine is an automated framework that allows the administrators to express and enforce usage policies that dictate how remote users can gain access to the resources and use them. Primarily, this promotes the owners to exercise absolute control over their resources. These policies get evaluated from the user side to ensure that the user is authorized, as dictated by these policies. Any unsuccessful evaluation of at least one of the policies denies access to use the remote resources governed by these policies. Currently, this policy engine has been implemented in Java and uses CoG Kit [8] services for proxy creation, policy file transfer, authentication with remote GRAM server etc. We now explain the components and mechanism using which the policy evaluation is accomplished.

4.1   Policy Files

Standard UNIX files are used as the medium to express policies of the remote site. They reside on the remote machine that accepts job request through the GRAM server. Only the administrator or the policy specifier are given write permissions to change these files. The files can be specific to user or group depending on how the polices are devised. The policies are specified as attribute value pairs, which for instance, might have parameters like allowed usage start time, end time as attributes and the time slots as their corresponding values. Other typical parameters include amount of resources that can be used, usage credits remaining, priorities etc.

Support for policies specified from the user's perspective, which could indicate the lifetime of proxy, sites to which it can be delegated to etc., is provided as well. The files are made readable by the user in order for the policy engine to fetch it on behalf of the user from the remote site, if needed. A typical policy file specified at the remote site could be as shown in Fig. 1. This dictates how, when and in what quantity can a user with the identity as the subject name access the resources under the mapped login name. This could be stored at /tmp/policyu476 which indicates that this file is specific to the user with ID 476. Optionally, a timestamp can be appended to the file name in order to easily examine the time of recent modification of the file.

```
    machine:'/O=Grid/O=Globus/OU=sp.uh.edu/CN=n017.sp.uh.edu'
    subject:'/O=Grid/O=Globus/OU=sp.uh.edu/CN=Babu Sundaram'
       login:'babu'
   startTime:'2001:5:1:00:00:00'
     endTime:'2001:5:31:23:59:59'
    priority:'medium'
         CPU:'6'
      memory:'256'
 creditsAvail:'24'
```

Fig. 1. Policy File with Attribute:Value Pairs for User with UID 476

Hence, the above set of specifications hold details about how the user can access the resources at the IBM SP2, University of Houston. The above set of policies dictates that the user identified with the subject /O=Grid/O=Globus /OU=sp.uh.edu/CN=Babu Sundaram would be mapped onto the local user as 'babu' and his access time starts on May 1 st , 2001 at midnight and ends on May 31 st , 2001 just before midnight. The user can request for 6 CPUs and 256 MB memory at the maximum and his jobs be granted medium priority. Also, if access is granted, the usage should not 24 usage credits where the accounting metric is agreed between the user and the site. Any violation of the above policy such as job request at a time not in the allotted slot, request for resources more than the allowed limits would result in authorization being denied.

Such a design gives the flexibility to the administrator to specify and modify policies at his will and the policy engine framework, on the user side, automatically ensures that they are satisfied before making a job request to the GRAM server. This set of policies can be specified independent and in addition to those enforced by the local resource managers. Further, the model could be extended to make the users and the site administrators agree on separate cost and accouting models for the resources. This helps in avoiding the need to have a single, rigid cost model between sites. Also, this allows the Broker to uniformly compare two resources based on their usage credits, though the individual cost models and accouting policies could, potentially, be different.

4.2 Policy Evaluation

The policy engine automatically evaluates all the attribute and value pairs in the policy file based on current time, user specifications about the job and machine settings. All policies must evaluate to true in order to obtain successful authorization. One added advantage could be that the user might have multiple logins with differing priorities, in which case the one with successful authorization and maximum priority, based on need, is identified automatically.

One important feature of this module is in that it always ensures that the most recent set of policies is the one examined for. In detail, during the very first job submission trial, the remote policy file is fetched to the local site (from where the user initiates the job request) and stored locally. This transfer of file from the remote site is done through GASS service provided by Globus toolkit. This is achieved by starting a local GASS server at a random port number between 45000 to 60000 and running a small Globus job, which then gets the policy file from the remote site. Then, appropriate policy evaluation is made. Other modes of fetching the file, for instance, GSI-FTP could be used as well.

For any future job submission evaluation for the same user (to the same site), the last modification time of the remote policy file is examined. If this is found to be no later than the latest fetch from that site, then the locally available file can be considered intact and evaluation can proceed. Otherwise, a GASS or GSI-FTP session, as mentioned above, is initiated to transfer the most recent version of the remote policy file and the local file gets overwritten.

Once the policy file is ensured to be available locally, the attribute parser reads and records it into attributes and their corresponding values. Appropriate attribute manager is then triggered to examine the respective policy. For example, the time attribute manager checks for the authorized time slot. If the current time is after the authorized start time and the job would complete before the authorized end time (based on the estimated run-time of the job), then the time policy is satisfied. Other managers that we have designed include the resource limit manager, credit manager, priority manager etc., All the managers need to evaluate to success in order to gain successful authorization.

The use of such managers facilitate the formation of any arbitrary and new policy by the administrator, which is typical. In essence, the policies are not restricted to a small set of attribute and value pairs. Any new appropriate policy can be defined on the fly and still the evaluation framework would work just fine and the entire system remains unchanged. Also, the user is relieved of the complexity involved with manually examining the usage policies at each site before proceeding with job submission.For the policy file shown, the time at which the authorization is requested is noted. If this falls between first and last days of May 2001, as specified in the file, then time attribute manager returns a success value. Then, the resource limit manager examines the job specifications made by the user to ensure that the allowed maximum limits are not exceeded. If this succeeds too, the resource limit manager returns success. In a similar fashion, all the managers need to return success based on the evaluation of their respective attributes and values in order for the site to be on the feasible list for the broker. The emphasis here is that the owners enjoy ultimate control over their resources and are assured of maximum priority.

5   Role in EZGrid System

EZGrid permits the user to carry out manual and automated resource selection and job submission. It supports manual submission by making static and dynamic information on grid resources available to the user via a single interface. This information includes such user-specific details as accounts, and the policies governing them. The user is relieved of the complexity involved with manually examining the usage policies at each site before proceeding with job submission.

The broker kernel is the component that decides on the best choice of resources that match the job specifications made by the user. The user drives this process by making specifications about the time and cost constraints. Then, the sequence of operations carried out by the broker includes refining the set of resources available to the user on the grid.

During the decision-making phase, the broker invokes the Policy engine in order to determine the sites accessible to the user and examines them for qualification based on the usage policies specified by the administrator. The feasible set of machines is narrowed down to only those whose policies are wholly satisfied based on the current time, user specifications about the job, available credit and machine settings, and any other policy components defined. Thus, the policy engine plays a critical role in ensuring that the usage terms for the remote sites are always satisfied and the owners are given the maximum priority.

After policy-based filtering of sites, the broker kernel then proceeds to filter the sites based on their queue lengths, CPU loads and other dynamic parameters, a discussion of which is beyond the scope of this paper.

6   Future Work and Open Issues

Future work includes refining the core of the engine to include support for user specified policies based on the work specified in [11] . This provides additional flexibility for the users as well to gain more protection against stolen credentials. More relevant attribute value pairs would be identified and included into the system to ensure minimal modifications to the system, in case of new policies being identified. Means to support different cost models between sites and users need to be developed in order to characterize the resources better in terms of accounting and cost credits. This model would then be incorporated into the policy engine so that handling cost related policies for the user would be more meaningful. Also, methods would be identified in order to ensure that whenever the owner gains access to his resource, if he desires, the remote user's job are check pointed and migrated elsewhere, as decided again by the broker. Further research is required to develop or identify suitable policy languages that would emphasize expressing and evaluating user and site policies over a grid environment. Some work has been dedicated to this area in examining Classad as policy language in Globus proxies. Other suitable alternatives need to be compared and the best medium needs to be identified.

7 Conclusions

Grid computing necessitates the sharing of heterogeneous resources owned by various autonomous domains. We have designed and implemented a policy-based framework for expressing and enforcing the usage restriction policies for authorization at a remote site. This facilitates the owners and the administrators to enforce fine-grained control and enjoy maximum priority over their resources. Expression of policies is achieved through simple files and this mechanism is flexible enough that the administrators can specify and change policies at their will and this framework automatically ensures the users that the most recent version of the policies are examined for authorization. Also, identification and inclusion of new policies by the administrators does not necessitate any significant change to the system. This mechanism can be used independent of the applications and heterogeneous target domains.

References

1. J. Bester, I. Foster, C. Kesselman, J. Tedesco, S. Tuecke, "GASS: A Data Movement and Access Service for Wide Area Computing Systems," Sixth Workshop on I/O in Parallel and Distributed Systems, May 5, 1999.
2. R. Butler, D. Engert, I. Foster, C. Kesselman, S. Tuecke, J. Volmer, V. Welch, "A National-Scale Authentication Infrastructure," IEEE Computer, 2000.
3. B. M. Chapman, B. Sundaram, K. Thyagaraja, S.W. Masood, P. Narayanasamy, "EZGrid: A Resource Brokerage System for Grids," http://www.cs.uh.edu/ ezgrid.
4. K. Czajkowski, I. Foster, N. Karonis, C. Kesselman, S. Martin, W. Smith, S. Tuecke, "A Resource Management Architecture for Metacomputing Systems," Proc. IPPS/SPDP '98 Workshop on Job Scheduling Strategies for Parallel Processing, 1998.
5. I. Foster and C. Kesselman, "Globus: A Metacomputing Infrastructure Toolkit," International Journal of Supercomputer Applications, Summer 1997.
6. I. Foster and C. Kesselman, "The GRID: Blueprint for a New Computing Infrastructure," Morgan Kauffman Publishers, 1999.
7. M. Litzkow, M. Livny, and M. Mutka, "Condor - A Hunter of Idle Workstations," Proceedings of the 8th International Conference of Distributed Computing Systems, pages 104-111, June, 1988.
8. G. von Laszewski, I. Foster, J. Gawor, W. Smith, and S. Tuecke, "CoG Kits: A Bridge between Commodity Distributed Computing and High-Performance Grids," ACM 2000 Java Grande Conference, 2000.
9. R. Raman, M. Livny, and M. Solomon, "Matchmaking: Distributed Resource Management for High Throughput Computing," Proceedings of the Seventh IEEE International Symposium on High Performance Distributed Computing, July, 1998.

10. T. Ryutov, B. C. Neuman, "Representation and Evaluation of Security policies for Distributed system Services," Proceedings of the DARPA Information Survivability Conference and Exposition, January 2000

11. B. Sundaram, C. Nebergall, S. Tuecke, "Policy Specification and Restricted Delegation in Globus Proxies," Research Gem, Super Computing 2000, Dallas, TX, November 2000.

Performance Contracts: Predicting and Monitoring Grid Application Behavior

Fredrik Vraalsen, Ruth A. Aydt, Celso L. Mendes, and Daniel A. Reed

{vraalsen,aydt,cmendes,reed}@cs.uiuc.edu

Department of Computer Science
University of Illinois
Urbana, Illinois 61801 USA

Abstract. [1] Given the dynamic nature of grid resources, adaptation is required to sustain a predictable level of application performance. A prerequisite of adaptation is the recognition of changing conditions. In this paper we introduce an *application signature model* and *performance contracts* to specify expected grid application behavior, and discuss our monitoring infrastructure that detects when actual behavior does not meet expectations. Experimental results are given for several scenarios.

1 Introduction

Computational grids have emerged as a new paradigm for high-performance computing [5]. Given the dynamic nature of grid resources, both distributed applications and the underlying infrastructure must adapt to changing resource availability to sustain a predictable level of application performance. A prerequisite of adaptation is the recognition of changing conditions.

In this paper we present an approach to predicting application performance and enabling the detection of unexpected execution behavior. We summarize related work, introduce a *performance contract* where commitments are specified, and put forward an *application signature model* for predicting application performance. We describe a *monitoring infrastructure* that detects when behavior does not fall within the expected range, and show experimental results for several execution scenarios.

2 Related Work

Predicting application performance on a given parallel system has been widely studied [12, 9, 3]. Recently the studies have been extended to distributed systems [7, 10]. The traditional focus of performance prediction methods is accuracy. Given the variability in a grid environment, we believe it is not practical

---
[1] This work was supported in part by the National Science Foundation under grants ASC 97-20202, EIA-997502, and the PACI Computational Science Alliance Cooperative Agreement, and by the Department of Energy under contract W-7405-ENG-36.

to pursue maximal predictive accuracy. Our techniques derive acceptable performance bounds and evaluate whether observed performance falls within those bounds.

Quality of service approaches seek to guarantee a minimum level of resource availability by reserving resources [6]. Our work does not rely on reservations or make guarantees. Instead, we use monitoring to determine when performance expectations are violated, signaling other agents to take appropriate action.

3 Performance Contracts

A *performance contract* states that given a set of *resources* (e.g., processors or networks), with certain *capabilities* (e.g., floating point rate or bandwidth), for particular *problem parameters* (e.g., matrix size or image resolution), the application will exhibit a specified, measurable, and desired *performance* (e.g., render *r* frames per second or finish iteration *i* in *t* seconds). We use the term *contract specifications* to refer collectively to the resources, capabilities, problem parameters, and performance.

To validate a contract, one must continually verify that the contract specifications are being met. Strictly speaking, a contract is *violated* if any contract specification does not hold during application execution. In practice, some degree of imprecision in the specifications is expected, reflecting variability in the environment and imperfections in the models. For these reasons, the monitoring system should tolerate "minor" deviations from the contract specifications.

4 Application Signature Model

A *performance model* generates a performance prediction for an application based on specified resources, capabilities, and problem parameters. Possible sources of models include application and library developers, compile time code analysis, and historical observations. Achieved application performance reflects a complex interplay of application demands on execution resources and the response of those resources to the demands. We outline a new approach to decomposing this interdependence, enabling separate specification of application stimuli, resource capabilities, and the composition of these into a performance prediction reflecting resource response.

4.1 Application Intrinsic Metrics

We define *application intrinsic metrics* as metrics that are solely dependent on the application code and problem parameters. These metrics express the demands the application places on the resources, and are independent of the execution environment. Examples of such metrics include messages per byte and average number of source code statements per floating point operation.

An *application intrinsic metric space* is a multidimensional space where each axis represents a single application intrinsic metric. Consider N metrics, each measured at regular intervals, for each of P parallel tasks. For each task, the measured values specify a trajectory through the N-dimensional metric space. We call this trajectory, illustrated in Figure 1, the *application signature.*

Some applications exhibit timing-dependent behavior and the application signature varies across runs. For others, values computed during runtime control the execution path and the application signature cannot be known in advance. However, we believe that, for a large number of important applications, the application signatures are not affected by timing or runtime dependencies.

By selecting metrics that capture critical resource demands, we can characterize the load an application places on the environment. The ability of the resources to service the load determines the performance of the application.

4.2 Execution Metrics

An application signature describes application stimuli to execution resources but does not quantify expected performance. We now consider the performance of the application on a given set of resources, and refer to achieved application performance in terms of *execution metrics* that express rates of progress. Examples of execution metrics are instructions per second and messages per second. An application traces a trajectory through the *execution metric space* as it runs, and we call this the *execution signature.*

The execution signature reflects both the application demands on the resources and the response of the resources to those demands. The execution signature may vary, even on the same resources, due to resource sharing with other applications. Our goal is to generate an expected execution signature for a given application on a specific set of resources during a particular period of time.

4.3 Performance Projections

To generate the expected execution signature, we *project* the application signature into execution metric space using a scaling factor for each dimension. The projection scaling factors correspond to the capabilities of the resources on which the application will execute. Possible sources of capability information include peak performance numbers, benchmark values, predictions of future availability (e.g., via NWS [13]), and observed levels of service for previous executions.

In the following projection equations, the first terms represent application intrinsic metrics, the second represent projection factors based on resource capabilities, and the results represent performance expressed as execution metrics.

$$\frac{instructions}{FLOP} \times \frac{FLOPs}{second} = \frac{instructions}{second} \qquad \frac{messages}{byte} \times \frac{bytes}{second} = \frac{messages}{second}$$

An application signature projected into two execution signatures, reflecting different resource capabilities, is shown in Figure 2. In the projection shown as the solid line, the bandwidth is higher than in the projection shown as the dotted line. The computing capability is the same for both.

We use the term *application signature model* to refer to our method of predicting application behavior by projecting an application signature into execution space via resource capability scaling factors.

4.4 Performance Contracts

Relating the application signature model to the performance contract from Section 3, the contract problem parameters are encompassed in the application signature; resources and capabilities are reflected in the projection factors; specified measurable performance is defined by the model output as points in the execution metric space. Contract validation consists of determining whether application intrinsic and execution metrics, measured at runtime, lie within an acceptable range of the expected values stated in the contract.

For some applications, the signatures consist of tightly grouped points in the metric spaces rather than far-reaching trajectories. Standard clustering techniques can be used to partition the points into equivalence classes, yielding cluster centroids and variance factors in the N dimensions. Our clustering algorithm takes a single parameter that specifies the maximum distance between a point and a cluster centroid, effectively controlling the size and number of clusters it identifies in a given set of points.

When such equivalence classes exist, contract validation can be thought of as determining whether runtime metrics fall within an acceptable range of a cluster centroid. The "acceptable range" controls the level of violation that will be tolerated. Ranges can be tuned independently for each dimension based on a number of factors including computed cluster variance, confidence in resource capability values, and estimates of model accuracy. Figure 3 illustrates this concept of contract validation based on equivalence classes and degrees of tolerance.

5 Monitoring Infrastructure

Our monitoring infrastructure is based on *Autopilot*, a toolkit for application and resource monitoring and control [11]. When an application executes, Autopilot *sensors*, embedded in application or library code, register with an *Autopilot Manager*. Sensor *clients* query the manager to locate sensors with desired properties and attach to those sensors to receive measurement data. The sensors, managers, and sensor clients can be located anywhere on the grid.

Application signatures and projections define *expected* application behavior, and runtime measurements capture *actual* behavior. Given these, we must specify (a) a policy to determine when a measured value is sufficiently different from an expected value to raise a violation and (b) a mechanism for implementing this policy. We base our policy on the equivalence classes and ranges of tolerance described in Section 4.4, and use *fuzzy logic* as the implementation mechanism.

Fuzzy logic allows one to linguistically state contract violation conditions. Unlike boolean logic values that are either true or false, fuzzy variables can assume a range of values, allowing for smooth transitions between areas of acceptance and violation. Using Autopilot decision procedures, which are based on fuzzy logic, it is possible to change the rule set describing contract violation conditions to accommodate different equivalence classes and levels of tolerance.

A rulebase defining two fuzzy variables, *distance* and *violation*, and linguistic rules for setting the *violation* based on the *distance* are shown in Figure 4. Space

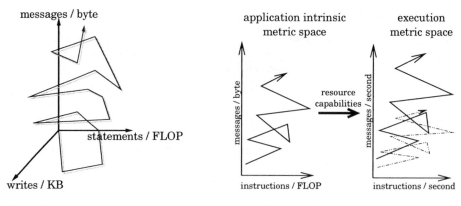

Fig. 1. Hypothetical Application Signature

Fig. 2. Performance Projections

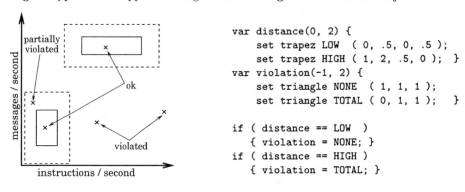

```
var distance(0, 2) {
    set trapez LOW  ( 0, .5, 0, .5 );
    set trapez HIGH ( 1, 2, .5, 0 ); }
var violation(-1, 2) {
    set triangle NONE  ( 1, 1, 1 );
    set triangle TOTAL ( 0, 1, 1 );   }

if ( distance == LOW )
   { violation = NONE; }
if ( distance == HIGH )
   { violation = TOTAL; }
```

Fig. 3. Equivalence Classes and Violations

Fig. 4. Contract Rulebase

constraints prohibit a full explanation, but intuitively each fuzzy variable has an associated transition function that maps "crisp" values to a degree of truth for the corresponding fuzzy members. The range of crisp values and the shape of the transition functions are controlled by the numeric values in the rulebase. We adjust the numeric values to implement the desired degrees of tolerance.

Our contract monitor receives sensor measurements and evaluates the fuzzy logic rulebase using these as crisp input. The distances for each dimension in the metric space are evaluated individually, and an overall violation level is obtained by combining the individual results. Given the violation levels, contracts could be marked as violated based on threshold values for individual metrics and overall behavior. Currently we report the violation levels directly as contract output.

6 Experimental Results

To verify the feasibility of the performance projection approach and contract monitoring infrastructure presented in Sections 4 and 5, we conducted a series of experiments using distributed applications on a grid testbed. All testbed sys-

Cluster Name	Location	Nodes	Processor	Network
major	Illinois	8	266 MHz Pentium II	Fast Ethernet
opus	Illinois	4	450 MHz Pentium II	Myrinet
rhap	Illinois	32	933 MHz Pentium III	Fast Ethernet
torc	Tennessee	8	550 MHz Pentium III	Myrinet
ucsd	San Diego	4	400 MHz Pentium II	Fast Ethernet

Table 1. Experimental System Environment

tems ran Globus [4] and Linux on the x86 processor architecture, as shown in Table 1. We inserted a call in each application to create Autopilot sensors that periodically captured data from the PAPI [1] interface (number of instructions and floating point operations) and from MPI event wrappers (number of messages and bytes transferred).

To simulate environments where applications compete for resources, we introduced two kinds of load external to the applications. A purely computational load was added by executing a floating point intensive task on one of the nodes, and a communication load was generated via bursts of UDP packets.

6.1 Master/Worker Application

For our first group of experiments, we created a program that executes a series of "jobs" following a master/worker paradigm. Each worker repeatedly requests a job, receives and executes the job, and sends the result back to the master. Parameters control the number and size of jobs, and their floating point intensity.

We executed the master/worker application on a virtual machine comprised of twelve nodes from the *major*, *ucsd*, and *torc* clusters, connected by a wide-area network. We captured application intrinsic metrics using sensors with a 30 second sampling period, and built the application signature shown in Figure 5a. This figure shows two types of node behavior. The master, represented by points to the right, executes few floating point operations as reflected in a higher number of instructions/FLOP. The workers, represented by points to the left, execute the bulk of the floating point operations. The messages/byte metric is constant for all nodes, reflecting the consistent size of the messages between each master/worker pair.

Based on the derived application intrinsic signature, we projected the performance behavior of the application for our particular virtual machine. Using computation and communication projection factors specific to the *major/ucsd/torc* clusters, we obtained the predicted execution signature shown in Figure 5b. Hardware differences among the clusters caused the workers to have different projected performance. We derived our projection factors by computing mean values for observed FLOPs/second and bytes/second, representing the computation and communication characteristics of each node.

The application and projected execution signatures define the expected application behavior on the selected resources. To obtain the parameters used for contract validation, we first clustered the points in each metric space to create sets of equivalence classes. In application intrinsic space, we used the cluster

160

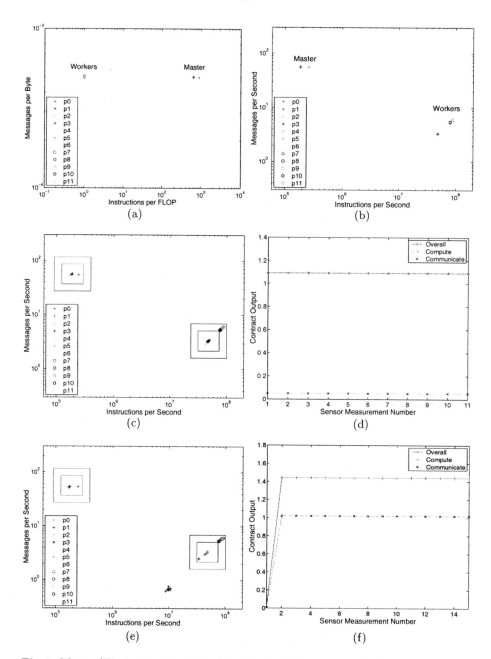

Fig. 5. Master/Worker Results: (a) application intrinsic signature (b) projected execution signature (c) baseline observed execution signature (d) intrinsic contract output for processor 9; plots of *overall* and *compute* overlap (e) measured execution signature under load (f) performance contract output for processor 3; plots of *compute* and *communicate* overlap

variance, reported by the clustering algorithm, to define the acceptable performance ranges. In execution space, we based the tolerance around the centroids on the variance in the projection factors.

Figure 5c shows the regions of acceptable performance for the master and for one of the workers, and the observed points captured from all nodes during the actual execution. The inner border for each region corresponds to no violation and the outer border to a total violation. Points that fall between the two borders partially violate the contract for that equivalence class. If an observed point lies outside the regions of all equivalence classes, a contract violation is reported. Since the parameters for the acceptable ranges of Figure 5c were derived from the same baseline execution, it is not surprising that most observed points satisfy the contract.

To determine whether the contracts we developed were able to detect contract violations, we repeated the master/worker execution under different operating conditions. We executed the program on the same machines, but configured the jobs assigned to nodes 6 through 11 to perform fewer floating point operations, testing our ability to detect violations in the application intrinsic space.

We applied the application intrinsic contracts and consistently detected violations on nodes 6 through 11. Figure 5d shows the contract output for processor 9. Computation, communication, and overall violation levels are shown separately, with higher values corresponding to more severe violations. The computation and overall contracts were consistently violated, while the communication contract was always satisfied.

In our next experiment, we reran the master/worker program with the original job mix and introduced an external floating point load on processor 3 of our virtual machine shortly after execution began. Because there was not any communication between workers, we expected the external load to affect only the performance of the worker on the node where the load was placed. This was confirmed by the measured execution signatures, presented in Figure 5e. While the signatures for most workers were the same as in Figure 5c, the performance of processor 3 no longer fell within the predicted range. Our monitor correctly detected the violation, as indicated by the contract output shown in Figure 5f.

6.2 ScaLAPACK Application

For our second group of experiments, we used the *pdscaex* application from the *ScaLAPACK* package [2], which solves a linear system by calling the *PDGESV* library routine. We executed an instrumented version of *pdscaex* with matrices of size 10000 and 20000, which were sufficiently large to highlight interesting behavior, but small enough to make parametric experiments practical.

We began our ScaLAPACK tests by executing on a virtual machine with four nodes from each of the *major*, *opus*, and *rhap* clusters at Illinois, using a 10000x10000 matrix and a sensor sampling period of 60 seconds. Following the same procedure described for the master/worker application, we conducted a baseline execution to obtain the application intrinsic signature. With that signature and the mean projection factors computed for the execution, we derived

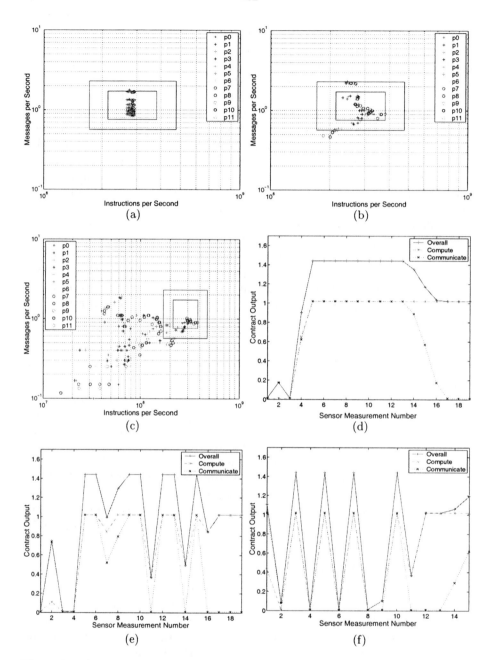

Fig. 6. ScaLAPACK Local Area Results: (a) projected execution signature (b) baseline observed execution signature (c) observed execution signature under load (d) contract output for processor 3 with computational load on processor 3 (e) contract output for processor 9 with computational load on processor 3 (f) contract output for processor 9 with network load

the projected signature and bounds of Figure 6a. Figure 6b shows the actual application performance, with the bounds derived in the previous step. Note that even in the baseline execution a few observed points lie outside the expected performance range indicated by the rectangles. In cases like this, one could adjust the fuzzy logic rulebase to increase the degree of tolerance.

In addition to the baseline described above, we conducted two other *pdscaex* executions in this environment. First, we added a computational load to processor 3. Figure 6c shows the observed execution signatures for all nodes in this run. Because of implicit synchronization in the algorithm, the performance of all nodes decreased while the additional load was present. Furthermore, both the communicate and compute performance metrics were affected, as the synchronization effectively links the two dimensions. The performance violations were detected by the contracts for each node, as shown in Figures 6d and 6e for node 3 and node 9, respectively. Violations were very consistent for processor 3, the node with the additional load, indicating that it never was able to achieve the expected level of performance when sharing compute resources. Although delayed when unable to get input, processor 9 did occasionally execute sufficient instructions per second to avoid severe levels of violation.

Our last *pdscaex* local-area test was run while a heavy communication load was active between nodes *amajor* and *rhap6*. These nodes were *not* participating in the execution, but shared the network with nodes that were. The contract output for the various *pdscaex* nodes indicated that performance was degraded by the network load. The contract output for processor 9, presented in Figure 6f, shows periodic violations throughout the execution.

We extended our ScaLAPACK tests to a wide-area grid environment consisting of machines at Illinois and Tennessee. We selected six nodes from each of the *rhap* and *torc* clusters, used a matrix size of 20000x20000, and set our sensor sampling period to 4 minutes to capture both compute and communicate activity in most periods. We conducted our baseline *pdscaex* execution under these conditions.

To simulate an external perturbation in our execution environment, we repeated this *pdscaex* execution and introduced a floating point load on processor 8 shortly after the beginning of the execution. This load ran concurrently with *pdscaex* for 50 minutes before being removed. The measured performance metrics for this run are shown in Figure 7a.

Figures 7b and 7c show the contract results for nodes 4 and 8, respectively. As with the earlier local-area run with an added computation load, the contract output for the loaded node (processor 8) showed constant violations while the load was in place. The performance of other nodes (e.g. processor 4) was also affected, but not as consistently.

Figure 7d shows the observed FLOP rates for a subset of the processors and offers insight into the behavior of *pdscaex* when one node is a bottleneck. The FLOPs/second for the loaded processor plateaued below its expected performance level when the load was in place. In contrast, the FLOPs/second measurements for other processors oscillated between expected values and zero, in-

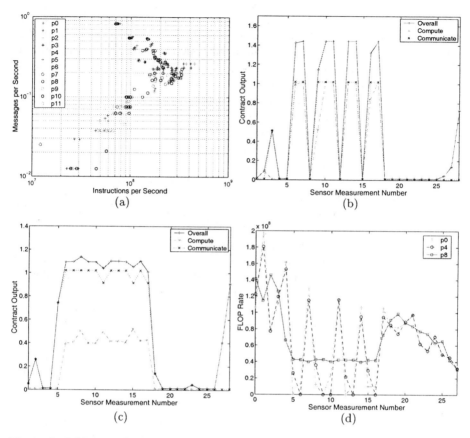

Fig. 7. ScaLAPACK Wide Area Results: (a) execution signature with load on processor 8 (b) contract output for processor 4 with load on processor 8 (c) contract output for processor 8 with load on processor 8 (d) FLOP rate for selected processors

dicating that the processors were either computing at the projected rate or idle while waiting for data from another processor. These FLOP rate behaviors are reflected in the contract violations shown in Figures 7b and 7c.

7 Conclusions and Future Work

In this paper we described performance contracts and a performance model based on application signatures, demonstrated the use of these with our monitoring infrastructure, and showed that we could detect unexpected grid application behavior. Our results indicate that this is a promising approach, however much work remains.

We plan to investigate other application intrinsic and execution metrics to capture computation, communication, and I/O characteristics for a wider set of applications. We are studying "global" contracts based on overall application behavior, rather than on per-process commitments, and will extend our violation policy to tolerate transient unexpected behavior. To handle application signatures with no equivalence classes over the entire application, we will explore periodic projection and clustering. Finally, we are considering how to extend our technique to cases for which baseline executions are not available, possibly using data collected during the current execution as a source for later predictions.

This work is the result of fruitful collaborations with the GrADS [8] team, notably Fran Berman, Andrew Chien, Jack Dongarra, Ian Foster, Lennart Johnsson, Ken Kennedy, Carl Kesselman, Rich Wolski, and many staff and students.

References

1. BROWNE, S., DONGARRA, J., GARNER, N., LONDON, K., AND MUCCI, P. A Scalable Cross-Platform Infrastructure for Application Performance Tuning Using Hardware Counters. In *Proceedings of Supercomputing 2000* (2000).
2. CHOI, J., ET AL. ScaLAPACK: A Portable Linear Algebra Library for Distributed Memory Computers - Design Issues and Performance. In *Proceedings of Supercomputing 96* (1996).
3. FAHRINGER, T. *Automatic Performance Prediction of Parallel Programs*. Kluwer Academic Publishers, 1996.
4. FOSTER, I., AND KESSELMAN, C. Globus: A Metacomputing Infrastructure Toolkit. *International Journal of Supercomputer Applications 11*, 2 (1997).
5. FOSTER, I., AND KESSELMAN, C., Eds. *The Grid: Blueprint for a New Computing Infrastructure*. Morgan Kaufmann Publishers, 1998.
6. FOSTER, I., ROY, A., SANDER, V., AND WINKLER, L. End-to-End Quality of Service for High-End Applications. *IEEE Journal on Selected Areas in Communications Special Issue on QoS in the Internet* (1999).
7. KAPADIA, N., FORTES, J., AND BRODLEY, C. Predictive application-performance modeling in a computational grid environment. In *Proceedings of the Eight IEEE Symposium on High-Performance Distributed Computing* (1999).
8. KENNEDY, K., ET AL. Grid Application Development Software. http://hipersoft.cs.rice.edu/grads/.
9. MEHRA, P., ET AL. A Comparison of Two Model-Based Performance-Prediction Techniques for Message-Passing Parallel Programs. In *Proceedings of the ACM Conference on Measurement & Modeling of Computer Systems* (1994).
10. PETITET, A., ET AL. Numerical Libraries and The Grid: The GrADS Experiments with ScaLAPACK. Tech. Rep. UT-CS-01-460, University of Tennessee, 2001.
11. RIBLER, R., ET AL. Autopilot: Adaptive Control of Distributed Applications. In *Proceedings of the Seventh IEEE Symposium on High-Performance Distributed Computing* (1998).
12. SAAVEDRA-BARRERA, R. H., SMITH, A. J., AND MIYA, E. Performance prediction by benchmark and machine characterization. *IEEE Transactions on Computers 38*, 12 (1989).
13. WOLSKI, R., SPRING, N. T., AND HAYES, J. The Network Weather Service: A Distributed Resource Performance Forecasting Service for Metacomputing. *The Journal of Future Generation Computing Systems* (1999).

Production-Level Distributed Parametric Study Capabilities for the Grid*

Maurice Yarrow[1], Karen M. McCann[1], Edward Tejnil[2], and Adrian DeVivo[1]

[1] Computer Sciences Corporation, Mail Stop T27A-1, NASA Ames Research Center, Moffett Field, CA 94035, USA
{yarrow,mccann,devivo}@nas.nasa.gov
[2] Eloret Institute, Mail Stop T27B-1, NASA Ames Research Center, Moffett Field, CA 94035, USA
tejnil@nas.nasa.gov

Abstract. Though tools are available for creating and launching parameter studies in distributed environments, production-level users have shunned these tools for a variety of reasons. Ultimately, this is simply a result of the inability of these tools to provide anything more than a demonstration-level capability, rather than the flexibility and variety of industrial-strength capabilities that users actually require. In addition, despite the difficulties of creating parametric studies without specialized tools, users still demand that such tools be intuitive, easy to use, and versatile enough to support their particular experimental procedures. We show some solutions to real problems encountered in users' parametric experiments, and simultaneously show how the success of grid computing in general will rely on the ability of grid tool developers to provide a much greater level of capability and generality than users have seen in current grid-tool demonstrations.

1 Motivation and Background

The ILab parameter study creation and job submission tool [1, 2] was developed to fulfill several goals. First, it had to be grid-enabled. Currently, ILab can launch parameter studies onto remote resources either with or without metacomputing middleware such as Globus [3]. Second, ILab had to be easy and intuitive to use. To accomplish this we constructed a sophisticated graphical user interface (GUI). We equipped it with current user interface paradigms and conveniences, including a special purpose parameterizing editor, file browsers, "previous-and-next" dialog widgets, built-in help for all screens, a graphical data-flow-diagram mechanism for constructing complex processes, etc. ILab had to be modular and easily extensible, so we developed ILab in object-oriented Perl (an excellent language for rapid-prototyping) with Perl/Tk for the GUI components. We also developed a separate GUI generator to facilitate the rapid construction of new GUI components. For extensibility, we designed ILab as basically a front-end which collects the many specifics of a user's experiment, and a back-end, consisting of five different "job models" (described below), which are modular code generators that produce Korn

---

* To appear at the Grid 2001 Workshop, Denver, Colorado, November, 2001. © Springer-Verlag.

shell scripts. Currently, these job models build the scripts which constitute the set of individual jobs comprising a user's parameter study experiment. Adding a new job model is relatively straightforward.

The five current job models are (1) a Local job model for an experiment which will run entirely on the local machine on which the user is running ILab; (2) a Remote job model, where each job in the experiment consists of a script that runs locally and chooses a remote machine from a list of candidate machines to which it will migrate a second script which actually runs the user job on the target machine, either under control of a job scheduler such as PBS or without; (3) a Globus job model similar to the Remote job model, but leveraging the Globus toolkit of command-line functions; (4) a Restart job model, which we will describe in detail below; and (5) a Condor job model, under development.

Having developed a powerful tool for parameter study creation and launching, we endeavored to attract real users from the NASA community of aeronautics engineers and researchers. Users were impressed to find that ILab, ostensibly a research tool written for experimenting with grid middleware, distributed computation models, and user-interface issues, was more sophisticated and capable than they had expected. Nevertheless, they could not use it for their highly specialized parameter studies for a variety of reasons. During our design phase for ILab, we specifically solicited user input from our potential user community. Users initially described a usage scenario with simple common needs. We naively assumed that users would be able or willing to accept a simplified view of their parameter study experiments. When we presented the developed product to these users, almost all of them nevertheless stubbornly decided to continue to use the specialized shell or Perl scripts that they had developed or had had developed for their needs. These scripts invariably were so specific that they lacked generality in terms of what engineering codes they could run, the layout of the file systems that they used, the parameterization of the input files for running, etc. Thus, these users' scripts were not usable for any problems except their own. On the other hand, the models for parameter studies experiments which ILab supported, sensible as they were, failed to address functionality critical to individual user environments. We will give just a few examples.

Some users required a large number of PBS options not supported by Globus. For example, many PBS users require PBS flags which allow them to get mail notification of job completion depending on completion status, to designate specific nodes on a given machine which should be used for their computations, or to specify a time after which a job is eligible for execution. Thus, it must be possible to specify any number of arbitrary PBS options, including any number of resources in a PBS resource list.

Some users needed to be able to rename groups of files with a common prefix or a common suffix. That is, a program run might have to rename all files of the form q.1.1000, q.2.1000, etc, to be of the form q.1.restart, q.2.restart, etc. This is an operation for which no particular shell command capability exists. It is a fairly specialized rename operation, and not easily accomplished, especially for the general case of a rename of all files of form1 to be in form2, where form1 will contain wild cards, and form2 may need to contain wild cards.

Some users needed to be able to obtain input files and executables from a variety of locations on arbitrary remote machines. Subsequent to completion of computations, users had to be able to send output to arbitrary archive facilities. Since such facilities are not within the Globus testbed, this posed a problem. Many users needed to be able to specify that the individual jobs comprising their parameter study should run in a particular scratch directory partition. However, the name of this partition could vary from machine to machine. For example, on machine1 it might be /scratch/username but on machine2 it might be /SCR/username.

Though some of the specialized needs of users might be addressable by skillful shell programming on their part, ILab makes the assumption that a user has no scripting knowledge. However, ILab does permit the entry of arbitrary shell commands, but does not assume that users wish to address specialized functional needs via the shell.

Another important and challenging issue was a "restart" capability, which many potential users required. (This is not to be confused with a checkpointing capability.) Users need this capability for two primary reasons. First, real production environments require that jobs be submitted through a scheduler, but many users have job runs that require hundreds or thousand of hours of computation. Such jobs will typically be of low priority and will not be given a run state by the scheduler for days in real environments. Users therefore wrote PBS scheduler scripts which would request less compute time but would resubmit themselves to the queue upon completion. In this manner, jobs could be configured to fit in a queue with relatively high priority and the entire run could be expedited.

There is a second and related issue. For many of the fluid dynamics computations common within NASA, various solver parameters (not physical parameters) need to be adjusted or "ramped" during the computation, and many of the legacy flow solvers did not provide a mechanism for specifying a schedule that automatically modified these solver parameters during computation. To accommodate this, it should be possible for solver parameters to be changed in conjunction with job restarts. This amounts to a variety of computational steering.

Because of the need for these functionalities, users rejected ILab in favor of the more cumbersome and specialized scripts developed for their parameter studies. As a result, we decided to add many of these user-requested features.

2 Addressing the User Need for a Restart Capability

The simpler specialized needs of users, such as generalized bulk file renaming, file archiving issues, etc., were addressed largely as ILab user-interface issues. Solutions for some of these were straightforward options added to ILab in such a way as not to violate our rule of "no user programming required". The generalized bulk file renaming, for example, required both a graphical-user-interface option, and underlying support in the form of a complex Korn shell function added to the shell scripts that ILab generates. By far the most complex capability added was the "restart" option. This required added extensive GUI capability, considerable additional internal data structure support within ILab, and a completely new job model for shell script generation, including a server script for launching the restarts. We will explain in detail how this capability was implemented with respect to this new job model, the nature of communication occurring between the generated shell scripts, and the server required to perform these restarts.

The RestartJobModel, like both the RemoteJobModel and the GlobusJobModel, generates Korn shell scripts. Currently, inter-machine functionality within these scripts is implemented using the secure shell "ssh" command and the secure copy "scp" program (or "rsh" and "rcp", if the user requests these). This job model is not implemented using Globus because too few production and archive machines of users' choice are members of the Globus testbed, and so-called "third-party delegation" would be required on all remote systems for implementing the restart functionality.

For each separate job in the user's parameter study, two shell scripts are generated, one being a script which runs locally (i.e., on the originating machine), and the other being a script which is migrated to, and runs on, the remote system that is chosen for computation by the local script. The local script performs the following functions. First, it queries remote systems from the list of candidate machines that have been selected by the user. Via ssh, the local script then interrogates the PBS queue on each system in turn, until it finds a suitable system onto which it can submit the job with hope that the job will start immediately. If all systems have queued jobs belonging to the user, the local script will go into a polling loop, and periodically repeat the queue interrogation for the system list until a suitable candidate machine is found. When such a system is selected, the local script, again via ssh, first creates an appropriate directory and subdirectory on the remote file system partition indicated by the user, and then, via scp, migrates the second shell script to that subdirectory. The local script then submits the migrated script (which includes whatever PBS directives are required) to the remote PBS queue, and terminates.

This is similar to the sequence of operations that occur in the RemoteJobModel and in the GlobusJobModel, with the following important difference. The very first of the local scripts to run launches a server script which will run for the duration of the parameter study (see Fig. 1). It is the function of this server to poll for the presence of semaphore files sent to the originating machine by each of the parameter study jobs upon their completion. This is how the server will know which job and which phase to restart.

When PBS runs the remote script, the following sequence of operations occurs. First, files required as input for the compute executables are obtained from their source locations using cp if local or scp if non-local. Next, the parameterized input files are copied from the originating machine, in particular, the input file associated with the first phase (restart "0", as it were). The compute executables are run, each preceded by the staging of appropriate input files. Upon completion of computation, all files, both input and output, are archived to a user-designated archive system and are placed into a directory structure (created by the remote script), which is comparable to the directory structure in which the remote script itself ran. An additional archive subdirectory structure is created to accommodate the distinction between files required by, but not changed by, the computations, and files changed or created by the computations (output files). The final act of the remote script is to send a semaphore file to the originating machine which indicates which restart stage of which job in the parameter study experiment has just completed. It is this semaphore file from which the restart server will

170

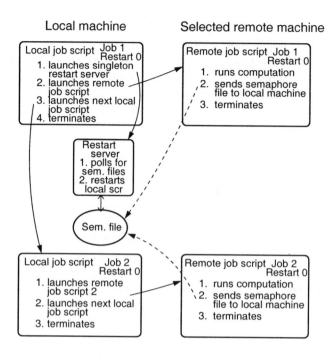

Fig. 1. Restart job model scripts, for restart 0

determine the correct local script to re-run (see Fig. 2). This appropriate local script then repeats its search for the best-candidate remote compute machine, and resubmits the remote script to that machine, this time for the next phase of the computations (restart 1 through final restart) of this particular job in the experiment. When this job restarts, it knows its own restart number, and thus knows from which archive directory to obtain the appropriate input files so that computation can be resumed.

A special case of this processing is when the user requests of this job model that no restarts be performed (restart "0" only). In this case, only one stage of computation is performed, followed by archiving of all output files, making the RestartJobModel perform like the simpler RemoteJobModel.

3 Lessons Learned from the Restart Job Model Implementation

At first glance, it would seem that the restart capability is a very specialized mode for distributed parameter study usage. Indeed, only a subset of all users wishing to run parameter studies will need the restart capability, though at NASA's Ames Research Center, that subset is surprisingly large. Discussions with production users revealed that very few researchers and engineers who wished to generate parameter studies were content with simple models for issues such as archiving, schedulers, etc. Our conclusion is that real users have complex and varied needs which made almost every aspect of their interactions with production-level systems non-addressable by demonstration

Local machine Selected remote machine

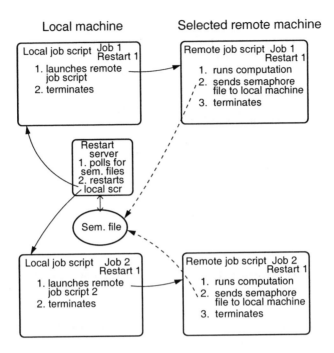

Fig. 2. Restart job model scripts, for restart 1

level tools. Grid-enabled tools for distributed tasks most often make use of simplifying models for conducting their business. These have limited practical utility. We have found that designing usable models which do not require any programming expertise from users is a considerable challenge. The success that tool designers and architects have in meeting this challenge is going to have a significant impact on the long-term success of computational grids and the underlying middleware.

4 Some Additional Production-Level Issues

We list here several additional issues that have been encountered in our production computing environments. We are considering or implementing solutions to these issues at this time.

Copying of files from source system to target compute system, and from compute system to archive system, is accomplished with the Unix secure copy command "scp" and, for the GlobusJobModel, with the "gsi" enabled version of scp. We have seen the scp command stall when archiving files. We are considering accompanying each scp command with an additional background process to monitor the progress of file copying. Then, if the scp process stalls for some period of time, the monitor process will terminate the copy. An additional attempt at copying could be made, or this entire particular job in the Experiment can be declared non-viable and aborted.

Many supercomputer systems are actually accessible only through a "front-end" system. Currently, some aspects of our job models require the ability to invoke the "ssh" command directly onto the compute system in order to perform resource discovery or to submit a job onto a batch scheduling system. On our local systems at the NAS division at Ames Research Center we have been able to issue ssh commands directly onto compute engines only because the duration of these commands is brief. Were these commands to last any significant time, they would be terminated by "skulker" programs monitoring command traffic to these systems. We will have to build into ILab a new layer of resource configuration data and control in order to accommodate indirect front-end access to arbitrary compute server systems.

ILab is currently incapable of automatically terminating all remote jobs in an Experiment. Since this could be very costly to a user in the case of an incorrectly configured Experiment, we will be adding the ability to terminate all Experiment jobs and clean up all appropriate disk systems.

These are only a few examples of problems that must be addressed when computing on the grid.

5 ILAB's CAD (Computer Assisted Design) screen: Directed Graph

Fig. 3 displays a Directed Graph whose nodes are units of user's ILab Experiment. The current icon units are Experiment, Process, FileList, FileHandling, and Restart; we anticipate adding additional icons for Loop, Condition, and Branch.

For each Experiment data set, there is one Experiment icon, representing global data for the Experiment: systems for running the Experiment, remote root and archive directories, etc. For each Process in the Experiment, there is one Process icon, which represents data specific to a Process: original path, meta-environments used, command line arguments, etc. If a Process has any associated files, a FileList icon is placed beneath the Process icon; the associated data is a list of file paths and names necessary for that process. If there is to be any handling (renaming, archiving, moving, etc.) of any of the files in the Process File List, a FileHandling icon is placed below the Process icon, to the right of the FileList icon. If user wishes to restart the Experiment, a Restart icon is placed beneath all Process icons, and connected to the first and last Process icons. The associated Restart data specifies number of restarts, data to be changed for each restart, restart stop conditions, etc.

Note that a restart is not the same as a loop; a loop would mean repeating the execution of one or more processes, while a restart means the repetition of all Experiment processes.

The set of icons representing Experiment data is interconnected by arrows which signify the flow of execution within the Experiment, and also by straight lines which signify attached data and/or conditions.

The CAD screen has a dual functionality. First, for Experiment Editing, the directed graph is generated from pre-existing Experiment data when user chooses "CAD Screen" from the "Edit Experiment" pull-down menubutton. User can pop-up editing dialogs from each of the icons, or can add and remove icons as necessary. Second, for Experiment creation, a user can initialize an Experiment, and then add icons and enter data for each icon. (Icon display is color-coded to signify whether necessary data

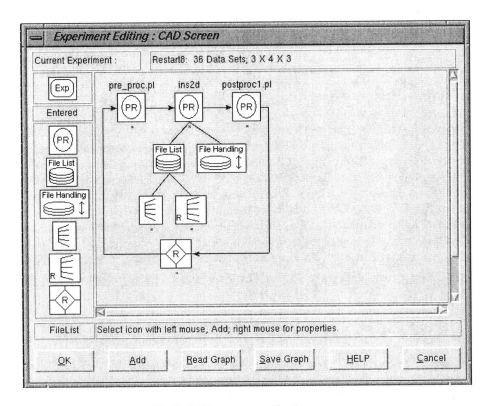

Fig. 3. CAD process specification screen

has been entered.) As each icon is added, the corresponding Experiment data structures are generated; when all necessary data has been entered into these structures, user can save the Experiment data to disk, and/or execute the Experiment. The CAD screen also functions as an organizational aid in Experiment execution and tracking; it is easier to visualize the parts of the Experiment and the flow of execution from the CAD screen, than from the wizard-dialog-based entry of the same data.

The form of the CAD screen layout was heavily influenced by practical considerations, since there are two non-trivial problems to overcome in order to create a visually effective display. The first problem is the placement of icons in such a way that no icons overlap. We solved this problem in two ways: by placing icons automatically in a simple 2-D "grid" type layout, and by providing, as a backup where the first method might fail, user ability to move icons, and their attached lines and arrows. In this way, if any icons overlap, user can easily and quickly adjust the icon positions in order to get a "neat" display.

The second problem we had to face was the likely proliferation of icons for real-world Experiment layouts: we wanted to avoid the situation where the directed graph would get so large that only a small portion of it could be displayed at once on a computer screen. Our approach was to make the icons represent "high level" data and operations, as opposed to "atomic" data and operations: each icon accurately reflects the internal structure of the major ILab data objects. This approach is both intuitive and effective, since a very large graph might provide more detail, but would fail in the effort to give user a reasonably effective visual cue to the organization of an ILab experiment.

6 Future Development of the CAD Screen

The inclusion of branching and loops is planned for the next release of ILab. Branching can be caused by multiple levels of parameterization, or by repeating the output of one process to several different subsequent processes. Conditional loops are repeated executions of one or more Experiment processes, where the repetition is terminated by either file existence, a process return value, or the execution of a predetermined number of repetitions. All of these conditions represent non-linear paths of process execution. It is anticipated that ILab's script generation algorithms will have to be significantly extended, perhaps by generating layers and/or sets of execution scripts, in order to handle these cases. We also plan to include the directed graph display in ILab's Logbook pages, for user convenience in referencing the Experiment results, and the construction of reports.

7 ILab's Interface to Condor: Under Development

We are collaborating with A. Globus (NASA Ames Research Center, Computer Sciences Corporation) to add ILab options for the Condor High-Throughput Computing System [4]. This aspect of ILab development is currently of interest, since the Condor pool at the NAS systems division at Ames Research Center now contains approximately 350 systems, and more systems are being added. We anticipate that ILab-generated Condor experiments will be of use to the scientific community, especially in the area of genetic algorithms, which need many runs to generate results. A user who already has Condor installed on his/her system will be able to use ILab to create large sets of program runs and automatically gather the output back to the originating system for processing. ILab will generate directories, appropriate lists of input files, and multiple Condor submission scripts. For significantly large runs, this assistance will be non-trivial, since creating file lists and Condor scripts "by hand" is quite onerous, time-consuming, and error-prone.

The Condor system has built-in monitoring and restart capability, but currently lacks a simple way of executing more than one process in sequence. If several separate programs are submitted to Condor, Condor guarantees that each program will be executed, but does not guarantee the order of execution, since Condor implements run-once-and-only-once semantics. In ILab, we generate scripts which execute all processes in user's Experiment in sequence, and each script is itself submitted to Condor as a Condor process, by a separately generated Condor "submit" script. In order to execute the set of scripts, the Condor "universe" must be specified as "vanilla", meaning that a script cannot be restarted from an interim point in case of failure, but must be re-executed from its beginning. This means that ILab's "Restart" option is not usable in Condor experiments. However, this should not be an issue for Condor jobs, since the restart option has been designed for use on multi-processor supercomputers with queue time limits, and

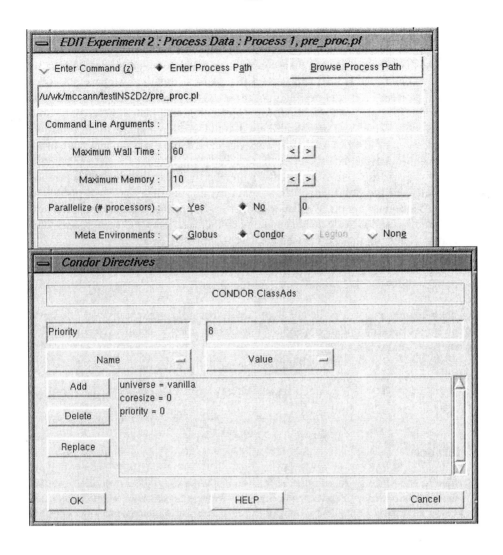

Fig. 4. Condor job model screen

for the specific case of Computational Fluid Dynamics (CFD) flow solvers that need to ramp-up certain internal parameters. We will also investigate the new Condor extension "DAGMan", which refers to a directed graph sequence of processes, as an alternate solution to this problem.

Setting up a Condor experiment in ILab is very simple, and involves two steps. First, users must choose the Condor "MetaEnvironment" in the Process specification dialog (see Fig. 4). Second, from the the Condor Options pop-up dialog, user must enter Condor "ClassAds" specifying execution environments, memory requirements, core size, etc. Some necessary default ClassAds are supplied by ILab. Since the number of ClassAds is rather large, and their construction fairly complex (users may specify logical "and" and logical "or" within each ClassAd), at this time we have not added extensive error-checking and user aids for the ClassAds. Instead, ILab presumes that a Condor user already has background knowledge regarding the construction of Condor submission scripts, and users are referred to the Condor web site for information. Nevertheless, entry of ClassAds is still very easy, and some ClassAd names are available from pull-down menus for user's convenience. After choosing Condor and entering necessary ClassAds, users will proceed as with other ILab experiments: the generation of parameterized files, and the generation and monitoring of scripts, will operate as for other MetaEnvironments. We plan to further implement the Condor option in a few months, and we will provide documentation that includes sample ClassAds, and some basic instructions, for those users who are unfamiliar with Condor.

8 Conclusions

We have labored much over details here largely because production-level grid computing cannot be accomplished without strenuous attention to details. Users justifiably demand services well beyond the demonstration level. We have described some typical user requirements and corresponding solutions which involved considerable development effort. We believe that the "Grid" is now at a critical juncture where this level of effort is necessary. It will be the production-level users whose acceptance will determine the success of the Grid.

References

1. Yarrow, M., McCann, K. M., Biswas, R., Van der Wijngaart, R.: An Advanced User Interface Approach for Complex Parameter Study Process Specification on the Information Power Grid. Grid Computing - GRID 2000, First IEEE/ACM International Workshop on Grid Computing, Bangalore, India, December 17, 2000, Proceedings.
2. DeVivo, A., Yarrow, M., McCann, K. M.: A Comparison of Parameter Study Creation and Job Submission Tools. Available at http://www.nas.nasa.gov/Research/Reports/Techreports/2001/nas-01-002-abstract.html.
3. Foster, I., Kesselman, C.: Globus: A Metacomputing Infrastructure Toolkit. Intl J. Supercomputer Applications, 11(2):115-128, 1997.
4. Litzkow, M., Livny, M.: Experience With The Condor Distributed Batch System. IEEE Workshop on Experimental Distributed Systems, Oct. 1990, Huntsville, Al. Available at http://www.cs.wisc.edu/condor/publications.html.

The D0 Experiment Data Grid – SAM

Lee Lueking, Lauri Loebel-Carpenter, Wyatt Merritt, Carmenita Moore,

Ruth Pordes, Igor Terekhov, Sinisa Veseli

Matt Vranicar, Steve White, Vicky White

Fermilab, P.O. Box 500, Batavia, Illinois 60510[1]

Abstract. SAM (Sequential Access through Meta-data) is a data grid and data cataloging system developed for the D0 high energy physics (HEP) experiment at Fermilab. Since March 2001 , D0 has been acquiring data in real time from the detector and will archive up to 1/2 Petabyte a year of simulated, raw detector and processed physics data. SAM catalogs the event and calibration data, provides distributed file delivery and caching services, and manages the processing and analysis jobs for the hundreds of D0 collaborators around the world. The D0 applications are data-intensive and the physics analysis programs execute on the order of 1-1000 cpuseconds per 250KByte of data. SAM manages the transfer of data between the archival storage systems through the globally distributed disk caches and delivers the data files to the users batch and interactive jobs. Additionally, SAM handles the user job requests and execution scheduling, and manages the use of the available compute, storage and network resources to implement experiment resource allocation policies. D0 has been using early versions of the SAM system for two years for the management of the simulation and test data. The system is in production use with round the clock support. D0 is a participant in the Particle Physics Data Grid (PPDG) project. Aspects of the ongoing SAM developments are in collaboration with the computer science groups and other experiments on PPDG. The D0 emphasis is to develop the more sophisticated global grid job, resource management, authentication and information services needed to fully meet the needs of the experiment during the next 6 years of data taking and analysis.

1. Overview

During the past decade the D0[2] experiment processed and analyzed 30Terabytes of data collected during 'Run I'. The central analysis system provided data to the analysis programs from a shared file system of 300 Gigabytes, operator mounted tapes, and a traditional batch system which scheduled jobs based on the number of compute seconds required. Allocation of the disk and compute resources across the 20 or so Physics Analysis groups was done through meetings and administrative agreement. Several dedicated FTEs were required throughout the several years of data analysis to monitor, manage and coordinate the disk space, and control and schedule the analysis jobs. Data tapes were copied and sent through US mail to collaborators around the world. Lack of access to the ancillary calibration and run information, and the lack of ability to synchronize and coordinate the data sets and code versions, made the analysis of data at anywhere but Fermilab extremely difficult. The above constraints resulted in data delivery bottlenecks that were difficult to resolve and an inability to use efficiently the available compute resources.

D0's second major data taking period – Run 2 - started earlier this year. The experiment will archive about 1/2 Petabyte of data a year. Run 2A will last for five or six years and is expected to be followed by Run 2B with up to an eight fold increase in data. The resulting Petabytes of data that must be processed and analyzed to produce publishable physics results consist of the raw data collected directly from the detector (about ½ the dataset), 100s of Terabytes of simulated data needed to understand and check the collected data, and successive levels of "refined data sets" of sizes ranging from a few Gigabytes to a few tens of Terabytes, which are analyzed many times over to understand and extract the final physics signals (and hopefully discover the Higgs!).

For the initial processing of the data, compute farms of about 20,000 SpecInt95s are deployed. For the analysis the physics groups will consume whatever resources are readily available and from which reproducible and defendable results can be obtained. Initially a minimum deployment of 30,000-100,000 SpecInt95s is planned[3] The collaboration of over 500 physicists is spread over 3 continents. Analysis facilities in England, the Netherlands and France are already being established, as well as at several universities in the US.

Given the experience of Run 1, the immediate challenges facing us for Run 2A and the anticipated needs for Run 2B – augmented by the simultaneous need for Run 2A analyses and Run 2B data processing - the D0 experiment has developed a fully distributed data handling and management system Sequential Access Using Meta-Data (SAM)[4]. While the system design and requirements were specified several years ago[5] SAM has been developed over the past few years as a production system to meet the immediate needs of the experiment for simulated data production, archiving and processing, and for development and testing of the final data acquisition and data processing systems. It has been in production use for over 2 years with robustness, automated recovery, and monitoring features built in from the beginning. SAM is used on many D0 systems at Fermilab[6] as well as handful of offsite institutions both in the US and abroad. The SAM requirements and design for remote data access, global disk caching and automated file replication, distributed job scheduling and resource management map well onto the current and ongoing Grid requirements and research activities. The D0 physics data processing and analysis applications are providing a good example from which to gain experience in the support of a production data grid and providing information for performance evaluation and tuning and management decisions.

Now that data taking has started and the initial data processing pipelines are in place and becoming stable, we are turning our efforts, as collaborators on the Particle Physics Data Grid[7] (PPDG) project to include research, design and implementation of the more sophisticated issues of data replication, global authentication, and job and resource management to meet the collaborations data analysis needs. Clearly, the continued and increasing use of SAM by the end users is giving us valuable feedback and input to the research and development directions. Aligned with the goals and strategies of PPDG, the D0 data distributed data management system provides an available deployment of end-to-end services ready to make use of new grid components as they become available.

2. D0 Applications: Distributed Analysis

D0 applications include data collection and archiving, data processing or reconstruction of physics triggered events from raw detector information, and event analysis. The analysis activities are organized as groups by physics topic. There are of the order of 10 such groups, each including several subgroups. D0 analysis applications process a collection or "dataset" of events selected by an pre-defined set of criteria. Generally, datasets are defined through have equal or related "physics trigger" or physics event type, or were originally acquired in a single sequence or "data taking run" or common detector configuration. The application is submitted to a batch system or run interactively. SAM delivers the files of the data set to the application asynchronously from the data consumption, in order to make optimal use of the available delivery resources (e.g. all files on the same tape before all files on another tape). Tunable parameters control the amount of disk cache available for the User Group running the application, the refresh algorithms for the disk cache, preventing the delivery of unneeded files if the application falls behind in the consumption of data already delivered etc. The D0 application infrastructure provides for the unpacking of data files to deliver event objects to the end user code.

A particular physics group will typically define common "reference" data sets and will run many applications whose data sets overlap or are in common. For large datasets – of the order of 10s of Terabytes – the physics groups will coordinate their applications and process the data files in parallel as the files are delivered to a local cache so as to increase the total analysis work achieved. Traversing a large dataset may require several weeks of computation, where only a

subset of the files need to be available on local disk cache on any one day. An individual physicist may define many of her own datasets for algorithm development and individual research. Users typically reprocess small datasets many times over the course of a week or a month especially for the most refined datasets where physics parameter "cuts" are being made to provide the final histograms and physics results. While many of the analysis jobs run as efficiently as sequential executions, some of the applications are benefit from being parallelized and incurring the extra overhead of combining the generated results.

This paper presents an overview of the SAM system with pointers to the more technical details published elsewhere [8].

3. The SAM system

SAM includes a rich metadata catalog, a set of distributed servers which communicate via Corba interfaces, interfaces to storage management systems and to file transfer services, command line and application program interfaces to user applications and the catalog, an interface to batch systems, and a set of services to provide management and scheduling of the job and resource requests. The meta-data catalog (which is currently centralized but given its implementation in Oracle can be distributed as needed) tracks "all information about all things" and is continuously being extended with new information. To date it includes:

- The Replica Catalog, the location(s) of each data file on disk and/or tape, contents, generation and processing history, physics signatures or "tags";
- Job Processing History, the information about each user job - time, duration, files processed, location, resource usage ;
- Collection Catalog, the definition and history of all datasets (collections of files).
- Ancillary Information Catalog, calibration and other bookkeeping information necessary to analyze each data file;
- Configuration Information, versions, environments, users, groups etc.
- Information Services - monitoring and status information about the files, jobs and users to allow analysis of the usage and performance of many aspects of the system.

Each collection of hardware (site) – locally distributed disk, cpu etc – in the globally distributed system is known as a "station" and managed and tracked by a "station master " server. SAM manages the movement of data files to and from archival (tape or disk) storage to the station disk caches, as well as the lifetime of each file e.g. "pinned" by application request; or subject to cache replacement policies. SAM supports multiple locations of any file, and provides for the efficient routing of files from existing locations to the disk cache local to the users application. Additionally the user interface includes features to automatically map logical file names to physical locations based on experiment rules and conventions.

The user interfaces for SAM include command line, C++ and Python APIs for user applications. Extensive interfaces to the database which support management of the users and infrastructure, definition of datasets through a "physics-aware", domain specific, query language etc. D0 experimenters use SAM integrated into their traditional data processing and analysis programs; and make extensive use the definition and query capabilities in the coordination and management of the physics groups.

4. Technologies Used

All SAM client-server interfaces are defined in IDL and use Corba as the underlying infrastructure. We have been using Orbacus[9] until very recently. Recently we have started to investigate the use of OmniOrb[10] in an attempt to improve the performance when large amounts of data are transferred, and we are investigating some instabilities in the Orbacus nameserver. SAM servers are implemented in C++, with clients in C++, Python and Java. The data set definition interface and language is implemented in Java, C++ and python, using the TomCat[11] java servlet implementation. A sophisticated perl cgi-script is used as a general tool for web based database queries. There are many administrative scripts for system startup, shutdown, restart, status and error logging implemented in shell and python.

Access to the data is controlled through private protocols between the SAM clients and servers and user roles for access to the meta-data catalogs. As part of the Fermilab "strong authentication" project some parts of the system incorporates wrappers to integrate enable its use in a Kerberos realm.

5. Distributed Data Caching and File Delivery

SAM is responsible for providing transparent user access to data via file delivery and management over a globally distributed disk cache[12]. It includes generic interfaces to storage resources and file transfer services and has been interfaced to mass storage systems at Fermilab[13], IN2P3 and Nikhef. SAM supports file transfer via rcp, ftp and bbftp, with GridFTP next on the agenda. The central replica catalog keeps a full account of the multiple locations of the physical files and is used to determine the optimal location from which to retrieve a requested file.

When a Station Manager requests files, delivery may be done through multi-stage movement of the data between caches, or by copying of the file from another stations disk cache, if it is determined that this will provide the quickest access. Global and local configurations can be used to control algorithms to affect how file replication will occur. Each machine controlled by a station has locally mounted disks. When a file is authorized for transfer, the station's cache manager allocates space from the available pool of local disk and issues requests to the associated station stager to deliver the files.

A station's disk cache is allocated among the physics groups. If a cached file is requested by a second physics group any existing local replica is used. D0 applications in general have no dependence on the order of delivery of the files in a dataset and invariably are computing on the data of only one data file at a time. Thus SAM moves files in the most efficient order to achieve sequential delivery of the complete dataset. Once a file has been consumed by the users job it is eligible for deleting from the local cache if noone else is requesting to use it and as cache replacement policies dictate. Users can pin a file in cache on request, and subject to the policies of a particular physics group. From an application perspective the management of the global disk cache is transparent. A user merely issues a request to "get_the_next_file" and when such is available a callback is executed.

6. Resource Management Research and Development

We are continuing to research and develop the global resource management and scheduling layer in SAM, in particular as mentioned above as part of PPDG. The end goals of the job control and data management are to ensure "fair" resource allocation by certain user categories, subject to the collaboration's policies, and maximization of the overall job throughput. In the data intensive world, both goals require approaches that fully incorporate the data management issues. To attain the first goal, the system uses fair share scheduling; for the second, the system performs resource co-allocation.

As discussed earlier, in general physics analysis applications are data-intensive. Given the data set sizes and storage capabilities for D0 Run 2 system, data delivery from tape is treated as expensive in terms of the number of tape mounts and tape reading time. Job scheduling decisions must be made depending on relative cost of data delivery and of increasing the job latency.. We must take account of such issues as use of tape robot arm, bandwidth of tape drive, and network bandwidth, which typically combine to result in the delivery of data being an "expensive" operation compared to the cost of delaying execution of the job such that it can be run using existing local data. The results of the comparison in cost of delivery vs delay may change as the execution of other applications may result in the delivery of useful data files.

Additionally, since applications from the same physics group typically access the same sets of data, coscheduling of these user jobs may increase the total work achieved by the system.

We are approaching job and resource management in SAM using the concepts of "computational economy". Work done for a user application is understood in terms of benefit and the resources used in execution of this work incur a cost. Many different resources, with differing worth or value, will be used in the execution of a user job – tape mounts and tape reads, network transfer, local disk caches, cpu etc. The benefit to a user or physics group is defined by the files processed and takes account of the experiment policies and priorities for these groups, as negotiated by the collaboration. Given insufficient resources to achieve all requested analysis processing – a given in all HEP experiments to date - the goal is to get the most analysis done ensure the priority tasks are achieved with the necessary time, get as much analysis done as possible, and use the available resources as efficiently as feasible. Allocation of the available resources must be responsive to the sociological and political goals of the collaboration, as well as dynamic in responding to the prevailing and changing conditions. This is a challenging area of exploration in such a complex system. The SAM meta-data catalog, log file and information services (fed from instrumented servers) provide extensive information that allows us to track the performance of the system in detail, measure and analyse the results of our decision making and resource management models. Computational ecomonics is providing a good metaphor to allow us to define and manipulate our metrics quantitatively to enable decision making and actions. As an example, we are studying and balancing the relative costs of dispatching a job at a site with computing resources, but not data, available a priori versus queuing the job at a ``busy" site where the data is available. Using a local distributed analysis cluster as an example, it is evident that the initial availability of (some) of the project's data at a machine is only one of the several factors to affect the job placement.

We plan to develop a formal language to allow us to describe the requirements and acceptable tradeoffs of a job and of the available resources. This PPDG work is planned as a collaboration with the University of Wisconsin Computer Science Department most notably with the Condor team[14]. The Job and Resource Definition Language must have rich enough semantics to communicate the full vocabulary needed to support the dynamic scheduling, flow control, and monitoring of tasks specified by job control or ad hoc analysis requirements across the globally distributed system. Its function is to allow the job management system to coordinate the allocation and management of compute resources, communication resources and storage resources to match the needs of the large number of simultaneous clients and to follow local and global policies. We are working with the Condor group to apply and extend the ClassAd language[15] and the matchmaking framework to meet these needs.

7. Conclusion

As data pours in, the collective needs of the D0 analysis jobs will far outstrip the available resources, especially as the physicists are freed from detector commissioning and start mining the vast data sets for new physical phenomena. We anticipate that the complexity of the events collected for Run 2 will result in more computationally intensive applications as time progresses. There is anecdotal evidence from Run 1 that such new analyses were attempted. If we can solve the issues of configuration management , versioning and tracking of all parameters, the experimenters will feel more comfortable recalculating intermediate results from re-delivered data files, and not storing all intermediate datasets.

As D0 experimenters return to their home institutions having completed commissioning of the detector, the need for PhD theses increases, and the number of analyses explodes, SAM will be an essential component in the experiments ability to deliver timely and reliable physics analyses and results. It will be relied on to provide fast, robust and complete data access, information cataloging and management of the computational resources. We can already see features that will become useful as the overall load of the system increases. As an example, since resources required and available are captured and the job execution scenario determined, it is possible to return to the user an estimate of the length of time to scheduling or completion of the job. Although this is an area of ongoing research and not a service we plan to incorporate soon, we decided that we will design every component of the SAM system to support estimation of the services they provide.

The design of SAM allows us to extend and increase the sophistication of the services it offers as we continue with our research and development as part of PPDG. Working with the Computer Science group at the University of Wisconsin we enable us to take advantage of their research and experience and deliver a system which can be used as a model and test bed for other high energy physics experiments data handling.

8. Acknowledgements

This work is done as part of the SAM and the D0 Particle Physics Data Grid project. We acknowledge input and support from many people in the Computing Division at Fermilab and the D0 Collaboration.

References

1. This work is sponsored by DOE contract No. DE-AC02-76CH03000
2. http://www-d0.fnal.gov - the D0 experiment.
3. http://runiicomputing.fnal.gov/runIIdocs/NAG/cdrun2needs.ps CDF/D0/CD Run II Data Management Needs Assessment Document
4. SAM Overview and Operation at the D0 Experiment", submitted to The International Conference on Computing in High Energy and Nuclear Physics (CHEP 2001), September, 2001. home page: http://d0db.fnal.gov/sam
5. http://d0db.fnal.gov/sam/doc/requirements/sam_vw_req_arch.ps - Requirements for the Sequential Access Model data access system, J. Bakken et al
6. ~20 stations listed at http://d0db.fnal.gov/sam_data_browsing/
7. Particle Physics Data Grid Proposal – www.ppdg.net/docs/scidac01_ppdg_public.pdf
8. SAM overview and operations at the D0 Experiment, Resource Management in SAM - the D0 Data Grid to be presented at the Computing in High Energy and Nuclear Physics conference, September 3 - 7, 2001 Beijing, P.R.China
9. http://www.ooc.com/ob/
10. http://www.uk.research.att.com/omniORB/omniORB.html
11. http://jakarta.apache.org/tomcat/
12. SAM for D0 - a fully distributed data access system", I. Terekhov et al, presented at VII International Workshop on Advanced Computing and Analysis Techniques in Physics Research (ACAT 2000), Oct. 2000, Batavia, IL, in proceedings.
13. Enstore mass storage system http://isd.fnal.gov/enstore/; SARA mass storage system http://www.sara.nl/; IN2P3 HPSS http://doc.in2p3.fr/hpss/;
14. http://www.cs.wisc.edu/condor/ - Condor High Throughput Computing
15. http://www.cs.wisc.edu/condor/classad/

Author Index

Athey, Brian D., 133
Aydt, Ruth A., 154

Beck, Micah, 124

Cannataro, Mario, 38
Chapin, Steve, 99
Chapman, Barbara M., 145

Darlington, John, 26
Denis, Alexandre, 14
DeVivo, Adrian, 166

Field, Tony, 26
Foster, Ian, 51, 75
Furmento, Nathalie, 26

Gannon, Dennis, 1
Gawor, Jarek, 2
Grimshaw, Andrew, 99

Hacker, Thomas J., 133
Humphrey, Marty, 99

Iamnitchi, Adriana, 51

Katramatos, Dimitrios, 99

Laszewski, Gregor von, 2
Lee, Byoung-Dai, 63
Loebel-Carpenter, Lauri, 177
Lueking, Lee, 177

Mayer, Anthony, 26
McCann, Karen M., 166
McGough, Stephen, 26
Mendes, Celso L., 154

Merritt, Wyatt, 177
Moore, Carmenita, 177
Moore, Terry, 124

Newhouse, Steven, 26

Pérez, Christian, 14
Parashar, Manish, 2
Plank, James S., 124
Pordes, Ruth, 177
Priol, Thierry, 14

Ranganathan, Kavitha, 75
Reed, Daniel A., 154

Sarangi, Anuraag, 111
Shankar, Avinash, 111
Shriram, Alok, 111
Srinivasan, Pramod, 87
Sundaram, Babu, 145

Talia, Domenico, 38
Tejnil, Edward, 166
Terekhov, Igor, 177
Trunfio, Paolo, 38

Verma, Snigdha, 2
Veseli, Sinisa, 177
Vraalsen, Frederik, 154
Vranicar, Matt, 177

Weissman, Jon B., 63, 87
White, Steve, 177
White, Vicky, 177

Yarrow, Maurice, 166

in Computer Science

Vols. 1–2151

ookseller or Springer-Verlag

Vol. 2152: R.J. Boulton, P.B. Jackson (Eds.), Theore Proving in Higher Order Logics. Proceedings, 2001. X,395 pages. 2001.

Vol. 2153: A.L. Buchsbaum, J. Snoeyink (Eds.), Algorithm Engineering and Experimentation. Proceedings, 2001. VIII, 231 pages. 2001.

Vol. 2154: K.G. Larsen, M. Nielsen (Eds.), CONCUR 2001 – Concurrency Theory. Proceedings, 2001. XI, 583 pages. 2001.

Vol. 2155: H. Bunt, R.-J. Beun (Eds.), Cooperative Multimodal Communication. Proceedings, 1998. VIII, 251 pages. 2001. (Subseries LNAI).

Vol. 2156: M.I. Smirnov, J. Crowcroft, J. Roberts, F.Boavida (Eds.), Quality of Future Internet Services. Proceedings, 2001. XI, 333 pages. 2001.

Vol. 2157: C. Rouveirol, M. Sebag (Eds.), Inductive Logic Programming. Proceedings, 2001. X, 261 pages. 2001. (Subseries LNAI).

Vol. 2158: D. Shepherd, J. Finney, L. Mathy, N. Race (Eds.), Interactive Distributed Multimedia Systems. Proceedings, 2001. XIII, 258 pages. 2001.

Vol. 2159: J. Kelemen, P. Sosík (Eds.), Advances in Artificial Life. Proceedings, 2001. XIX, 724 pages. 2001. (Subseries LNAI).

Vol. 2161: F. Meyer auf der Heide (Ed.), Algorithms – ESA 2001. Proceedings, 2001. XII, 538 pages. 2001.

Vol. 2162: Ç. K. Koç, D. Naccache, C. Paar (Eds.), Cryptographic Hardware and Embedded Systems – CHES 2001. Proceedings, 2001. XIV, 411 pages. 2001.

Vol. 2163: P. Constantopoulos, I.T. Sølvberg (Eds.), Research and Advanced Technology for Digital Libraries. Proceedings, 2001. XII, 462 pages. 2001.

Vol. 2164: S. Pierre, R. Glitho (Eds.), Mobile Agents for Telecommunication Applications. Proceedings, 2001. XI, 292 pages. 2001.

Vol. 2165: L. de Alfaro, S. Gilmore (Eds.), Process Algebra and Probabilistic Methods. Proceedings, 2001. XII, 217 pages. 2001.

Vol. 2166: V. Matoušek, P. Mautner, R. Mouček, K. Taušer (Eds.), Text, Speech and Dialogue. Proceedings, 2001. XIII, 452 pages. 2001. (Subseries LNAI).

Vol. 2167: L. De Raedt, P. Flach (Eds.), Machine Learning: ECML 2001. Proceedings, 2001. XVII, 618 pages. 2001. (Subseries LNAI).

Vol. 2168: L. De Raedt, A. Siebes (Eds.), Principles of Data Mining and Knowledge Discovery. Proceedings, 2001. XVII, 510 pages. 2001. (Subseries LNAI).

Vol. 2169: M. Jaedicke, New Concepts for Parallel Object-Relational Query Processing. XI, 161 pages. 2001.

Vol. 2170: S. Palazzo (Ed.), Evolutionary Trends of the Internet. Proceedings, 2001. XIII, 722 pages. 2001.

Vol. 2171: R. Focardi, R. Gorrieri (Eds.), Foundations of Security Analysis and Design. VII, 397 pages. 2001.

Vol. 2172: C. Batini, F. Giunchiglia, P. Giorgini, M. Mecella (Eds.), Cooperative Information Systems. Proceedings, 2001. XI, 450 pages. 2001.

Vol. 2173: T. Eiter, W. Faber, M. Truszczynski (Eds.), Logic Programming and Nonmonotonic Reasoning. Proceedings, 2001. XI, 444 pages. 2001. (Subseries LNAI).

Vol. 2174: F. Baader, G. Brewka, T. Eiter (Eds.), KI 2001: Advances in Artificial Intelligence. Proceedings, 2001. XIII, 471 pages. 2001. (Subseries LNAI).

Vol. 2175: F. Esposito (Ed.), AI*IA 2001: Advances in Artificial Intelligence. Proceedings, 2001. XII, 396 pages. 2001. (Subseries LNAI).

Vol. 2176: K.-D. Althoff, R.L. Feldmann, W. Müller (Eds.), Advances in Learning Software Organizations. Proceedings, 2001. XI, 241 pages. 2001.

Vol. 2177: G. Butler, S. Jarzabek (Eds.), Generative and Component-Based Software Engineering. Proceedings, 2001. X, 203 pages. 2001.

Vol. 2178: R. Moreno-Díaz, B. Buchberger, J.-L. Freire (Eds.), Computer Aided Systems Theory – EUROCAST 2001. Proceedings, 2001. XI, 670 pages. 2001.

Vol. 2180: J. Welch (Ed.), Distributed Computing. Proceedings, 2001. X, 343 pages. 2001.

Vol. 2181: C. Y. Westort (Ed.), Digital Earth Moving. Proceedings, 2001. XII, 117 pages. 2001.

Vol. 2182: M. Klusch, F. Zambonelli (Eds.), Cooperative Information Agents V. Proceedings, 2001. XII, 288 pages. 2001. (Subseries LNAI).

Vol. 2183: R. Kahle, P. Schroeder-Heister, R. Stärk (Eds.), Proof Theory in Computer Science. Proceedings, 2001. IX, 239 pages. 2001.

Vol. 2184: M. Tucci (Ed.), Multimedia Databases and Image Communication. Proceedings, 2001. X, 225 pages. 2001.

Vol. 2185: M. Gogolla, C. Kobryn (Eds.), «UML» 2001 – The Unified Modeling Language. Proceedings, 2001. XIV, 510 pages. 2001.

Vol. 2186: J. Bosch (Ed.), Generative and Component-Based Software Engineering. Proceedings, 2001. VIII, 177 pages. 2001.

Vol. 2187: U. Voges (Ed.), Computer Safety, Reliability and Security. Proceedings, 2001. XVI, 249 pages. 2001.

Vol. 2188: F. Bomarius, S. Komi-Sirviö (Eds.), Product Focused Software Process Improvement. Proceedings, 2001. XI, 382 pages. 2001.

Vol. 2189: F. Hoffmann, D.J. Hand, N. Adams, D. Fisher, G. Guimaraes (Eds.), Advances in Intelligent Data Analysis. Proceedings, 2001. XII, 384 pages. 2001.

Vol. 2190: A. de Antonio, R. Aylett, D. Ballin (Eds.), Intelligent Virtual Agents. Proceedings, 2001. VIII, 245 pages. 2001. (Subseries LNAI).

Vol. 2191: B. Radig, S. Florczyk (Eds.), Pattern Recognition. Proceedings, 2001. XVI, 452 pages. 2001.

Vol. 2192: A. Yonezawa, S. Matsuoka (Eds.), Metalevel Architectures and Separation of Crosscutting Concerns. Proceedings, 2001. XI, 283 pages. 2001.

Vol. 2193: F. Casati, D. Georgakopoulos, M.-C. Shan (Eds.), Technologies for E-Services. Proceedings, 2001. X, 213 pages. 2001.

Vol. 2194: A.K. Datta, T. Herman (Eds.), Self-Stabilizing Systems. Proceedings, 2001. VII, 229 pages. 2001.

Vol. 2195: H.-Y. Shum, M. Liao, S.-F. Chang (Eds.), Advances in Multimedia Information Processing – PCM 2001. Proceedings, 2001. XX, 1149 pages. 2001.

Vol. 2196: W. Taha (Ed.), Semantics, Applications, and Implementation of Program Generation. Proceedings, 2001. X, 219 pages. 2001.

Vol. 2197: O. Balet, G. Subsol, P. Torguet (Eds.), Virtual Storytelling. Proceedings, 2001. XI, 213 pages. 2001.

Vol. 2198: N. Zhong, Y. Yao, J. Liu, S. Ohsuga (Eds.), Web Intelligence: Research and Development. Proceedings, 2001. XVI, 615 pages. 2001. (Subseries LNAI).

Vol. 2199: J. Crespo, V. Maojo, F. Martin (Eds.), Medical Data Analysis. Proceedings, 2001. X, 311 pages. 2001.

Vol. 2200: G.I. Davida, Y. Frankel (Eds.), Information Security. Proceedings, 2001. XIII, 554 pages. 2001.

Vol. 2201: G.D. Abowd, B. Brumitt, S. Shafer (Eds.), Ubicomp 2001: Ubiquitous Computing. Proceedings, 2001. XIII, 372 pages. 2001.

Vol. 2202: A. Restivo, S. Ronchi Della Rocca, L. Roversi (Eds.), Theoretical Computer Science. Proceedings, 2001. XI, 440 pages. 2001.

Vol. 2204: A. Brandstädt, V.B. Le (Eds.), Graph-Theoretic Concepts in Computer Science. Proceedings, 2001. X, 329 pages. 2001.

Vol. 2205: D.R. Montello (Ed.), Spatial Information Theory. Proceedings, 2001. XIV, 503 pages. 2001.

Vol. 2206: B. Reusch (Ed.), Computational Intelligence. Proceedings, 2001. XVII, 1003 pages. 2001.

Vol. 2207: I.W. Marshall, S. Nettles, N. Wakamiya (Eds.), Active Networks. Proceedings, 2001. IX, 165 pages. 2001.

Vol. 2208: W.J. Niessen, M.A. Viergever (Eds.), Medical Image Computing and Computer-Assisted Intervention – MICCAI 2001. Proceedings, 2001. XXXV, 1446 pages. 2001.

Vol. 2209: W. Jonker (Ed.), Databases in Telecommunications II. Proceedings, 2001. VII, 179 pages. 2001.

Vol. 2210: Y. Liu, K. Tanaka, M. Iwata, T. Higuchi, M. Yasunaga (Eds.), Evolvable Systems: From Biology to Hardware. Proceedings, 2001. XI, 341 pages. 2001.

Vol. 2211: T.A. Henzinger, C.M. Kirsch (Eds.), Embedded Software. Proceedings, 2001. IX, 504 pages. 2001.

Vol. 2212: W. Lee, L. Mé, A. Wespi (Eds.), Recent Advances in Intrusion Detection. Proceedings, 2001. X, 205 pages. 2001.

Vol. 2213: M.J. van Sir Protocols for Multimedi XII, 239 pages. 2001.

Vol. 2214: O. Boldt, plementation. Proceeding

Vol. 2215: N. Kobayashi, Aspects of Computer S 561 pages. 2001.

Vol. 2216: E.S. Al-Shaer, .. (Eds.), Management of Multimedia on the Internet. Proceedings, 2001. XIV, 373 pages. 2001.

Vol. 2217: T. Gomi (Ed.), Evolutionary Robotics. Proceedings, 2001. XI, 139 pages. 2001.

Vol. 2218: R. Guerraoui (Ed.), Middleware 2001. Proceedings, 2001. XIII, 395 pages. 2001.

Vol. 2220: C. Johnson (Ed.), Interactive Systems. Proceedings, 2001. XII, 219 pages. 2001.

Vol. 2221: D.G. Feitelson, L. Rudolph (Eds.), Job Scheduling Strategies for Parallel Processing. Proceedings, 2001. VII, 207 pages. 2001.

Vol. 2224: H.S. Kunii, S. Jajodia, A. Sølvberg (Eds.), Conceptual Modeling – ER 2001. Proceedings, 2001. XIX, 614 pages. 2001.

Vol. 2225: N. Abe, R. Khardon, T. Zeugmann (Eds.), Algorithmic Learning Theory. Proceedings, 2001. XI, 379 pages. 2001. (Subseries LNAI).

Vol. 2226: K.P. Jantke, A. Shinohara (Eds.), Discovery Science. Proceedings, 2001. XII, 494 pages. 2001. (Subseries LNAI).

Vol. 2227: S. Boztaş, I.E. Shparlinski (Eds.), Applied Algebra, Algebraic Algorithms and Error-Correcting Codes. Proceedings, 2001. XII, 398 pages. 2001.

Vol. 2229: S. Qing, T. Okamoto, J. Zhou (Eds.), Information and Communications Security. Proceedings, 2001. XIV, 504 pages. 2001.

Vol. 2230: T. Katila, I.E. Magnin, P. Clarysse, J. Montagnat, J. Nenonen (Eds.), Functional Imaging and Modeling of the Heart. Proceedings, 2001. XI, 158 pages. 2001.

Vol. 2232: L. Fiege, G. Mühl, U. Wilhelm (Eds.), Electronic Commerce. Proceedings, 2001. X, 233 pages. 2001.

Vol. 2233: J. Crowcroft, M. Hofmann (Eds.), Networked Group Communication. Proceedings, 2001. X, 205 pages. 2001.

Vol. 2234: L. Pacholski, P. Ružička (Eds.), SOFSEM 2001: Theory and Practice of Informatics. Proceedings, 2001. XI, 347 pages. 2001.

Vol. 2237: P. Codognet (Ed.), Logic Programming. Proceedings, 2001. XI, 365 pages. 2001.

Vol. 2239: T. Walsh (Ed.), Principles and Practice of Constraint Programming – CP 2001. Proceedings, 2001. XIV, 788 pages. 2001.

Vol. 2240: G.P. Picco (Ed.), Mobile Agents. Proceedings, 2001. XIII, 277 pages. 2001.

Vol. 2241: M. Jünger, D. Naddef (Eds.), Computational Combinatorial Optimization. IX, 305 pages. 2001.

Vol. 2242: C.A. Lee (Ed.), Grid Computing – GRID 2001. Proceedings, 2001. XII, 185 pages. 2001.